Blossoms
of the lower
Branches

A Hero's Journey
through Grief

By
Rebecca Guevara

REBECCA GUEVARA

First edition
ISBN 978-0-9793958-3-3
April 2011
Text copyright © Rebecca Guevara

All rights reserved. No part of this publication may be reproduced or transmitted in any form or by any means, electronic or mechanical without written permission from the publisher, except brief excerpts for the purpose of review.

Non-fiction, Memoir, Self-Help

This is a Panoply Publishing product
Printed and bound in the United States

Acknowledgements

No one suffered on this path of the hero's journey through grief as much as my mother, Gloria Spiking. I hope the good memories sustain her enough to be peaceful with the pain of life. It is her guidance through my childhood that provided me with the spiritual beliefs and views that have brought me peace. Alongside me through all of this were my husband, Sam and son, Zachary. They have always faced life well and I have learned much from them. Sam has been very supportive by encouraging me to get this work to people who may find solace in it during their hero's journey.

Lori Giovannoni Roper inspires through how she manages her own life, career and her way of enveloping her devoted group of friends. She accepts, nurtures and brings out the best of what each one of us can offer. Thank you, Lori, for your belief.

Published writing is also benefited by people a step away from the drama with clear vision, thoughtful suggestions and practical talents. A too often rambling, wild, repetitious manuscript was first read by Susan Vogel, so she needs a special thanks of courtesy for patience. Later readers were Karen Wilson and Judy Wolf, special women who I knew would read with heart as well as a critical and informed eye. Thank you.

REBECCA GUEVARA

Also published by Rebecca Guevara

The Trading of Ken
Juniper Press

*Write Your Book -- A Writer's Guide
to Combining Creativity with Project Planning*
Panoply Publishing

*My Family, Mi Familia,
A Young Anglo Woman's Journey
into a Mexican-American Family*

BLOSSOMS OF THE LOWER BRANCHES

TABLE OF CONTENTS

THE CALL TO THE HERO'S JOURNEY   1
GRIEF'S BLOSSOMS OF THE LOWER BRANCHES   7
TRAVELER'S ROAD SIGNS   14
THE FIRST CHALLENGE – Initiation to the Underworld   23
    Underworld First Guards – *Beyond them is darkness*
    Altered Consciousness – *The day of my father's funeral had also been my nineteenth's birthday*
    Dreams, Ghosts and Voices – *Morpheus' visit*
    Sensuality – *Making love, the supreme remedy for anguish*
    Premonitions – *To play my appointed part*
    Relief of Death – *But oh, God, tenderly, tenderly*
    God's Place – *A hard-hearted lot you are, you gods*
    Belly of Whale – *Swallowed into the unknown*
THE SECOND CHALLENGE – Refusing the Trials   77
THE THIRD CHALLENGE – Accepting the Trials   82
    Symbols, Talismans and Amulets – *Tempered in fire by dwarfs*
    Time Needed for Recovery – *Demeter's wandering*
    Why Me? – *Buddha's mustard seed*
    Overcoming vs. Accepting – *Jonah's fear*
    Tell Everyone or Tell No One – *Iona's little horse*
    Outside Support – *Baba Yaga's question*
    Revenge vs. Justice – *Hamlet's choice*
    At the Gate of Trials – *Kali's invitation*

Table of Contents II

THE FOURTH CHALLENGE – Society's Trials	142
Watching Others Take Risks – *Icarus' flight*	
Reaction of Others – *But, you must know, your father lost a father*	
Deflecting Conversations – *Gilgamesh's question*	
Reassessment of Value – *Salt Woman's lament*	
THE FIFTH CHALLENGE – Inner Trials	165
Changed Memory – *Mimir's Well*	
Imagine Death – *The River Styx*	
Personal Responsibility – *Three-headed dragon with the killer tale*	
Genetics – *Trickster's primal creativity and pathological destruction*	
Family Damage – *Halcyon's loss*	
Sadness and Anger – *Vasalisa's corn and poppy seeds*	
Compensation – *The armless maiden's baby*	
APOTHEOSIS AND BOON – Sighting the First Blossoms	217
THE CHOICE TO RETURN	224
Visiting the Grave – *My friend becomes a part of me!*	
The Martyr – *Phaeton's sisters*	
Allowing Happiness – *And so I kept my grief*	
RETURN TO LIFE – The Blossom's Fruit	248
The Deep Abiding – *A sea of peace serene*	
Non-profits and Activists – *I know something of the misery of man*	

TABLE OF CONTENTS III

Compassion – *Odysseus' smile*
Redemption – *Recovering rightful heritage*
Forgiveness – *Grace for Cupid*
Joy – *Mwindo's sorrow*
Closure – *Gilgamesh finds an end*

THE HERO'S END OF THE JOURNEY 295
   Traveling Between Two Worlds – *Learn until our brains all rot*

SUGGESTED READING AND REFERENCES 304

The Call to the Hero's Journey

Did the universe know the collected notes, pens, paper, and calendar of writing deadlines would be my sacrifice to grief? Unsure and tentative, I was writing an article for a local monthly and relying on the closeness of notes and pens to urge sentences from a frail, guarded inner self. When I heard a car door shut, I looked out the front window and saw my mother and grandmother coming up the walkway. We are not a family to visit one another without warning, but without curiosity, I walked to the front door.

I felt a timeless, serenely indifferent thought wave crest and roll around, through and beyond the house when I opened the door, forever to leave me in an endless wake. Their faces were grim. We heard my husband, Sam, and son, Zachary, coming from the TV room. Mother stood in front of me, Grandma Spiking to the side.

"You don't have a brother anymore," Mother said.

I stepped back and stiffened, "No." It was a forceful denial of what I was experiencing in the thought wave's endless wake. A vision appeared of my brother, Jody, wearing a blue shirt and holding a gun. He was among tall pines in a small clearing. He held the gun in his right hand, pointed it through his ribs and fired. A rush of heat went through my right chest and out my left, neither pleasing nor painful, only very hot and final. His legs gave first, before his hips sagged under falling torso, and then his handsome head with wild curly hair the color of summer's wheat hit dirt.

The five of us were silent and mindless. "How?" I asked.

"He did it himself, but we don't know. The police chaplain was waiting when I came home from work. That's all I know. I have to call Donna now." Mother called her sister, said arrangements needed to be made and the police still had him. *Still had him.* I felt a sliver of self the width of a hair leaving. Mother and Grandma, who had said nothing, left.

On August 7, 1979, I was called to the unwanted hero's journey through traumatic grief.

※

The hero's journey is the first form of story, dating back to at least 2500 B.C. when it is believed the Sumerian tale of *Gilgamesh* was written in stone. Buried in ruins in Nineveh, the tablets were unearthed in the mid-1870s. The literary hero's journey is told to strengthen group beliefs in an interesting, usually uplifting way. Heroes are people others want to be like because they show courage, strength of body, character, leadership, and intelligence. Heroes are loved because they can right a wrong, face adversity, save the helpless, and then be humble shy folk embarrassed by the showering of gifts when they are thanked. They face obstacles or trials, and their victories often reach far beyond their own lives as they become our examples and leaders.

Two hundred items have been listed as part of the hero's journey in scholarly study, but a basic description is:

They live a routine life.
They receive a calling to a quest.
They face challenges and learn from them.
Others benefit from what the newly designated hero learns.

"Gilgamesh was king of Uruk, a city set between the Tigris and Euphrates rivers," is the first line of *Gilgamesh*.

"Once upon a time" begins fairy tales of princes slaying dragons and kissing fair maidens to awaken love before living happily ever after. Once upon a time tells what is going on when the hero receives the call to action. "Once upon a time there was a prince. He wanted a princess, but she had to be a real princess," starts *The Princess and the Pea* by Hans Christian Andersen.

Human heroes also start their journey with simple words of how it was. In his memoir, *Night*, Elie Wiesel, a survivor of Hitler death camps gives a description of his tranquil boyhood in the village of Sighet. "My parents ran a shop. Hilda and Béa helped them with the work. As for me, they said my place was at school." My routine before the call was, on a Tuesday work day, before preparing dinner, I was working on an article I hoped would launch a more interesting career. Life was pleasant and normal.

Mythical and historical heroes often appear to be leaders from the beginning, and we enjoy following their stories and admiring their strength. The first lines written by Homer to describe the hero Odysseus in *The Odyssey* tells us all we need to know to believe in him. "This is the story of a man, one who was never at a loss. He had traveled far in the world, after the sack of Troy, the virgin fortress; he saw many cities of men, and learnt their mind; he endured many troubles and hardship in the struggle to save his own life and to bring back his men safe to their homes."

The tales of Odysseus, Gilgamesh, King Arthur and the Norse god Odin are from long ago and have become myth. Jesus Christ, Muhammad, Buddha and other religious figures have a hero's story. The Ugly Duckling and Thumbelina come from fairy tales. Dorothy in *The Wizard of Oz* and Harry Potter are recent fictional heroes.

The hero's journey is a template holding the stories of life. Falling in love and marrying, raising children, and creating a career can be told as a hero's journey. And, of course, love, raising children and a career don't always end happily. Living has many challenges and not all of them are settled in a way that makes people proud or peaceful. Challenges are not always successfully met and sometimes a would-be hero falters. Shakespeare's *Hamlet* and William Styron's *Sophie's Choice* are compelling stories of tragedy that have all the elements of the hero's journey, but along the way the protagonists fail.

Contemporary stories of grief's hero journey that are used in this book can be found in many lives. The call for C.S. Lewis, author of *The Narnia Chronicles*, came when his wife died of cancer. Candy Lightner, who founded Mothers Against Drunk Driving (MADD), lost her daughter when she was hit by a drunk driver, and Nando Parrado survived a plane crash in the Andes that killed his mother and sister.

While in my thirties, over a five year period, my only sibling, my mother-in-law, Grandma Spiking and my father died. Reasons were suicide, cancer, old age and complications from surgery. They were all important people I continue to love in memory and given a choice, I would have all of them back in my life. I still remember the endearing and aggravating things each one did to create their niche in my heart and memories. Not once in all that time did I think of myself, or anyone else who lost a loved one, as a hero.

Grief's emotions were different with each one. Sam, Zachary and Mother also had different emotional and intellectual good-byes. Jody's was the most traumatic for me and I know, for our mother. Only in the last years has Jody's memory obtained the patina of long, thoughtful polishing that is comfortably warm and an indelible part of who I have become. Recovery shouldn't have taken so long. It's easy to say suicide created the guilt, regret, shame and sadness but looking back, I know there is more.

Traumatic is not always unexpected. The hero's journey also

includes those who have tended a loved one through illness or the results of an accident. This grief is not about how the person died. It is about the person who continues to live.

Sam's call to his mother's death was when he was told she had cancer and was going in for surgery within the week. Sam, Zac, Mother and I struggled during this time of the five deaths, sometimes with each other, and sometimes alone.

Being told devastating news of someone we love irrevocably changes our life's path. The news sets an opening scene, but it does not make anyone a hero. Odysseus was not a hero when his call came to leave home to fight the Trojan War. King Arthur was not a hero when he pulled Excalibur from the rock to prove himself a leader. The title of hero is given only to those who complete the trials presented to them. However well grief's hero's journey is completed, survivors of traumatic death understand why Mother still says when she wants to talk of her son, "Before Jody left …."

Hearing of death from doctors, strangers in military uniform, police or religious dress is a difficult rite of passage to begin the hero's journey. More inviting and charming was Harry Potter's unexpected letter addressed to his sleeping quarters under the stairs urgently calling him to school. All calls change a person's life.

Grief's Blossoms of the Lower Branches

When someone unexpectedly or publicly dies away from home and hospitals, chaplains or police knock on front doors or call in night's darkness and say irretrievable words. Mother was told by a stranger waiting in a car when she arrived home. I was told by her as I weakened into a near catatonic state.

MADD founder Candy Lightner was told by her ex-husband, Steve, when she returned home after waiting for her daughter who didn't show. "'What's wrong?' I asked. Steve said, 'Honey, we've lost Cari.' I patted him on the back and said, 'It's all right, we'll find her.' I was about to suggest that we check with the neighbors but he didn't let me continue. 'You don't understand,' he said. "She's been killed. She was run over and she's dead.'"

In *East Toward Dawn*, Nan Watkins recalled, "In the black of a winter night, the phone woke my husband and me from sleep. It was a stranger calling to tell us our son was dead. He had been lying on a sofa watching the eleven o'clock news with a friend, when his heart, inexplicably, stopped beating. Peter was just twenty-two ...." Joseph Campbell defines the call in *The Hero with a Thousand Faces*. "[T]he call brings up the curtain, always, on a mystery of transfiguration—a rite, or moment, of spiritual passage, which, when complete, amounts to a dying and a birth."

Moses, the adopted son of a pharaoh's daughter, had a dramatic call. In a spontaneous burst of anger he murdered an Egyptian overseer of Jewish workers after witnessing him beating a slave. He fled to the desert and began his hero's journey, culminating in the Ten Commandments.

Buddha's quieter call came when his charioteer, Channa, took him for rides out of the confines of his sheltered, wealthy life. First he saw a bent and broken old man. Next he was shown poverty and disease. He saw his first corpse and was told that is how life ends. Lastly he saw a monk. Puzzled by the inequities of life, he began his quest by choice.

In 1427 Joan of Arc was an uneducated fifteen year old daughter of a tax collector in a small French village. At first she discounted the visions of light and internal voices. After several events she started believing, but kept it a secret. When she trusted her call, she never wavered again as she led France to victory over the English.

The call is clear, but the ways it presents itself are endless. Originally the hero's voyage, as scholar David Adams Leeming describes it, was shrouded in mystery and studied by few, but that has changed. "Mythologists are now anthropologists, philologists, etiologists, ethnologists, and perhaps most of all, psychologists. And crossing these disciplines are ritualists, diffusionists, structuralists, Jungians, Freudians, and culturalists, who, in turn, are not always mutually exclusive." The hero's journey is the property of all humankind.

In the first days after Jody's death, I was in a disorienting fog of everything happening at once and felt drowned by the serenely indifferent void that swept through the house when Mother told me. I was on a precipice, near personal mental obliteration when I would be suddenly swept back, gasping at the simplicity of life, the silliness of someone's anger.

Hours, then days and weeks of sadness mixed with doing laundry, laughing with joy, feeling deep love, hearing voices, planning a picnic, questioning everything, filling the car's gas tank, doubting reality, going to my son's school event, believing without question, reading a mystery, being sad, dancing alone through the house, quietly thinking, going to work, making love, cleaning the refrigerator, laughing at a joke and starting all over again.

Through this schizophrenic tumbling of emotion I slowly regained a surer footing in the routines of life, and like most people, kept serious mourning private. Within months I told myself it was over, nothing could be done and I needed to put grief aside as soon as possible. I told myself I understood the silence of friends and acquaintances because I didn't want to spend endless hours talking about death either. I was busy convincing myself I needed to recover and that took private, intense work, though I couldn't even name all I felt. I only wanted it all gone, and sometimes it was. Within the first week there was genuine reason to laugh. Yet, ten years later I could still cry as though it was yesterday. It was baffling that everything I thought and felt seemed a perpetual and unreliable roller coaster.

Privately I listened to stories and tried to piece life together. It was slightly before the popularity of support groups, and I'm not a person to automatically consider professional or religiously trained help, so I relied on books of meditation, the new age comfort of Leo Buscaglia, Ruth Montgomery, and reading of Buddha, Walt Whitman and philosophers from saved college text books. Elizabeth Kübler-Ross had published the famous *On Death and Dying*. Some issues overlapped with mine, but its clinical prescription of clear passages felt remote. Interspersed were escapist novels that spoke to an emptiness that needed to rework itself into a life I could handle.

Later, an emotional weight settled so gently on my shoulders that by the time several years passed, I thought it was mine right along with my heart. I believed myself healed and as I saw a change in public attitude about death issues, it was from the distance of remembering a long ago nightmare and being pleased it was now easier for others. Psychologists on book tours, radio shows and public health announcements were making a needed difference.

Then, on a spring day, I was reading a magazine article with a newspaper beside me open to the movie section and the television blaring in front of me. An ephemeral flash of an idea flitted through my mind. The article was a writer's view of the mythical hero's journey, the newspaper had a large ad for the upcoming movie of the flawed hero Batman, and on television commentators were talking about the Tour de France. Spontaneously, I saw similarities in recovery through grief and the hero's journey. An imperceptible emotional weight I hadn't realized lifted as though five pounds evaporated. I sat straighter. In the next instant I told myself, "Yah, right, me and Lance Armstrong. Heroes. Get real." Emotional weight re-settled and my shoulders fell.

A month later I was in my garden late at night. My Salt Lake City house backs the slope of a mountain and a winding path leads to a deck. I went out to enjoy the quiet night air and on the way I passed a six-foot yucca in full bloom. I looked at the tall, evenly-spaced arms of horizontal flowers so heavy their branches sagged while the creamy white blossom heads turned to sing to the moon. The desert yucca, which can live through snowy winters and hot summers with little rain, was planted level with my knees and I couldn't reach its upper flowers. They were framed by night sky and busy with their song. In exultant joy, as the favored among the hundreds of beautifully arranged flowers, they didn't turn toward me. I stared at them.

My gaze shifted to the lower blossoms. The air was darker, closer to earth. My heart understood. What I learned in the depth of me from my brother's death was from the less visible blossoms of the lower branches. His death began and still is in the darkness with many things I don't understand. Things beyond both of us that had nothing to do with his death and everything to do with causing me to think.

Again I felt the weight lift, but this time I was ready to understand. Yes, I had painfully taken myself through recovery from a devastating loss, but I had also blindly accepted the definition society had of that slow recovery. My tale was one of loss that at best strengthened endurance with nothing to be proud about. I live in a country that understands engraved two-feet high silver cups, gold medals around necks of athletes, curving Emmys held by beautiful people, and Nobel prizes received by the gifted and educated. Deservedly so, they hold the gifts of the blossoms of the higher branches, the gifts easily seen and well-applauded.

As a society, we do not understand or acknowledge the gifts that come from the blossoms of the lower branches. Gifts that are also hard-won and life affirming. It doesn't matter that they aren't acknowledged by roaring approving audiences, but it does matter when what is learned and gained by the person is called only a tale of loss.

Gilgamesh's story shows grief, and the eventual making of peace with death as a legendary tale from the earliest stories. Accepting death is a task that is accomplished without desire and perhaps never in complete peace. Acceptance is lonely and an unwanted compromise. But, when loss is finally stared at and reluctantly accepted, the blossoms of the lower branches can give sustenance and growth.

When Jody died I hoped to regain a footing in life so strong, clear and alive that it would be as though it never happened. I wanted grief to clean and scrub me with bleach and brushes until I felt innocent and loved for goodness never tested. I wanted everything undone and my brother back where he belonged. I wanted to be as those top flowers so sure, so lovely, so happy, admired and blithely enjoying being above the darkened and dying lower flowers now giving their youth and innocence for the blossoms above.

I am now less afraid of death, more compassionate, less judgmental, more grateful, less fragile, more developed, and less sure anything will stay mine. What I now feel more deeply about myself is because of walking through the steps scholars outline as the hero's journey. This book is an invitation to any person locked in the arms of grief who would like a more aware and positive look of where they have been, where they are and where they are going.

Odysseus did not return home to Ithaca triumphant from victory in Troy. He wasn't on the shoulders of comrades in a parade where petals dusted his shoulders and citizens hailed his bravery. Instead, he was carried as he slept by sailors who were instructed to leave him on a blanket on the sand with enough food and water to continue alone. His challenges with the cyclops, Circe, the sirens and more, were behind him. It was time to decide how to return to a normal life and understand what he had learned. But first, the challenges must be lived, observed and understood by a potential hero.

Traveler's Road Signs

Mourning begins as an incomprehensible dream where little is recognizable. The hero is suddenly on a road not knowing where she is going, why or how long it will take. Everything is unfamiliar though she may be standing in her own kitchen. To make this trip, it is important to read new road signs so the journey slowly winds to the traveler's chosen destination. Alice was not so lucky when she followed the rabbit and fell down the rabbit hole. Lewis Carroll wrote in *Alice in Wonderland* that Alice was not very surprised to see a rabbit talking to himself on that hot summer afternoon when she felt sleepy and stupid. But when the rabbit took the watch out of its waistcoat, she followed without thinking and fell into the phantasmagoric wonderland.

She wasn't given any clues or map to follow, but travelers along the path of blossoms on the lower branches can be told the experience of others who have gone before.

There isn't a schedule

Every traveler is held to confronting the issues, but some will be settled early while others linger for years. Perhaps it will be only two weeks before it is comfortable to say a spouse has died, but it may take years to resolve the anger that is felt. Grieving can be brief or prolonged and neither is superior. The real point is whether life is resumed in a healthy, productive way.

Mourning and grieving

Mourning is a time to accomplish the duties of death and openly express sorrow. A mourner is operating within the time period of society's accepted bereavement, handling of business matters and settling the estate. The accepted time for public display is fuzzy but often abruptly comes to an end within a week or month.

The mourner then turns into a griever. Grieving is feeling deep sorrow or distress in a poignant life changing way. Grief does not have a definite end. Mourning and grieving will both be used in the beginning, but as the mourner walks the darkened path, she will find herself alone in grief and that word will be used through the rest of the journey. Grief is an unmarked time when mourning falls away and the story is the griever's alone.

There are continuums and waves

A sea of tears to only enough to water a cactus is a continuum, and it means little to the outcome of the journey if issues are honestly and consciously confronted. Not eating to the point of becoming skin and bones or gaining weight well beyond healthy limits is a continuum, and both extremes show an area the hero needs to confront. Continuums are often referred to when talking of challenges like sensuality, crying and talking. Continuums allow for the variation of human stories and, I believe, they allow a picture of seeing the same motivation can result in different human action. Continuing the example, a sea of tears and no tears come from the same need to heal, but different people use different methods, believing they are doing what is best.

Emotional waves are hallmarks of mourning. They are shattering onslaughts in the beginning, but they can continue as gentle wavelets for the rest of life. Great, perhaps majestic theatrical grief correctly reigns in the beginning. The more emotion that gets out the better, but oddly, it is often kept in check from destroying the mourner by evaporating completely for short periods of time—thus, the wave.

An early mourner may wake up from a distressing dream feeling sad, a few minutes later in the shower there are moments of concentrating on washing that dissolve sadness. When the hero looks in the closet at what to wear, she sees the beloved's hat on the top shelf and bursts into tears, then goes to the refrigerator and calmly notices the need to stop at the grocery store for milk. There are tears all the way to the office, but a quick wipe of the face before leaving the car prepares her to sit at the computer, turn attention to work and genuinely laugh at a co-worker's joke. Off and on, on and off emotions swing in waves through days, weeks and months. The same wave action can hold true of individual problems. The need to be around people versus alone can move up and down the scale with ferocity never felt before.

There is not a specific order

There is a beginning call, but beyond that every story is its own. Internal rhythms of how emotions and issues are confronted will vary tremendously. Some mourners rush headlong into being angry this could happen to their loved one or to them. Others may not feel its strength for a year, while others never feel anger with a boiling intensity.

Elizabeth Kübler Ross defined five stages of recovery, grief therapist Elizabeth Harper Neeld named seven in her book, *Seven Choices*, starting with impact and ending with reconstruction. Psychologist Catherine Sanders listed five from shock to renewal. In academics they sound clear, but experience is a messy journey with one overriding question. When will it be finished?

Everything happens at once

Regaining life is a jumbled process comparable to putting together a thousand piece puzzle. A griever will start without any direction or a single piece of information that helps. Only with time, patience and a willingness to continue do a few puzzle pieces finally come together. There may be a transporting moment while looking at a sunset, or a birth of a new family member, and for that short time we pick up a piece of life and unconsciously link it with another, and maybe six months later with another, until more and more pieces fall into place.

Everything happening at once explains the feeling of being recovered for an hour within the week of death and an hour of feeling newly bereaved ten years later. Grief is not a simple story easily told. It jumps and reflects as a house of mirrors. That is why my story is not told in calendar time. I spent the night with Mother the day of the funeral, but that story isn't told until later because it took years to realize what the experience meant, though its benefit was immediate. I was helped by that night, but I only realized it in retrospect.

Positive for one can be negative for another

Some people are seamless talkers who may say as many words in a day as written in *Moby Dick*. Their counterparts would be horrified to talk that much and would lose their voice in the effort. That's simply the variety of human beings expressing individuality. More important is whether emotion and thought are reaching the griever's brain and heart, not how few or how many words it takes to hear it. Personality differences are to be respected.

Everyone has different problems

Traditional hero Hercules would call them battles. They feel like battles of the heart seeking to overpower sadness, anger and all of life's changes. Emotional ability and desire to redefine life will also be different. Many mourners feel it is necessary to plunge into work that fights the reason for the loved one's death. They join MADD, run consumer campaigns about helmets, rush to form a support group. Others would find all that activity not only self-sacrificing, but a distraction from better ways of healing for them.

There will be problems that are not mentioned in the following pages. By observing, asking and studying, I listed as many as possible, though not all of them were important to me. A very common one is a sudden anger or shift of feeling toward God. Rabbi Harold Kushner had many questions after the death of his son and his struggle resulted in writing *When Bad Things Happen to Good People*. In his search he consulted with others and found, "They had answers to all of their own questions, but no answer for mine." When I read or listened to the hurts and angers of others toward God, I was baffled by their torment and I was relieved my questions of the hereafter were not as agonized. Just as Hercules faced the nine-headed serpent, the beast of death is in front of us, but it looks different to everyone.

Because I believe everyone walks the hero's journey at some point in life, I want to be inclusive in descriptions. Hero is intended to include men and women, but I found it difficult to decide whether to use "he/him" or "she/her" when referring to a person. It felt awkward and exclusionary to rely entirely on either gender, so I compromised by alternating every other sub-chapter.

Myths, religious leaders, fairy tales, academics, literature and biographies overlap

I use examples from many sources. Religious leaders and people who study mythology and folktales have overlapping points with psychologists and psychiatrists. Fiction and biographies show timeless examples of the human struggle of life and the infinite variety of stories that reflect repeating patterns. Scholars and philosophers give drier analysis and morsels of thought that hearts tend to overlook under emotion's sway.

Some sources are mentioned once, others are examples a number of times. It is a purposeful tool to show consistency and variety of what traveling heroes face. In *The Odyssey*, Homer outlined a classic hero's journey, but as Roger Abrahams points out in *African Folktales*, the epic of Mwindo also follows traditions. So do *The Aeneid* by Virgil, *The Wizard of Oz* and the adventures of Harry Potter. Contemporary lives of C.S. Lewis, Nando Parrado, Candy Lightner, Mikal Gilmore and Eli Wiesel have parallels to the hero's journey. The literature of Shakespeare's *Hamlet* and William Styron's fictional Sophie in *Sophie's Choice* show the journey's difficulties and describe why some sufferers never return to a full and good life.

Some stories are true and others are not; some are new, others old. The strength is in the overlapping similarities through time as heroes on journeys of all sorts face and explain living in grief.

A personal storyline

The hero's journey is a template, a menu, capable of changing into infinite variety. What it means is up to the person who lives it, but a hero ends with a story involving learning, grace or peace. Carol S. Pearson writes in *The Hero Within*, "The reward for the hero's inevitably solitary journey, then, is.... At the end of the journey, the hero feels and is at home in the world."

My story is weaved through as an example of returning from deep sorrow to feeling at home in the world. It is a spiritual journey using examples from the adventure of Odysseus, magic of fairy tales, worldwide headlines of Parrado, the tragedy of Hamlet, and stories of established religious beliefs. Their common elements have convinced me that human beings experience life in endlessly different stories that are the same.

My full story is not told. I didn't want to splay myself or anyone around me for others to judge. Nor is it unique, though it easily fits the journey's template as an example of one more life seeking to live well and come to terms. I've told what I wanted or could, which is the definition of any memoir. It is true to my life, but there is always more in any writer's memory, and often a great deal more in the memories of those around the memoirist.

Reading the road signs

All journeys begin with a personal hero's call, which is a definite stop sign. A stop sign alerts a traveler there may be a pedestrian, car, bike, train, truck, bus or scooter coming. The driver's job is to stop, look, listen and proceed with caution. No one needs to tell the experienced driver how to decide to cross the street. Desire to live and experience will guide. Every traveling hero will assess the danger and proceed her way. There is not a single answer or way to dissolve grief. My purpose is to present options and show what others have done, not dictate a strict path unaccommodating to the differences in every searching traveler.

I am a fellow traveler who has made many mistakes. All I can do is present a simple map, one not well marked, but clear enough to point a way. I visited a mythical underworld and for a time refused the call, believing I was continuing well. I lived in the belly of the whale where everything looked the darkest. Finally, I accepted and prepared for the journey, where I faced social and personal demons before experiencing a thoughtful return to a renewed life.

I wish I could call every person who suffers the traumatic loss of a loved one a hero. But that is not a freedom I, or anyone has, when traveling the hero's journey. Heroes emerge from the completion of the the trials, not because they took a first step. What's worse, the trials are difficult, lonely and very hurtful. That was true for Gilgamesh, grief's first hero's journey, and it is true for everyone who has followed. The most I can do is wish you the best on your travels down this darkened path and let you know there is a silent legion of fellow travelers walking beside you.

THE FIRST CHALLENGE

Initiation to the Underworld

Nando Parrado's initiation into the underworld began in 1972 when he woke from unconsciousness after a plane crash in the Andes. Strewn around him amid luggage and airplane parts were a few surviving passengers, rugby teammates, and the dead. Close by were his dying sister and dead mother. Alone on a mountain peak in one of the most isolated ranges on earth, the handful of survivors would endlessly suffer for seventy-two days before reaching help.

In mythology the underworld is a place that resembles hell. In grief the underworld is a state of mental hell. I was thrown into a mental underworld of surreal experiences when told of Jody's death, while knowing I was alive in a three dimensional space that only moments before had felt reliable and clear. It is a temporary, but profoundly mentally shattering experience.

Grief's underworld is a tormenting descent into the self with unpredictable consequences. The experience is so unbelievable, that at first it isn't believed. Days, perhaps weeks after the traumatic death, it is natural and normal to expect the sound of a returning car in the driveway with a loved one easily explaining his absence. A baby's plaintive cry for food or comfort can wake a parent in the night, just as it did before death. Weeks after a funeral it can be momentarily surprising that grandma forgot to invite us to Thanksgiving.

Parrado explains grief's underworld. "[I] was so baffled by the dreamlike strangeness of the place that at first I struggled to convince myself it was real." Grief therapist, Kathleen O'Hara received a call that her college age son was missing with his roommate and blood was found in their rented house. "With every detail, my shock increased. I was shutting down. Terror was forcing my old life out of me, and I felt like I was suspended in the middle, between the world I had known and a shattered, out-of-control universe."

I began shutting down into the underworld while hearing Mother. The August day's topaz sky was turning to darkening evening as I drove the freeway to Mother's house. The setting sun was broken into sharp luminescent swords plunging through threatening clouds coming from the west. When I pulled up to the house on 1300 West, I parked under the linden tree and turned to mindlessly gaze at the small red brick, post WWII house Mother, Jody and I had moved into when I was fifteen and he was ten.

I spent the early years at Wasatch Elementary on South Temple and then Bryant Junior High on First South. During that time, a basement apartment on the top of Fourth South by

Eleventh East gave way to a white Cape Cod two story house by the city cemetery on N Street, built before electrical cords were tucked behind walls. Grandma refused to help with the down payment, so Mother set aside a dollar at a time until she was able to put the several hundred dollars down. A mixture of pride and anger slides across her face when she talks of the fight with her mother and her determination to get a house for her children. Then her shoulders slip a bit and she reluctantly admits it was her father's strong business reputation more than the pittance of a down payment that won her the loan from a local bank.

We lived in the house for five years when Mother decided she wanted a sturdier, newer home with a garage. Jody left fifth grade at Wasatch and I left Tenth at East High, two schools on the "good" side of town. Jody started at Backman Elementary. When I started West High my walks to school changed from passing South Temple mansions with towering, graceful trees to walking in back of the Fairgrounds, along streets of small clapboard houses with crooked chain link fences, under the I-15 freeway and over railroad tracks.

Over fifteen years later it was still a neighborhood bordered by industry. I looked south through trees. Four blocks away were lights of the electrical plant on North Temple, just beyond that I-80 West, stretching past the airport and then through the desert to San Francisco. I opened the car door and went inside. Mother's sister, Aunt Donna, her husband, Dick, their four children, Grandma and Mother had gathered and were writing the obituary. They read it to me and I insisted our four younger cousins be named. The oldest cousin, then eighteen, and Dick were appointed to take the obituary with a photo to the newspaper. The phone rang and Mother picked it up. "Yes, this is Gloria." A few seconds passed and she let out a lonely, tortured cry so long and dark it still occasionally cries its mother's pain through me, waking me in deep night.

"They are holding him for tests." No one said anything. People wandered, talking in quieter tones. Occasionally there was a muffled embarrassed chuckle at an absurdity, a remembrance. Because it happened in a public picnic area, it was reported on television and they wanted to watch the ten o'clock news. Jody had been dead nine hours and I had known for four.

I opened the front door, closed it behind me, and sat alone on the front porch. The light of the moon was bright enough to cast Mother's garden in umber, violet and silver shadows. A sweep of stars in their August path looked so far away and safe, I wished to dissolve into molecules and glide between them. I looked to the garden where spiky cleome arms bobbed gently above the other flowers.

I watched the cleomes. Perhaps the police were on the way. They could come get me, I thought, I was involved in his life and death. I participated. I held responsibility. I was an accessory. The cleomes still moved. The trees did not stir. The stars were silent. Inside the house stiff human voices knocked each other like a rocked bin of nails but I couldn't hear the words through door, screen, brick and window.

That morning my living brother passed the cleomes on his last walk from this childhood home to his car. Did the wind of his strong man body cause them to stir as they did for me as I watched and could see nothing else move? Yes, the police could come get me. I would answer any question they asked if they could make this not real. I would walk to their car to greet them and sit in their car with hands behind my back.

Normal behavior of the bereaved can range from rising beyond the situation and appearing flawlessly in control and capable, to suddenly catatonic and incapable of remembering to bathe or undress for bed. Either extreme or anything in between hides an internal melting. Grief's initiation is not easy.

Gilgamesh suffers inconsolably after the death of his dear friend and best warrior, Enkidu. They emotionally say good-bye during Enkidu's last breaths when he whispers his concern for Gilgamesh before his eyes close for the last time. Gilgamesh plunges into disbelief. "The word Enkidu roamed through every thought like a hungry animal through empty lairs in search of food. The only nourishment he knew was grief, endless in its hidden source yet never ending hunger. In his silence he reached out. To touch the friend whom he had lost."

Grieving Gilgamesh was plummeted without warning. Half-goddess Circe informed Odysseus his visit to the underworld would be a challenge, where among other tasks, he would burn slaughtered bodies of souls of the dead, thus granting them peace.

In The Wizard of Oz, Dorothy's journey begins when she and her dog, Toto, are lifted by a cyclone and carried toward Oz. She did not know where she was going or how she was traveling as they sped to Oz and inadvertently killed the Wicked Witch of the East when the house landed. Without warning, her old world of Kansas was left behind and she was met by the odd-looking, otherworldly Munchkins. In the first printing in April 1900, L. Frank Baum explained his purpose in his introduction. "It aspires to being a modernized fairy tale, in which the wonderment and joy are retained and the heartaches and nightmares are left out." The heartaches and nightmares cannot be left out of grief's journey, but the wonderment and joy of Baum's story are used here to remind the mourner they can be refound.

Underworld First Guards – *Beyond them is darkness*
The time of funeral planning and burial is the house of the underworld's first guards. Campbell calls them custodians who watch the passageway and let the hero through only after passing a test of courage. He writes, "Beyond them is darkness, the unknown and danger ...." Getting past these days is a first test of courage inevitably leading to darkness, the unknown and the danger of grief.

Grieving Gilgamesh wished to travel in the underworld to ask his long dead father the secret of eternal life so he could carry it to his friend, Enkidu.

When he arrived at the mountains of Mashu,

BLOSSOMS OF THE LOWER BRANCHES

Whose peaks reach to the shores of Heaven
And whose roots descend to Hell, he saw
The Scorpion people who guard its gate,
Whose knowledge is awesome, but whose glance is death.

Though frightening, when confronted the underworld first guards let the hero through. The Scorpion man, Utnaphishtim, laughed at Gilgamesh's request, and as he opened the gates he told him there would only be more grief. His wife kindly told Gilgamesh to be careful of the darkness.

The Aeneid, by Virgil, is the story of Aeneas whose warriors lost to Odysseus in Troy. Odysseus returns home as victor while the defeated Aeneas searches for a new home. Aeneas also wishes to visit his father in the underworld and is given instructions by a prophetess. The guardian he must pass is very different than the Scorpion people. It is a sacred tree with leaves of gold and if a bough breaks for him he will be allowed to pass, otherwise he will not.

Funerals and disposal of property gain the mourner entrance to the underworld. There is no escape, turning back or denying work must be done with some consciousness to finish the business of a loved one's life. Through these gates are sometimes horrifying experiences, and always heartbreaking ones that begin the grieving process.

In the otherworldly landscape of Oz, the underworld guardian, the Witch of the North, gives Dorothy directions, presents her with the magical slippers of the Wicked Witch of the East, and gives her a kiss on the forehead that leaves a round, shining mark. With two magical protections she and Toto begin their walk.

Altered Consciousness – *The day of my father's funeral had also been my nineteenth birthday*

"Someday it will be ten years from now," was my first thought on waking the first morning. Mother received a call from the coroner who released her son, my brother, to the funeral home. Arrangements started the night before needed to be finished that day. Sam needed to be in the office. We ran a small graphic arts company where magazine and printing deadlines did not give way to death. After taking Zac to be with friends, I drove to the funeral home to meet Mother and Donna. On the walk inside Donna showed me the clothes they had chosen, including white briefs. I wondered if Donna or I was the most deluded. Without saying so, I doubted the underwear would be put on his now stiff legs and lifted under his hips. There might be an ever-growing pile of underwear reaching to the ceiling of the mortuary brought by relatives still wanting propriety. Underwear and modesty felt ludicrous. Let him be stark, roaring naked before God, me and eternity. It wasn't important.

"Triumphant, triumphant! I want the music triumphant," Mother shrilled, her eyes wide, her body leaning toward the mortician without compromise. He nodded but his head bent and his eyes questioned. We were led down stairs to a basement room where caskets lined the four walls. I stood inside the door, unable to walk, incapable of comparison shopping. All the caskets would be filled, all of them were waiting for people moving, living, breathing in the city around me. I felt suffocated. "This is the first one," the mortician gestured. "Rebecca, what do you think?" Mother looked at me. I nodded. "This is oak with satin," the man pointed, urging us to the next one. "This one," Mother said pointing at the first. "Are you sure?" Donna asked. I couldn't look at the empty caskets and began walking out of the room.

A mile from the mortuary we turned left on N Street and headed north to the city cemetery, passing where we had lived for five years. Our old home was now a parking lot for an apartment building. We drove under the arch leading to the sexton's office. My brother and I had walked past this building when the ground was soggy from melting snow, when flowers planted by widows bloomed, when the earth began cooling until it froze under winter snows, locking skeletons in their place. We had played and lunched among the graves and under the trees. The sexton laid down a map of a block in the northeast corner of the cemetery. It was a far corner Jody and I seldom visited where most of the real estate was still for sale. I think it was me who pointed to an open spot that would give him space to stretch and distance to watch.

We seemed to need familiar chairs and a private quiet. I went home to rest, heavy from the morning's business. We agreed to meet at a restaurant for a late lunch before going to the police station to pick up things the police said were now ours.

I don't remember going home or what I did, but on the way to the downtown restaurant I drove the freeway. "Take her off the road!" "Run her off the freeway!" "Let's get her, too." "Come on, die!" Spritely mischievous voices filled the inside of the car. I felt I was half seeing squat men looking like sailors and pirates, and there was almost, but not quite, a pressure on my arm to move the steering wheel and careen into the median. They danced about, teasing, as in a dream. It felt as if they were trying to convince me, and gain approval of a shrouded male figure in the periphery.

Wouldn't it be great? Two from the same family! Read the papers!" a voice continued. Should I? My mind was motionless, altogether devoid of my history. It felt blank and stilled. They seemed to laugh at me. I held the steering wheel harder and opened the window for air. They flew out, away and above the city, laughing and rolling at an inhuman speed until disappearing to the low northern sky.

After the stop at the police station there was still day left, time that would not leave unlived. We looked at the paper and decided to see a Herbie movie at the Tower Theatre. I remember picking up Zac to go with us and Sam's impervious face as he watched us leave. He didn't like what was going on. Mother, Grandma, Zac and I sat in the theatre surrounded by laughing children who could not sit still. They bounced up and down, making chairs creak, alternately growing tall and sinking in front of us. They stretched to see and slunk to sip their drinks and nudge a neighbor. Energy and muffled laughter surged in the room, and Herbie flew through the sky on the screen, while three women were grounded only by their sounds and the soothing company of their younger blood, Zac. My brain felt clogged and only dimly working. I was in connection with life only through laughter and being with my son.

When Zac and I were home from Herbie, Sam insisted he call my father in Balikpapan, Borneo to tell him of his son's death. Reluctantly, I gave him the number in Jakarta: 373323, operator 1571. I had avoided it. Did I think I could keep it a secret? Perhaps always tell him Jody was just too busy to come to the phone? I felt shame I was the surviving child without the beautiful son.

Our father. The relationship felt as fragile as threads of spun glass. Jody and I did not know him through childhood and we had re-united only three years earlier when he called during a road trip through the west with his wife, Chamsie. We met in a downtown restaurant that evening where he learned he was a grandfather. We had a charming, Southern belle step-mother of Lebanese descent who had been a model in New York and department store clothes buyer in San Francisco. We looked forward to seeing our father once a year though we ran out of conversation in half an hour. We wanted his approval and to be a success in his eyes, but felt incapable of pleasing this larger than life person who easily moved in the world outside Utah, a life I only experienced before age six, and Jody never experienced at all.

The grin that made strangers smile when he said hello, the

broad shoulders that led his walk, the jingling sway of his hips like gypsy bracelets that carried him along sidewalks as people turned to notice. There was an assurance in his near six-foot stance and a stride that perhaps wasn't there when I knew him as a child, but now it was and it resonated in his voice.

During his visits he told us of his early working years as a construction project manager for the Idaho company Morrison and Knudsen, and now he worked for Lummus, a British firm. Much of his career was in Southeast Asia, where he was currently representing U.S. interests in a joint project with the British to build a fertilizer plant in Balikpapin. "When we can, Chamsie and I go to Singapore to visit the dentist and relax," he said, making a trip to the dentist glamorous.

We heard about buying jewelry in Singapore. We looked at his ruby ring in 24 kt gold and all of us held Chamsie's heavy gold bracelets. He wore a light blue custom-made suede jacket by his favorite tailor that fit his tall, over two hundred pound frame. It rustled over his white shirt sounding like brocade over satin. Eager, but overwhelmed to hear his stories and hoping a little glamour dust would fall on us, Jody, Sam, Zac and I settled into silence. How tiny our lives, how provincial and routine. Would his travels, his practical way of dealing with the world have made us stronger, brighter, more able to match his shine? Or was his career a tribute to the loss of us, just as mother's relentless years in a pre-anti-discrimination office had been because of us?

Sam made the call, gave the news and as I listened, I could

tell he would soon be on his way to Salt Lake. The next morning I stopped on my way to the funeral and bought a single red rose surrounded with white baby's breath. I removed the rose from its bouquet and florist tissue and held the long green stem. Jody had given me a red rose surrounded with baby's breath for my birthday eight months earlier.

The funeral home hall was dark after walking in from the Rocky Mountain sun. His name was on a chest high sign written with plastic letters stuck in felted grooves, Joseph Jarman Phillips, II. Named after his father. Phillips. A name Jody and I grew up with and didn't know another person attached to it.

When Jody was a boy Mother and Grandma Spiking argued over changing his last name to Spiking. Mother said the one Phillips we had known was long gone and refused to send money to raise his own children. Our father, Joseph Jarman Phillips, was born to Lois Williams Jarman and Irving William Phillips, who we were told, worked for the power company. After being electrocuted he spent his last years in a coma at a VA hospital until he died when our father was fifteen. What memory I have of Lois is constant movement as she cooked, cleaned, cared for chickens, kept a vegetable garden and nursed her two elderly, near bed-ridden parents.

"On the other hand, Daddy had a respected name," Mother continued her argument with Grandma. Orvin Spiking's Swiss immigrant father died when he was a boy, leaving his mother to raise him and a younger brother. She worked where she could and sent Orvin out to sell. An entrepreneur by necessity, and from the results also by talent, he began by selling flowers door-to-door from his uncle's floral shop. With money he borrowed from grandma's mother he built his own greenhouses. They still stand at 1522 East 3300 South, next door to the house where he and Grandma raised their children. Seeing another opportunity, he built and ran the Spiking Motor Lodge on State Street in the late forties. Shortly before he died both companies were sold, leaving sufficient income from investments that grandma lived comfortably for thirty years, before leaving a nice sum to each of her two daughters. I don't remember the arguments for not changing Jody's name, but it never happened.

The heavy double doors to the room where my brother's body lay were closed. I inhaled and walked in. I had not been told where the bullet struck, and the closed casket was in front of me. Already I regretted agreeing to the choice. I didn't like its color or finish. I took the handle, lifted it and swayed with a dizzying sensation of Jody's arrival between two attending angels. He was reluctant to be there. The angels looked ahead. He felt above and below me. His face was perfect, his body still as an oil painting. He was whole and dressed in a suit. I did not feel for wounds. I tucked the flower deep under his right arm.

"Triumphant! I want the music triumphant," Mother repeated to the organist sitting on her bench. She was silent for a few moments before beginning to play. I don't know what she played, but it was neither triumphant nor heavy with a funeral's slow sadness. Family sat in front. People came. Mother had two speakers. The first was a neighbor who was a minister for a fundamental Christian church who spoke kindly of Jody and talked of God. The second was a minister with a new age church who spoke about love, forgiveness and a timelessness.

Mother, Donna, Grandma and I did not speak as we rode in the black car up N Street, passing our old house. I stared at the asphalt parking lot. Mother looked away. Sam and Zac watched.

I spent that night with Mother. The next morning we were sitting on the back patio when she placed a pineapple muffin on my plate. "Jody ate one Tuesday morning. He was sitting where you are." Her voice had the flat tone of shock. My stomach closed, unable to accept food. I looked down at the golden muffin with twigs of fresh pineapple. "A last supper," I silently reasoned, "I must eat." I took a few bites.

Mother frantically hoped all loose ends could be taken care of before she left the next day for a river rafting trip planned months earlier on Idaho's Snake River. The trip that was planned for pleasure was now a place to flee. So busy there was little time for real grief to intrude, we spent the morning obtaining a death certificate and going to the social security office. In the afternoon we gathered her sleeping bag, packed a few items and talked in monotone voices about what else she needed to take, interspersed with, "I'm sure Jody is all right," and "It was nice of so and so to send flowers."

Late afternoon I went home, where it was quiet and empty. I could almost feel the steady tremor of my father's airplane still over the Pacific Ocean heading to California. Saturday morning I rose early to take Mother to the bus station. We parted warmly with kisses and small assurances that things would be fine. Her cowboy boots clicked on the floor. Her jeans were western and tight, her face resolute.

Father came in later that day. I don't remember picking him up. Perhaps Sam did. I remember very little of the visit. He, Sam, Zac and I sat in the living room making small talk with awkward starts and stops. Jody was barely mentioned, though I remember him saying, "I've never seen anyone hit a golf ball as far as he did." Sam and Zac left the room so we could talk. What little I started to say was hollow and sounded like a midway fortune teller machine with an inserted quarter reciting a most unhappy future. He stopped me, saying he hadn't the heart to hear it. He was here for me he said, looking surprisingly earnest into my eyes. I shrank inside, losing volume, moisture and life. I felt unworthy of sincerity and unprepared. I had nothing to offer back.

I mentally returned to being the child I was at seven when life was disintegrating. Since I seldom yelled or cried in tearful fits, neither of my parents were aware I was capable of feeling utter loss. They were wrapped in their drama and either didn't have enough energy to consider us or they thought our emotions were unripe fruit, a common belief of the times. Surely, they innocently thought, we would never know the difference.

Voices and half-felt visions appeared in air without notice or reason during the next months. When I heard a soft voice distinctly whisper by my side, as though it was a real person, that

BLOSSOMS OF THE LOWER BRANCHES

I should hold things like a piece of wood, my son's shoulder, or a sun warmed rock because they would heal me, it was no less real than hearing Sam and Zac. I looked at the walls in my house during this time and they dissolved into more space than substance. The atoms of the walls flitted before me in whirling stationary orbs of color.

Many people report similar sensations. Visiting angels, bodiless voices, music from nowhere, a touch to the skin when they are alone, smells without origination. Some call it delusion, others are sure it is contact from another dimension. Whatever the cause, it leaves its mark on anyone who experiences it. I respect the experiences though I don't understand them.

When psychologist David Treadway's mother died, he witnessed his sister's encounter with altered consciousness in the underworld. A few days after the funeral he received a call from her roommate. "[S]he hadn't slept or eaten. She had taken off most of her clothes and just paced the floor like a caged animal." When they checked her into a hospital she told the guards, "The Mommie bird is hurt. She needs me. I have to fly to her."

Juxtapositions of time and event feel otherworldly, or cruelly purposeful. James Baldwin writes in *Notes of a Native Son:* "On the 29th of July, in 1943, my father died. On the same day, a few hours later, his last child was born. A few hours after my father's funeral, while he lay in state in the undertaker's chapel, a race riot broke out in Harlem. On the morning of the 3rd of August, we drove my father to the graveyard through a wilderness of smashed plate glass. The day of my father's funeral had also been my nineteenth birthday."

Lost in the desert, Moses hears the voice of God in thunder and sees His face in a burning bush. Alone in a cave meditating, Muhammad feels held so tightly by an angel who wants him to write that he is almost breathless. Altered consciousness may produce more profound results among religious leaders, but the capacity exists in others.

Six days after Jody's death on Monday morning, Father left, Mother was on the Snake River and I went back to work.

Ghosts, Dreams and Voices – *Morpheus' visits*

King Ceyx of Thessaly, Greece was said to be the son of the morning star. He and his wife, Halcyon, were very much in love, but when his brother died it sent him into a tailspin of grief. King Ceyx wanted to consult with the oracle of Apollo for comfort, but he would need to travel by sea. Halcyon begged him not to go because she feared for his life. When he sailed Halcyon was left at the seashore waving good-bye until his ship disappeared in the horizon. At first the waters were calm, but of course, a mighty storm overtook and he and his men perished. After waiting beyond the time of his expected return, Halcyon sent a messenger to ask Somnus, the god of sleep, to send her a dream of Ceyx's fate. Somnus sent Morpheus to assume the dead husband's form and mannerisms in a dream that would tell Halcyon the truth of Ceyx's death.

Dreams are accepted as fact and honorably studied while ghosts and disembodied voices remain debatable. Ghosts and voices stir from a consciousness indistinguishable from imagination, memory and unknown sources. Grief's hero journey is not science, it tracks feelings, emotions, sensations and thinking from a trauma over time. Though science disregards ghosts and voices, if a griever uses these experiences as a guide, they must be addressed.

Ghosts, dreams and voices are time-honored tools of storytellers and artists. It does not matter to a mourner if they can be proved by science when she is suddenly dropped into the realms of their power or imagination. The ghosts, dreams and voices that occur shortly after a death are often described as experiences that verify, inform or assure. Halcyon's dream verified her husband's death, though the reader is told the messenger Morpheus is an impostor. Not all is as it appears. The shadows where dreams, ghosts and voices impress the consciousness are murky, questionable, unreliable and when experienced, feel real.

Shakespeare's *Hamlet* opens with two guards believing they are seeing the ghost of the recently murdered king. Hamlet's friend, Horatio, is told of the ghost but declares it fantasy. He is invited by the guards to be with them at night when it comes. A guard, Bernardo, asks, "Looks it not like the king?" Horatio replies, "Most like: it harrows me with fear and wonder."

Hamlet is told of the ghost and hoping to see his father, he also waits and then follows the beckoning figure. The ghost says, "I am thy father's spirit; doomed for a certain term to walk the night, and for the day confined to fast in fires, till the foul crimes done in my days of nature are burnt and purged away." The power of belief in the ghost sends Hamlet on a headlong journey of revenge.

My mother-in-law was again in the hospital a few weeks after Jody's death. Sam's sister, Linda, gave me the room number and warned a nurse might stop me if it wasn't visiting hours. I walked quickly and with purpose to find her room, 534C-L. Her head faced away and thin strands of dyed brown hair no longer hid the grey.

I sat facing her. Her eyes were open and I whispered, "How are you?"

"I'm fine. How are you, Beeckie?" Always she said my name with a long e of Spanish.

"I'm fine," both of us were clearly lying. Liquid dripped from a tube, entering her blood. Beside the bed was a urine bag. All life, I thought, enters, circulates and leaves. The end.

Suddenly a sheepish, confidential giggle lit her eyes, making her look thirty years younger, "Please tell the party in the next room to settle down. I can't get any rest. They keep coming through my room, the nurses, to get to the party."

I glanced around the room. I also was seeing the wall as vulnerably soluble in back of a slowly breathing roommate, "Yes, I'll tell them."

"Thank you, Beeckie," she grasped my hand and tried sitting up, but was powerless so she used the burning bronze of her eyes to keep my attention. "I saw Jody last night. 'Jody, you've made it back,' I said. 'Yes,' he said, 'I've made it back,' but when I turned to tell Manuel and Steve he was gone."

Strong drugs were easing her pain, so I knew she was vulnerable to delusion. I had stopped questioning whether the sensations and images I had been experiencing existed in everyday reality because I knew for others they did not. I had lost connection with the reality of my adulthood.

I saw the phantasm of Jody above the coffin and heard voices, but the only time I had a sensation of him was several weeks later. Alone in the car running errands for work, I looked to the passenger side and saw him. I burst into tears and the feeling vanished as I pulled to the side of the road to regain composure. During the first months, the more common feeling was confusion and hearing conversations that weren't real. They had to do with Jody and seemed to be swirling in a dangerous unworldly dimension.

Therapist and researcher Catherine M. Sanders calls momentary sight of the dead "flicker phenomenon." She describes it as a shadow often seen to the side that, when sight is moved to the area, flickers away. In her book *Surviving Grief*, she describes her comforting first-hand experience after her mother died. It seems related to seeing out of the corner of one's eye.

The morning after Jody's death, Zac, looking as surprised by his words as Sam and I were, announced Jody had visited him during the night. He had touched him on the shoulder to wake him and asked how people were doing. Zac watched as he slowly paced at the foot of his bed and answered he thought they would be fine. He then faded and Zac resumed a normal sleep.

The night of her daughter's death, Candy Lightner lay down next to her surviving daughter. While the daughter slept, Lightner saw the daughter who had died only hours before. "She was wearing shorty pajamas and had a look that was literally ageless. She silently communicated to me that she was okay."

In *Will the Circle be Unbroken*, social historian Studs Terkel interviewed Haskell Wexler, winner of two Academy Awards during a career as cinematographer that included *One Flew Over the Cuckoo's Nest*. After Wexler's brother passed away he began experiencing his presence. He wondered what was going on, but decided he enjoyed feeling his brother's company so much that, "Fuck it, let it happen."

Mikal Gilmore is the younger brother of Gary Gilmore, who was executed for murder in 1977. Norman Mailer won the Pulitzer Prize for *The Executioner's Song* about the murders, but it is Mikal's memoir, *Shot in the Heart*, that holds the heartbreak, devastation and answerless questions that can live forever with survivors of the perpetrators of tragedy. He describes a frightening apparition of a woman in white holding him down to his bed, kissing his ear and whispering, "I know you. You're the last one. I've taken everything from all of them, and now I've come for you."

In time, my dreams lost some horror and followed a pattern with variation. I am a teenager (or in my 20s or 30s), returning from a trip with luggage (or naked) and while standing at an intersection (or airport, boat dock or bus terminal), I need to decide whether to go to Sam and Zac or check on Mother and

Jody. I start toward Sam and Zac, then feeling dread, retrace to Mother's house. She is busy (washing dishes, vacuuming, reading) and Jody is sitting behind her. He looks at me with an expression so penetrating, I sometimes wake. Other times I talk to him and take him to his basement room where I tell him I love him and how good he was. Mother follows us down but leaves. His room is neat, clean, full of mementos (or scattered and dirty) and he looks amused (bored or sad) with me. I talk but he never answers. I see the moon through a window and skulls lying about on crusted snow.

Written down dreams lose some dread. The playing out of emotions, the venting through sleep, the touching of deepest hurts and fears are their power. Most people have a handful of deeply affecting dream memories. The oversized visual or emotional memories can be uncomfortable enough that the idea of keeping a dream journal is frightening. I found reducing the memory to ink on paper is instructive and freeing. Awareness of dreams has made me stronger and a bit more integrated and calm.

There are hundreds of books on dream interpretation, but most writers agree dreamers have personal symbols and inner knowledge of value. In his 1996 book, *Conscious Dreaming*, Robert Moss wrote that dreams are the property of the dreamer who is the final authority on meaning. Carl Jung believed in universal symbols, but the dreamer should also be consulted for personal validation. Nathaniel Hawthorne often used dreams as wells of inspiration, but he thought they are only one more way of being aware of the waking world and they could be unconscious self-deception.

I have respected dreams since I was twelve. Mother had a boyfriend she met not long after her divorce and they were together over twenty years. He was good-looking and respected in his profession. He did not care for Jody and me and endured our company on few occasions. Mother and he spent time together on dates, through weekends and on vacations when Jody and I could stay with Grandma, or later alone. Never physically cruel, he had a killing look and around us, an icy demeanor and often subtly cruel words. But, I saw he was affectionate with his daughters, the people he worked with, and his dog. I will call him Nameless. It is not respect, lack of it or fear that keeps me from naming him. It is the belief that eventually hurts and angers must be laid down in the interest of deeper meaning, learning and sometimes, forgiveness. Nothing is gained by continuing hurt, and I do not wish him harm, but I will not grant him access.

I dreamed I put money into a vending machine and pushed the button for a drink, but when I reached for it, it was a handgun. Methodically, deliberately, I turned, took aim and shot Nameless dead. Shocking at the time, I kept reviewing it, because it made me question myself. This was my first encounter with conscious, deep, abiding anger. Years later I also realized he had rejected me as surely as my father, plus permanently stepped between Mother and me and I felt powerless to do anything about it. I accepted the dream as a wish to rid him from us.

Many cultures would be baffled by our society's common fear or lack of interest in dreams. Southwestern Native Americans, the Iroquois, and Australian Aboriginals are a few who believe dreams should be respected and used in life. Looking at, discussing and accepting dreams diminish their power or positively re-directs them. Kept in the privacy of one head without the benefit of another's ear, or at least the friendship of ink on paper, magnifies nightmare qualities. Because they are so intimately intriguing and full of personal riddles, I respect what Carlos Castaneda wrote don Juan told him in *The Art of Dreaming*. "[I]f dreaming is overemphasized, it becomes what it was for the old sorcerers: a source of inexhaustible indulging." Over attention and no attention of the dream continuum can stall recovery.

Voices are curious. It is difficult to know where they come from. They could be a memory of the person, similar to remembering a detail like the texture of hair. Muhammad was said to have grieved deeply when his wife Khadija died, and the awareness of her voice would return him to temporary melancholy.

C.S. Lewis wrote *A Grief Observed* when his beloved wife passed away. He describes his experience of hearing a chuckle beside him in the dark, but acknowledges this sound may not be real. "I'm not mad enough to take such an experience as evidence of anything. Just an impression of her mind momentarily facing my own."

The inner voice is sometimes portrayed as an impish devil

that leaps to action by sitting on the shoulder during temptation. Occasionally, my experience feels so forceful that the voice could be residing in a bachelor apartment behind an earlobe where it gives directives, arguments and sentimental comforts. "Don't you remember how his hair felt?" "How his voice sounded?" "How he called you his little sister?"

There isn't a single belief about dreams, ghosts and voices. Experiences range from horrors to lasting comfort. Frequency, intensity and horror lessen through time, and I believe, they fade further as grief is faced and settled.

Sensuality – *Making love, the supreme remedy for anguish*

Last Tango in Paris, starring Marlon Brando, was billed as a romantic sensual movie. I didn't expect to cry as he began a sexual encounter. His wife had taken her life and the movie is about the first days after her death. I recognized his poignant desperate pitching between life and death.

Within a day of burying his mother, Albert Camus' protagonist, Meursault, in *The Stranger* begins an affair. Europeans are not afraid to openly say, write or portray it in movies. Death and sensuality are intertwined. Death creates an odd abandonment of routine use of the senses. Growing from the seed of altered consciousness, inner numbing of usual routines can create very different responses.

Literature is a window to look through that is able to put words to our deepest feelings while it protects us from having to admit we are anything like the characters we are reading about.

Blossoms of the Lower Branches

William Styron's popular book, *Sophie's Choice,* invites awareness with an unexpectedly stark description. The narrator, Stingo, tells of Sophie, a Polish Christian survivor of Hitler's death camps. She has lost her family in the war and is trying to start a new life in New York with her lover, Nathan. "Sophie's lust was as boundless as my own ... [B]ut it was also both a plunge into carnal oblivion and a flight from memory and grief."

Isadora Duncan was a flamboyant personality credited with being the founder of modern dance. Her two young children, Deirdre and Patrick, died in an automobile accident and within weeks her need to break the crush of death and feel life overcame her. While walking along a beach crying, a man approached and asked if he could help. "Yes," I replied, "Save me—save more than my life—my reason. Give me a child." She described the lovemaking as saving her and bringing her a step back to life.

Writer Toby Talbot writes of losing her mother with, "How to soften the pain of upheaval. Making love, the supreme remedy for anguish: To make love is to plunge into the world prior to birth, prior to the greatest separation. To unite and reunite, to generate birth and be reborn. It is to find again that deep slowness, that wordless rhythm, that tidal dissolve."

The underpinning of my desire was a primal need to assert life and verify my body could feel. Years later, after regaining a sense of humor, I believed my less literary experiences were a desperation to pee on the boundaries of life and scream at death to get away. Operating more on automatic than arousal to a specific, I had the sensation of giving death a blow by asserting sensuousness. With Sam I was alternately feverish and icy as I re-learned life and feeling.

Sensuality is also eating, exercise or burying oneself in art and music. They give proof of the body's ability to survive and enjoy. In the primal part of the brain where fight or flight originates, there is resistance to a power as strong, as shocking as death. Fight or flight resists shock to defend the body. News of the death of a loved one triggers the primal response, causing explosions of anger, tantrums or feelings of desperate hungering need of sex, food, drink or drugs, anything to feel the body.

Hearing music as never before was a sensual prod. Stretches within pieces arrested me. Classical, opera, jazz, blues, rock, all had notes, timbres, sounds I didn't understand as a musician, but I felt so deeply I almost believed the notes were fine thin silver hammers striking cells of unquestioned thinking that needed cracking and new air. Notes struck from the top of my head straight down and out my vagina and I loosened, melted, evaporated into walls and space. They left shards of awareness that hurt and I needed to stop making dinner, driving, or whatever I was doing and rest before I continued.

Nature jumped in front of me for attention. The coursing veined life of leaves on trees with light dancing through them flirted as I drove to work. Flower gardens waved, their colors sensuous patches simultaneously nourishing and emptying me and I didn't know how or why. Stout strong bushes leaned my way in nonexistent breezes to encourage me.

I noticed the perfection and fragility of the faces of the people I love as though seen for the first time. I recall the detail of my son's nine-year-old lightly freckled face at that time with its thick rows of dark lashes that quivered when I kissed his forehead. His breath was a gift, a tenuous blessing that made his sun brown skin smelling of dirt and sweat alive.

In the office, the sterile unmoving air of daily work was gagging. The telephone was an affront, the ring too loud, human voices remote and trivial. Perhaps because they were drummed out by the strong, sometimes guiding, sometimes threatening voices and feelings within.

Healthy, protective sensuality is at one end of grief's continuum. At the other end is questionable indulgence. Odysseus was the victor and Aeneas was the loser of Troy, but after battle they both rested for a time in sensual comforts. Circe recognized Odysseus' weariness from battle, his suffering, and that he was "not in tune with good cheer." Odysseus accepted her offer to stay and rest with her.

Dido, princess of Carthage, was smitten with Aeneas when he asked her for provisions and rest for his men. Ruinous and unhealthy relationships are easy to slip into. Dido did not realize her place in Aeneas' suffering heart. When they made love for the first time they retreated to a cave during a rainstorm and Virgil describe it as, "Lightning fires flash, the upper air is witness to their mating, and from the highest hilltops shout the nymphs. That day was her first day of death and ruin. For neither how things seem nor how they are deemed moves Dido now, and she no longer thinks of furtive love. For Dido called it marriage." It is not always the mourner left to suffer at the end of a relationship started from the depths of grief.

My unhealthy indulgence was wine. Drinking was a pleasure that never removed me from grieving, but relaxed my brain and heart to allow more painful thoughts and miseries than when I didn't drink. Liquor plunged me deeper for answers, comfort and reasoning because it allowed daily conscious and self-protecting habits to doze. More relaxed, I could probe, remember and return to sobriety with new bits that helped recovery. In a way I still don't understand, explain or defend, I felt a heightened sense of lucidity about managing grief. During that early time daily life and work felt like sleep and drink and sleep felt awake.

Some scholars maintain the relaxing ability of wine that promotes new thought was Dionysus' purpose in beginning the cult of wine and pleasure. David Adams Leeming writes: "His struggles with unbelievers were struggles to bring life to all peoples. This was the agon—the struggle between priest and unbeliever, actor and audience, to discover the truth of life however ecstatic, however painful."

Drinking, drugs, prescription or otherwise, or dangerous sex are not recommended to treat grief. At best they are temporary, and at worst they get out of hand. Eating, overworking or exercise also have healthy limits. None are suggestions to follow, but it is important to realize the magnetic pull there is to feel or not feel one's own body at the time of a dearly loved one's death. The need to feel and regain control can sweep through and feel so necessary that it's not until limits are broken that the second tier of damage is realized to ourselves or others.

More than the body, it is the mind that must settle grief. The body unquestionably wants to survive and regain equilibrium quickly. It reacts with knee jerk response by releasing huge fight and flight emotions. The body has a sensual rage to keep us alive and the victor over death.

Excessive denial of sensuous pleasure is a challenge at the other end of grief's continuum and it is riddled with the choice of the right to die. My taste buds temporarily closed down and I had zero interest in food. I maintained ninety pounds for years without effort, but being short and small I didn't look as hungry as it sounds. Only Mother eventually said I needed to eat more.

For many people sex is suddenly a least desired pleasure and if it is the lover who died, it may also feel unavailable or wrong. Returning to sex can be problematic. As with so many issues to be named, there is a need to see through the misty shadows of grief well enough to allow a good life to continue. During time in the underworld a good life can feel forever gone.

Consciously or unconsciously one of three choices will be made. Some people will fall into addiction and excess of any chosen indulgence. Others will emotionally retreat, refuse to feel too deeply and try to go on with life as though little has changed. That is the preference of U.S. society. Under the intriguing title of *The Pornography of Death*, Geoffrey Gorer argues death has become more taboo than sex. He explains everyone's discomfort and a griever's need to pretend everything is just fine. The first two choices will keep issues secretly hidden away, while some wounds heal and others quietly fester.

The third choice is to walk forward as wide-eyed as Dorothy did on the yellow brick road and treat the sensual experiences, along with all issues that leap in front of us as worthy of attention, thought and good decisions. Changed sensuality is often a task requiring deeper probing for suffering mourners during the long walk through the lower branches of grief.

Edward Abbey wrote *Desert Solitaire* during a summer as a park ranger in Utah's Arches National Monument. He was part of a search party for a missing man who was an amateur photographer and unfamiliar with life in the desert. After they found his body under a juniper tree and were carrying him out, Abbey considered the death. "Thus we meditate upon the stranger's death. Since he was unknown to any of us we joke about his fate, as is only natural and wholesome under the circumstances. If he'd meant anything to us maybe we could mourn. If we had loved him we would sing, dance, drink, build a stupendous bonfire, find women, make love—for under the shadow of death what can be wiser than love, to make love, to make children?—and celebrate his transfiguration from flesh to fantasy in a style proper and fitting, with fun for all at the funeral."

Premonitions – *To play my appointed part*

Premonitions feel like whispered warnings that could have

changed everything. Time spent in the underworld remembering them is dark and confusing. Premonitions are for religious prophets, overwrought zealous missionaries, myths, folklore and entertainment. It is easy to disregard the Aztec belief in Acpaxapo, a serpent living in water that periodically lifted its body with the face of a woman to foretell events. The Greek Delphic Oracle that induced revelations is a mythical storytelling technique. The snake at the zoo that winked at Harry Potter is dismissed as entertainment.

Premonitions are unscientific, fanciful and to western thinking, weaken or remove the power of self-determination. They are not clear, easy to categorize, define or settle. Master magician, Merlin, managed Arthur's education and preparation for kingship, but he could not stop the destiny he foresaw. "[King Arthur] gave Lancelot the honor of journeying in the King's name to bring back his bride from her father's Hall. Lancelot was the King's true man. But neither the King nor Lancelot himself could foresee the consequences of this task. I saw what was to come, but nevertheless had to play my appointed part …."

Premonitions gave me a mental picture of two sharply pointed swords together twisting skin at a single point to cause painful damage. One point is the accusation that I could have prevented Jody's death and all the pain it meant if I had acted sooner, making premonitions a tool I failed to use. The other sword point is there was never anything to be done, everything was inevitable and no one could prevent it. That is suggested in II Timothy 1:8-9 in the Bible. "…the power of God; Who hath saved us, and called us with an holy calling, not according to our works, but according to his own purpose and grace, which was given us in Christ Jesus before the world began."

From this view, a premonition could be a gift of whispered warning to shatter the human illusion of control. The Norse Three Fates, sisters Urd, Verdandi and Skuld, endlessly spun the life's fate of all people. It was believed the sisters did not weave from their wishes for humans. Instead they were "blindly, as if reluctantly executing the wishes of the eternal law of the universe, an older and superior power, who apparently had neither beginning nor end."

"I was watching Jody play," Mother told me, "and suddenly I felt directly told he would be taken from me as a young man. I would no longer have him." Jody was still a young bright smiling boy when she had this flash. She fought the idea, squirmed against it, but the memory never left. Perhaps such flashes are part of the force of love and connection to the mystical so deep and unconscious that we are blind to our own depth.

Mikal Gilmore writes of finding his mother staring at a mountain. "It is a proud and isolated thing, like Bessie Brown herself. 'Is that your mountain?' I asked. 'Yes, that's my mountain. I've been talking to it. I know how to hear the things it says, and this morning it is telling me that my father is not going to live.'"

In the last months of Jody's life, I often woke feeling caught in dark fearful dreams I purposely shook away. A dark robed man was on either side of me. They were rapt, watching what was before us, yet aware of what I did. I would sink beside their skirts, sickened by the scene in front of me. Whenever I looked away the man on the right poked my chin to look again. I could not stand on my feet, but I never fell from a powerless crouching half suspension. Dream movement was through a wavy substance similar to paint strokes in Edvard Munch's The Scream. Jody did feel a part of it and in flickering half memories so were Zac, Sam, Mother and others I didn't recognize. It felt like I was witnessing a panoramic horror without power to stop it. I partially connected it to Jody's difficulties at the time so dismissed it as a worry dream. The shadow hung over my days, and for months before his death I was unaccountably, near unconsciously, aware of a blackness, a horror laying a veil that choked tighter the more I kicked against it. My lack of insight to turn the dream to a useful tool is a regret, but I don't know if it should be.

A Greek myth is told of Old Mother Earth who is asked by her son-in-law, Zeus, to produce a beguiling flower. Unaware the flower she created would bring destruction to her daughter, Demeter, and granddaughter, Persephone, she created the narcissus. In *Gods, Heroes and Men of Ancient Greece*, W.H.D. Rouse describes the flower: "... one hundred blooms upon one stalk, that smelt so sweetly that heaven and earth and sea laughed for joy." Beautiful Persephone was attracted to the flower and when she picked it Hades, lord of the underworld, appeared and claimed her as his bride as he was promised by Zeus. Stricken with grief at the disappearance of her daughter,

Demeter is plunged into grief unaware of Zeus' part.

The morning of Jody's death I woke without the heaviness of forcing myself out of the dream. I felt peaceful, clear and happy to be alive. I felt lighter, without burden and with hope. It was weeks before I realized the witnessing dreams had fallen away.

Today, April 2, is Jody's birthday. Early spring can have any weather. This year it is wet and dark. Clouds hang low, snow that unexpectedly brought four inches fell two nights ago. Disappearing mounds of shoveled snow line sidewalks, roofs are clear at the peaks with white sliding blankets dripping at low edge. Streets are clear but wet from the gentle rain now falling and melting snow on lawns. Tulips are coming up but blooms are not close. Hairy finger buds are at the branch tips of aspens. Only a willow tree has the fuzzy green of a promised spring.

His last birthday was early spring bright with Easter egg blue sky, lemon yellow daffodils, peppermint green candy lawn. Bare tree branches appeared to twist and reach to each other forming a basket to hold earth's symbols of renewed life. That April I was squelching nightmares, unable to see what I was witnessing in sleep reflected in my brother's eyes, smells and posture as he sat on Grandma's couch receiving presents.

Premonitions hold a charge of awareness at a level difficult to read. Greek King Croesus received a Delphic Oracle that if he crossed the Halys River he would defeat a great kingdom. Only upon his defeat by the Persians does he learn the defeat is suffered by his own kingdom.

Many people who will soon die from an unexpected death

spontaneously take care of surprising details. Less than two weeks before a friend accidentally drowned in a raging spring's mountain runoff with his wife, he asked his sister to watch the children if anything happened to them. Another story in the local newspaper tells of a healthy, happy young woman on a family vacation. She makes a friend promise to tell her parents how she wants to be buried. The next day the friends are in a car with the girl's brother and there is a tragic car accident. The brother and sister both pass away, leaving only the friend to tell the stricken parents their daughter's request.

In *Man and His Symbols*, Carl Jung writes about dreams, premonitions and their many enigmas and contradictions of approaching death. "Experience shows that the unknown approach of death casts an adumbriato (an anticipatory shadow) over the life and dreams of the victim."

Within three hours of last talking with Jody and three hours before his death, a friend of Sam's called and invited us to meet for drinks on Thursday. Without thinking, I cheerfully responded, "Sorry, but I have other plans." Immediately, I wondered where my excuse came from because it felt genuine and was not meant as an excuse. I so confused myself, I told him I couldn't remember what the plans were at the moment but I knew I had committed to something. After the phone call I looked at the calendar but there was nothing planned for the day of the funeral. The lower branches line a dark twisted path through the obscured inner self.

Relief of Death – *But oh, God, tenderly, tenderly*

"I know there are not only tears to be dried but stains to be scoured.... But oh, God, tenderly, tenderly. Already, month by month and week by week you broke her body on the wheel whilst she still wore it. Is it not yet enough?" C.S. Lewis felt great pain watching his wife die of cancer, yet death's relief was of little comfort.

Over five years we watched the slow decline of Sam's mother, Lupe, with great hope when she was in remission after rounds of chemotherapy. For two years she held her own, but over time there was a steady loss of strength and softening of her resolve into quiet bearing of pain. The battle was wearing, her victories shorter.

Our first Thanksgiving without Jody was the last with Lupe. It was at her house with twenty people running here and there. A long table was set up in the living room and she was wheeled in on a rented bed on which she neither laid flat nor sat up; a frightful midway ride where one quick spin would send her round and round and round.

Still in her bedclothes, Lupe was placed by the table where she tried to not writhe in pain. The smell of medicines and illness mixed with turkey and cranberries. Television football games competed with loud voices calling for food and making jokes. No one acknowledged the pain of the woman at the head of the table and that seemed best.

For a time she lived with Sam's older brother Manuel and his wife, Marlene. Before Christmas Marlene could no longer lift her and her needs were too great to ever be left alone, so Lupe moved into a nursing home. An attempt at constant vigils was made, people didn't want her to be alone, but even with close to a dozen adults who loved her that was difficult.

Traditionally, Lupe gave a grandchildren's New Year's Eve party so adults could go out. Zac affectionately remembers the late nights with excited cousins when Chinese food was delivered before midnight. On this last New Year's, Sam decided to pick-up Chinese food and take it to his mother. As the three of us ordered it I had misgivings. Was it wise to flaunt good times in front of a dying woman? Was it absurd to approach normality in that stale nursing home setting of iron beds and sick people who may not know it was New Year's?

Our footsteps rang down the darkened hall at 9:00 p.m. It was so quiet it could have been 4:00 a.m. I looked in rooms and saw figures lying down and turned away, neglected and neglecting. There was no celebration here, only determined refusal or listless surrender. Ham fried rice, shrimp and chow mien mixed with the smell of urine, floor cleaner, age and death.

Lupe was propped in her bed, still in the day's half elevated position. She was surprised and pleased to see us, and excited to see the food. It was a good idea, a faint recalling of happier times, a symbolic salute to her life on this particular night of the year that showed her son remembered and that we were grateful for her history. She was not angry, bitter or hurt. She said she was happy to have met the goal of seeing in the new year.

I looked at Zachary having to say another good-bye in his

young life. Aware his parents could not overcome the deaths of others, he quietly accepted this last Chinese meal on his grandmother's deathbed. And what was Sam thinking as he saw his mother wasting away? She had always been the center of strength in his family. Slow deaths provide time for sincere understanding, true good-byes and heartfelt acknowledgement, though it is not less painful, nor is the loss of the person less important.

On May 5, Lupe left her body rigid and at last, without pain. Her five children gathered around her in the nursing home. Sam said the feeling of that moment was encompassing. Transporting. A moment he has hidden away and treasured, bringing it out to feel on only the most special of times.

The speakers had level voices at her funeral. They marveled at her ability to withstand the last years of pain. There was an occasional sniffle and a solemn air, but not a desperate clutch of passion or deep gasps in handkerchiefs. Shock did not stiffen mourners' eyes and the sweet clinging smell of gladiolas did not sicken the room. It was still a difficult good-bye. Final partings with people we care about always are. The day was endured, the motions accomplished, but the final acceptance was only one step along.

A month later, French wine freely poured from endless bottles to all desiring passengers aboard the Mexicana flight out of Denver. I enjoyed it completely, knowing exactly where the pleasant warm feeling could be found and maintained. Excitement pushed from my center to the skin, making it tingle.

I felt I would explode. There was wonderful life still!

Sam and I had booked the trip to Mexico City and Puerto Vallarta almost a year in advance. At last we were following the earth's curve, flying so high that mountains we could not climb looked miniature and insignificant. I remembered the words of a forgotten philosopher in a college textbook, "If I don't see it, how can I believe it exists?"

I paused, fingered the book, feeling the texture of the cloth cover and laid it down. Was someone really so self-assured, so self-important to believe only what he could personally verify existed? That the universe was only the small room of personal sight? How pompous to feel the world, all that was sensually touching, was personal imagination to entertain the self. Life could be handled with impunity, disregard, detachment, as an amusement.

"Suicidal souls are exhausting and emotionally draining to all who get near them. And I think, at a certain point, even those who love them completely just say, in deeds if not in words: So fine, blow your brains out. They don't expect it to happen. [I]t is also because of the large nature of the mental illness that the people close to them were as likely to feel resentful, exhausted, used, abused and angry by the end—and too far away and alienated to come running to the rescue that one last time." This quote is in *Bitch, In Praise of Difficult Women* by Elizabeth Wurtzel.

It seems beyond random chance I so often pick up a book or go to a movie for entertainment and find myself wrenched back into suicide and death. I expected to read about stand-up women shining in intelligence, sexuality and bravery. I didn't expect to read about craziness I recognized. But I understood it, and after reading about Courtney Love, Anne Sexton, Sylvia Plath, Margeaux Hemingway and Zelda Fitzgerald, I wondered. Had I been waiting?

Yes, there was more I could have done. I remember in detail the last time I saw him, the last time I talked to him on the phone. I regret I wasn't more aware and didn't do very much. But, I have faith in the goodness of a universe I do not understand. I also believe there was a pivotal time when Jody's life story entered its final path beyond my understanding, perhaps beyond his control. I wasn't relieved he died. I was relieved his suffering was over.

Linda Gray Sexton, daughter of poet Anne Sexton writes of her dramatic, creative and difficult mother in *Searching for Mercy Street.* She was called by school administrators to come as soon as possible, and during her walk she thought of her family. When told of her mother's suicide, her reaction was, "Thank you for not making it Joy, Daddy or Nana. I laughed, one short despairing beat. On October fourth my mother killed herself. Suddenly my childhood nightmare had a name and a date. It was reality—not just some wolf under bed."

Death stops the loved one's sadness and anger, ending the relentless suffering we have been unable to help. For them as well as for us. Death ends a drama and leaves quiet if not peace.

Robert Frost's family is one of the literary world's very

tragic stories. His grandfather, father and several of his children suffered mental illness. On his son Carol's wedding night his bride, Lillian, recalled he "announced to her that now his experience was complete, his life fulfilled, so he might as well kill himself." The marriage lasted seventeen years until a night when Lillian was in the hospital for a hysterectomy and Carol Frost woke his son, Prescott, and told him he was going to kill himself. Having heard this many times before, he went back to sleep. His father's one gunshot from the kitchen woke him.

The death of those with suffering minds is not always apparent suicide. Repeatedly self-destructive people too often curl their lives around alcohol, drugs and other dangerous habits. Deaths from automobile accidents, overdoses, fights and baiting police are often caused by people who do not pull the trigger, but they set the stage.

The days in Mexico City after Lupe's death were a sensuous wonderland and I was overcome by smells, textures, voices speaking in melodies, statues, boulevards, pulsating flowers, small dark Indians seeming to float as ghosts around sophisticated and urbane men and women in European fashion. It reignited early childhood excitement of lights, people and adventure, as fulfilling a drink as the wine. The last night in Mexico City we had dinner at a café a few blocks from the hotel. Sam began drinking an amount of gin that was enough to begin drowning sorrow, making us a toddly couple walking back to the hotel. He fell on the bed mumbling, rolling, first in a restless, then comatose sleep.

I sat in a green upholstered French provincial chair and looked out the corner windows, viewing two sides of Mexico City. The remote quiet of the high hotel room, excitement of twinkling city lights following to the horizon, all were far promises I remembered from a night before I had a little brother. My parents followed a woman around a vacant house to rent as I looked out the kitchen window, across dark fields and roads to Los Angeles lights. I danced in the kitchen, twirling and turning on every light and then turning them off when I couldn't see city lights. I pretended it was New York and just over there was the Plaza Hotel where Eloise lived from the Kay Thompson book. We didn't move there, but I kept the vacant house's ghost.

The fantasy of rejoining twinkling lights below a home in an isolated dark neighborhood that was quietly, fully and freely mine to dance in gathered in a dense compacted center. Lost to awareness, the memory was loosened with music's silver hammer, French wine and Mexico City. Now, watching lights stretching to the mountains, I knew the world was as foreboding as I imagined only Salt Lake to be. The choice was mine to play a minor character in a Hemingway novel by leaving everything behind and becoming a barmaid in Martinque where I would never speak of my history again, but I knew I wouldn't. There was no escape by merely changing surroundings. In deeper awareness, I began that night to transfer the bright lights beyond darkness to my son's life. No matter the unhappiness or bitterness I sometimes felt, there was not going to be any shortcuts or escapes from the small city and its people who held my life by its ankle with Sam and Zac.

This was the moment I walked beyond the halfway mark of the underworld.

In Puerto Vallarta a permeating rush of earthiness was in every breath. Silently and individually, Sam and I agreed to put aside our unhappiness and begin a real vacation. We spent hours on the beach, walking, shopping, driving, dancing, eating, loving. The flowering trees were succor, the music, colors and air a seductive call.

The plane lowered into Salt Lake, sucking me back. I wondered if waiting thought patterns hovered above cities, like lingering demons attaching themselves to unsuspecting travelers. The familiar mountains and valley glared from the ground as I glared at them from the window. The tie to Salt Lake on that third Tuesday morning in June was my son. Seeing his hair, touching his thin boy shoulders was validation there was good in me because Zac and Sam were still part of my life.

God's Place – *A hard-hearted lot you are, you gods*

It is easy to feel deserted. Life was operating with understood rules and liberties. Belief and faith learned, modified and solidified since childhood gave it meaning. When a loved one is ripped away it upsets structure and comfort, leaving mourners shaken to the core. Beliefs that gave solace and predictability evaporate into a chaotic and frightening underworld. God can suddenly feel as unreliable as a trickster. C.S. Lewis wrote of his wife's illness, "Step by step we were 'led up the garden path.' Time after time when He seemed most gracious He was really preparing the next torture."

In a 1963 interview Elie Wiesel said, "I have been digging in the history of religions ever since. Sometimes, I still go to the synagogue—with my teeth clenched, for I cannot help but indict God." Poet Sylvia Plath's father died when she was eight and her mother reported she announced, "I'll never speak to God again."

There is often one of three reactions. God can be (or is) cruel. God carried me through it, or God had nothing to do with it. People often feel unfairly abandoned by God as Lewis, Wiesel and Plath did, and it happens in myths as well. Odysseus was caught in a storm and almost swallowed by the sea's tempest as he headed toward Calypso's Island, "What clouds are these that Zeus has brought over the broad heavens! How he has stirred up the deep, how all the winds come sweeping upon me! Now my destruction is a safe thing!" When Calypso falls in love with Odysseus, but cannot keep him, she doesn't feel abandoned, she feels mistreated, "A hard-hearted lot you are, you gods …."

Mortician June Knights Nadle wrote in *Mortician Diaries* that a common reaction of her clients is to ask why God would take their loved one. In the book *Dead Reckoning* grief therapist Daniel Treadway admits, "I imagined myself saying directly to God, 'Why the hell did you let my mother die? She turned to you for help, you son of a bitch.'" Gordon Livingston, also a grief therapist, had two sons die. In his concise book *Too Soon Old,*

Too Late Smart, he writes, "I have forsaken my belief in an orderly universe and a just God." Sophie in *Sophie's Choice* said in her Polish immigrant dialect, "God who must be a monster, Stingo, if He exist. A monster!"

The second group sees God as their strength. Joan of Arc followed her inner voices with complete conviction. She believed herself chosen by God for a mission and didn't question her place in His plan. When she was sold to the British and put on trial she warned, "Consider well what you do, for in truth I am sent by God and you put yourself in great peril." She hadn't any patience, or perhaps any comprehension of allowing personal experience or human judgments to override her convictions.

Stranded in the Andes, Parrado and fellow survivors quickly began acknowledging their deepest beliefs to see them through. He asked Liliana why God would save some, and not others. She replied humans cannot understand God, but we can love and trust in Him. Days later he wondered aloud to a teammate, Arturo, what good was God if He leaves us to suffer. "Arturo answered, [B]ut God is beyond religion. The true God lies beyond our comprehension ... He didn't abandon us and He will not save us. He has nothing to do with our being here ... He simply is."

Arturo and Liliana's views are similar in believing God's inscrutability. Liliana believes there is much she does not and may never understand, but faith is used to handle the mystery. Arturo adds he is comfortable with the mystery and God's impersonal oversight.

My religious training was from Mother and Grandma. Summarized, I interpreted Mother's belief as, "Of course God loves you. He loves everyone. Only believe religious teachers who show love and respect for all and practice it on more than Sunday. Pray if you want. Don't if you don't." What others learned from sermons and religious books, I was taught through literature and life examples. Mercy was explained through Victor Hugo's bishop in *Les Miserables* when he protected Jean Valjean from the police after stealing the silver.

"We must learn the lessons of life," Grandma Spiking said many times. Nodding her head she indicated I was to understand whatever I suffered was a deliberate lesson to be remembered and put to good use in the great, unseen beyond. Whether the head nod followed discussing Frank Sinatra's love affairs, Jody and me asking why our father left us, or why we felt defenseless around Mormons, we were told it was a lesson in life. We, nor anyone else, were exempt from human consequences.

I would not trade the haphazard instruction of my two sometimes warring priestesses. Mother and Grandma taught reverence for true goodness, perseverance and the ability to be serene in paradox and mystery. I learned to respect churches and I'm awed by their human effort and beauty to comfort and portray majesty, but my comfort is God's mystery in nature and spirit.

While in the underworld, I reconsidered one of Grandma's lessons of life. I came away from childhood believing the trials of life were handpicked by God to make me miserable for specific reasons. From the first weeks after Jody's death a quiet whisper within murmured, "God is not punishing you." Eventually I heard the words clearly and realized two things. It required a surprising amount of self-importance to believe God would heap unsolvable life long trials on me and second, I would never do such a cruel thing to my son. God had to be better and more loving than me or why believe in Him?

More substantially, Sam softly slept next to me. I could touch him and I knew the hairs on his chest, the smell of his sweat. Zac still wanted me to say goodnight and make him cookies. The business was doing well, the roof wasn't leaking and leaves on trees were fluttering through their seasons. I never considered my view of God and eternity threatened or benefited by grief, but I did spend time re-thinking from the perspective of a new experience. Life was shaken, so beliefs were reviewed and modified.

Deep grieving is fertile ground for renewing and revising one's belief in God. It is understandable that someone who has been observant of beliefs and humble in faith would feel jilted and cheated. The Book of Job in the Old Testament of the Bible is pages and pages of Job wrestling with his grief after his family and possessions are taken from him. Terrified that he is losing faith and his place with God, Job confronts Him and his neighbors. In the end, in spite of all Job has said and felt, family and property again become his and he has a new, deeper relationship with God.

Belly of the Whale – *Swallowed into the unknown*

In the Hans Christian Andersen fairy tale, *The Ugly Duckling*, a cygnet is born into a family of ducks. At first the loving and dutiful mother duck defends the odd and homely child, but it becomes too much for her and its presence is a danger for his brothers and sisters. The ugly duckling is run out of duck and human society to make its way in the first dangerous winter of its life. All seems lost and hopeless to the cygnet when he enters the "belly of the whale" of his hero's journey.

Freezing and alone, the ugly duckling sat staring at the barren winter landscape. The griever now also sits alone, looks at a desolate life's landscape, and listens to the silence without comfort. Enough time has passed to realize death's full impact. Friends have resumed lives, flowers wilted long ago, and now re-assuming routines of responsibility is expected. Everyone expects the griever to return to previous good cheer and carry his load.

All roads in the underworld of traumatic death lead to this point. No matter the cause, religion, belief in God, or desire to continue on well and happily, the grieving hero pauses here. It is the low point where all appears lost; there are few if any coping mechanisms in place, and little or no vision of a good future. There may be endless tears or a stoic resolve, but both fronts feel despair and loneliness.

This is a curious time. From Jody's death in August to Lupe's in May, I experienced constant background noise, work, duty, and harrowing inner voices while I superficially acted in survival's automatic mode. Without warning, when Lupe died there was a settling to silence. An almost unbearable silence.

"We have no way of knowing that the funeral itself will be anodyne, a kind of narcotic regression in which we are wrapped in the care of others and the gravity and meaning of the occasion. Nor can we know ahead of the fact (and here lies the heart of the difference between grief as we imagine it and grief as it is) the unending absence that follows, the void ...," Joan Didion wrote of an entrance into the belly of the whale in *The Year of Magical Thinking.*

Inertia settles with no visible relief. It is easy to believe life will always be empty and under a shrouding pall. Yet, as I experienced the belly of whale I was gaining insight. It is like being stalled on a sailboat and seeing clearly to all horizons without a breath of wind to begin the journey. I was aware Sam, Zac and Mother were still alive and well in my life and that all of us were suffering with broken hearts. In our own way the four of us were more alive and lost to each other. I appreciated Sam, but I was no longer the same person in his life as I was before, and at times could not pretend even an appearance of caring.

I was pummeled with so many emotions and ideas that there was little energy left for effort. I was gaining small insights of joy and compassion along with the ability to act on them at the same time I was not able to see joy or compassion or give it to others. What small efforts I gave to find a way out were inadequate and half-hearted. The belly of the whale is near unfathomable.

Campbell's outline of the mythical hero's journey describes it as a time of being lost, almost discarded from the known world. He compares it to being lost in unknown territory and appearing to die. He writes of an overwhelming feeling of personal impending destruction. "The hero, instead of conquering or conciliating the power of the threshold, is swallowed into the unknown, and would appear to have died." In *The Denial of Death*, Ernest Becker adds the social games, psychological tricks, and personal preoccupations no longer work.

Heroes may wish they had died with their loved one, as Odysseus wished he had in Troy. "I wish I had died there, and found my fate on that day when a host of enemies were casting their sharp spears at me over the dead body of Achilles!"

The time in the underworld brings a weary, sad, perhaps beaten and angry hero to an impasse with a question that can be answered a thousand ways. How do I live now? The decision can be made quickly, slowly, with conscious deliberation or it can appear a person is flung into action by the unconscious. It can be decided and re-decided.

Life experiences, mixed with individual personality, begin to tell a unique story of either human victory or the beginning of a griever's defeat. During the first moments Stingo met Sophie in *Sophie's Choice*, he describes her face as "[T]the despair on her face worn....along with the premonitory, grieving shadows of someone hurtling headlong toward their own death."

Hamlet plunges headlong into action that irrevocably keeps

him in misery. "O! that this too too solid flesh would melt, thaw and resolve itself to dew .... How weary, stale, flat, and unprofitable seem to me all the uses of this world."

Sir Lancelot believes in the lofty goal of King Arthur's Round Table but he faces his belly of the whale when he lost the illusion of the glory of battle and sees he will never have Guinevere, the woman he loves. In one of the darkest moments of battle with Baldwin of Brittany, he is overcome by the sounds of his men dying and calling for help. As he bravely fights he glimpses quiet acts of great humanity on the battlefield. A crippled warrior leaps forward to protect a friend newly blinded in one eye, a wounded spearman defends a dying companion. Not long after, he witnesses the marriage of Guinevere to his beloved King Arthur. Both the protective reasoning of a killing warrior and the hope of being with the woman he loves are lost to him. Sadly and with resolve, he decides to honor his allegiance to King Arthur and forever live without Guinevere. He looks inward for consolation and new understanding, following Campbell's promise of transformation. "[T]he hero goes inward, to be born again."

In the continuing story of a mother's unending grief, earth mother Demeter disguises herself in rags and wanders the world looking for her lost daughter. Without Demeter's attending care, earth dries and is unable to produce crops. Drought is widespread with suffering, but Demeter is unable and unwilling to attend to her work. The phrase "belly of whale" perhaps comes from the Bible's story of Jonah, who reportedly lived in a whale, but the concept is in many legends.

In a Native American legend of the Nez Percé, all the animals of earth are swallowed by a creature whose body covers the Great Plateau of the Plains. Coyote enters the belly of the creature and fights to save the trapped animals. After a horrific battle, he at last frees them and thus the world is given the animal kingdom.

The belly of the whale finds Odysseus wishing he had died, Lancelot accepting and continuing with a human degree of peace, Demeter wandering lost and alone, and Coyote battling to give the world animals. Aeneas, though defeated by Odysseus, is one of the few who early on realizes a good future waits for him. While in the underworld his dead father tells him of the wife and son he will have. "[A]n Alban, his name is Silvius, your last-born son. For late in your old age Lavinia, your wife, will bear him for you in the forest; and he will be a king and father kings …."

The ugly duckling's journey was through a friendless and suffering winter. He learned perseverance, how to survive on his own and who he was inside. When spring broke he was at last found by his true family of beautiful and graceful swans. His transformation was complete. Human heroes may not believe Campbell's promise of rebirth is for them as they view the looming trials to be faced in their winter's journey. They only know one day follows another.

The Second Challenge

Refusing the Trials

Journalist Jim Sheeler walked with men charged with informing families of the death of loved ones in the military. In a radio interview he told of a mother who slapped him when she was informed of her son's death. Many exclaim, "No!" while pushing away. He came to understand they knew they were hearing the truth, but it was the only way to declare they did not like it. I said no to Mother as I pushed her away, while seeing a gruesome scenario in my mind verifying her words. I regret pushing her, but it was a refusal of death, not her.

Shocking news commonly results in disbelief too overwhelming to quickly absorb. Extremely good or bad news shoves people into denial. Victims who moments ago lost their homes in floods and tornadoes express disbelief. Newly expectant parents who have tried for years without success, will ask doctors, "Are you sure?" Many newly crowned Miss Americas have stunned looks of disbelief as they clutch roses and begin the catwalk. Shock during the early days, weeks or months is not a refusal to begin grief's recovery. It is necessary time to mentally accept before beginning open, sincere mourning.

Odysseus at first refused the call to Troy. He was happily married to Penelope, had a newborn son, Telemachos, and didn't want to leave them. When distinguished visitors came to call him to duty he acted deranged and pretended to be a peasant. As Odysseus continued his act while plowing his field, one of the visitors placed his infant son in front of the plow. To save his son he, of course, stopped plowing, and gave his attention to the visitors though he still didn't want to answer the call.

Another reason to refuse the call is the mourner's brutally new awareness that the loved one is not replaceable. There may be six billion people on earth, but not one of them replaces who has died. This awareness can result in subconsciously thinking, "Then I'll mentally stay right where I was when I last saw him." I soon learned there would never be a replacement for glancing at a man's eyes for the understanding I had with the brother I babysat, took to Saturday matinees and yelled at for doing so poorly in high school when I knew he was the smarter one. I did try.

To fill the void of Jody's birthday I invited Steve, Sam's younger brother, to go shopping. He was entering the job market after college and I took advantage of his need for new clothing to fill my need to buy a younger brother a birthday present. We chatted easily, he was appreciative and I enjoyed myself, but I realized Jody had taken his presence, personality, charm and idiosyncrasies and left crystallized memories that held only him.

Innocently, well-wishers do not realize the literal landscape new grievers grope through. They think they are being comforting by telling a griever they will find a new husband or have other children. Instead, they give a griever more hurdles to jump. They can either believe the loved one is replaceable and a good shopping trip will cure the problem, or be a warrior against the very idea someone would suggest it. Either fight is doomed because finally, the hero is forced to lay down the empty shopping bag or sword and admit that no one is replaceable as the unique person they were.

Refusing can also be a denial that prolonged grieving doesn't or shouldn't exist. Since society and those around us are reluctant to acknowledge the impact of traumatic death, survivors are often expected to do the impossible: disregard mourning, stand up, dust ourselves off and continue stoically. The stoic can believe they don't need to face grief, or there isn't the right to deal with something society believes shouldn't exist.

A poignant heartbreaking reason to refuse the call to recovery is being lost in a reality that is too painful to confront. That was suggested by Kathryn Harrison in *While They Slept*. She delves into the back story of Jody, whose brother killed their parents and younger sister. She must deal with overpowering grief for her whole family. A numbing princess sleep would be welcome and perhaps necessary before embarking on an arduous inner grief journey.

It is possible to mentally sleep under the glass case and wait for a prince's kiss, sleep in the poppy fields before reaching Oz, or like Rip Van Winkle, under a tree for a hundred years while life passes by. Grievers stay busy by pretending they can manage the hurt in the continuum of too much or no food, sex, work, liquor or drugs, feeling or not feeling.

Some grievers will think they've avoided grief if they learn to walk around it well and become blind to who they are. At first it can seem good to proudly refuse help, feel self-pity, anticipate our own death, scorn society for its stupidity, not assess personal responsibility, or hold revenge tight in the heart. None of these possible feelings help the griever, and will in time strangle inner growth of understanding, compassion, joy and what is most prized, peace.

Mourners of traumatic death are not cushioned. They are plunged without warning. The horrific shock can temporarily shut down normal response and cause a longer rest while refusing the call. It is a common disadvantage of this path of the lower branches, but it can be handled. Refusing the call is well padded with good intentions and sincere misunderstandings.

The hero's journey does not care whether we accept its call. Its possibility has plopped itself in the middle of life and we can look at it, make friends with it, or pretend it's not there. Life has given us a problem. The griever must either face the trials, or choose to kill a potential future as Odysseus would have killed his son.

Thumbelina, a girl no bigger than a thumb in the Hans Christian Andersen fairy tale, is abducted by a toad. Through a series of adventures and misfortunes she comes to rest under the care of a kindly field mouse. The neighbor is a mole, who over the following winter Thumbelina reluctantly agrees to marry. Secretly she nurses a bird, and when the bird is ready to fly in the spring he shows Thumbelina the sky she has not seen in a great while and invites her to go with him. She refuses saying she has a duty to the mouse that was so kind to her. Thumbelina has suffered after being stolen from her previous life, and is no longer able to act on her best interests. She mistakes accepting the trap she is in with duty to the circumstance that keeps her trapped.

The Third Challenge

Accepting the Trials

Within a month of Jody's death I began meditating and by the second month Mother and I signed up for a wine appreciation class. Meditation gave seconds of peace and the class gave cover by studying the difference between varietal and geographic wines. We developed a children of Dionysus' appreciation and understanding while swirling wine in glasses big enough for tadpoles and watching wine drips make skinny rivulets like Ichabod Crane's legs. I imagined smelling blueberry undertones, raspberry overtones and whiffs of vanilla infused with oak, promising delight when well-matched to the correct cheese and a palate cleansing water cracker. The class was our passable drinking excuse.

Food and drink were schizophrenic plunges in the continuum of sensuousness that promises body feeling and numbing at the same time. The conflicting desires to live and die were tinged with desperation, extreme and without awareness. Only in retrospect did I see strengthening through time.

Immediately, meals for Zac and Sam fell to an all time low for flavor and variety. Since I lost all interest in food and the use of most of my taste buds, I hadn't noticed until Sam complained. I forced myself to consider meals but it was irregular. Swinging on the continuum, I subscribed to *Bon Appetite* magazine and haphazardly followed recipes. *Bon Appetite* recipes aren't all nine-year-old boy pleasers, but the two of us devoted a Saturday to making a Dome Cake Lenotre, named after a renowned French chef.

It took both of us to carry off the three layer cake, dessert syrup and mousse café. Twelve eggs, beating egg whites (on two occasions), one pound of butter, Grand Marnier, a two quart bowl to bake the cake in, shaved chocolate and a heated skewer to sear the sugar on top are involved. We ordered pizza for dinner, but the dessert was one of the best I've ever had. The day with Zac remains a favorite memory.

Over the next several years I jumpstarted numerous times toward recovery with irregular attention to steamy novels, astronomy and religion classes, volunteering for non-profits, exercise and tap dance lessons. Subconsciously, each was aimed at a different area of my compromised life. I was living as a wife, mother, daughter and businessperson, jumping from one to the other, trying to fill time with activities.

Working toward recovery is not denying pleasure, as Thumbelina thought. There is pleasure in enjoying the company of others or learning a new activity. There is pleasure in renewing the responsibilities of relationships through work and play as Zac and I did with the cake. Gradually, the griever begins renewing the self with choices that guide life to new purpose; or perhaps unconsciously, as Thumbelina did, settling on varying degrees of self-pity, escapism or martyrdom that serve the ego, but do not nurture the deeper self.

When the challenge of trials is accepted, the hero's journey fully begins. Odysseus began when he went to war; King Arthur when he pulled Excalibur from the stone; Aeneas with his flight from Troy after defeat; Dorothy when her house lands on a witch far from home; and Harry Potter when he goes to school.

Many grievers have mental pictures of a sea to be crossed, a candle to be burned, tears to be cried, prayers to be offered or stones to be rubbed shiny and smooth to gain earth's wisdom. Some begin the trials with awareness, resolve and single-minded dedication; others are reluctant, while they feel alone, afraid or bitter in a situation they never wanted and don't know how to handle. Most grievers have responsibilities of children, a job or spouse that need attention. Others aren't aware enough to know they are at a door of expectation to continue, but they do know what all mourners learn. Days pass and life is not returning to before the call. Adjustments happen though acceptance may not. The first stages of facing the trials can be done as consciously as Parrado's descent off the mountain, or as reactively as when Dorothy started down the yellow brick road.

Parrado's airplane crash put his life in great peril and he needed to leave the scene of death. Weeks passed while survivors waited to be rescued until Parrado confronted his friend,

Roberto, to begin descending the Andes with him in the hope of finding help. Parrado consciously began a literal path.

Harry Potter's story builds when he reluctantly faced the three-headed dog and then slammed the door as quickly as he could. But that glimpse, and Hermoine's observation the dog was guarding something, gave Harry enough reason to pursue the mystery in his hero's journey.

After Parrado's decision and Harry Potter's glance, the next step was facing and living with the fear of what was ahead. On the evening before his walk for help, Parrado doubted himself and wondered if he should stay for rescuers to find them. But it had been too long and he knew that wouldn't happen. He would die if he didn't help himself.

Fledgling heroes seldom recognize the power in themselves that others see. The Wicked Witch in Oz is the evil force that for a griever represents a personal list of sadness, anger, guilt, regret or a hundred other negative things. Dorothy succeeded in facing the witch but didn't know how to kill her. She did not realize the power of her shoes or the mark of the kiss from the Witch of the North others see. The Wicked Witch laughed to herself, "I can still make her my slave, for she does not know how to use her power."

The size of the task feels overwhelming. Parrado's description of the Andes is a striking metaphor for all grievers. "[T]hat endless sky made me feel small and lost and impossibly far from home. In this primeval world, with its crushing scale, its lifeless beauty and its strange silence, I felt awkwardly out of joint with reality in the most fundamental sense, and that scared me more than anything, because I knew in my gut that our survival here would depend on our ability to react to challenges and catastrophes we could not now even imagine."

A first step in this strange land where everything happens at once, and in no particular order, can be an act as simple as cleaning. My brother's eight-year-old faded Malibu was picked up from the police impound lot, perhaps by Steve, and taken to Lupe's backyard. Mother wanted me to clean it, so on a late August afternoon I went to Lupe's. She was listless in her bed, the room dark except for the slats of light that jutted from the edges of pulled blinds. Standing at the kitchen window, I faced west to see the car in full sun. Jody last sat on that seat behind the steering wheel. Two months earlier we went to lunch at a sandwich shop on Ninth South that piled sprouts on thick slices of tomato and shared a fruit smoothie. I walked out, opened the door and sat on the seat. Smells escaped of skin, hair, forest air freshener, aging vinyl. For a few seconds I stared out the front and consciously breathed. Then I leaned and looked under the seats, ran my fingers between the seat and back, got out and did the same in the back seat. I walked to the trunk and saw a spare tire, tire iron, cleaning supplies and a chamois ready for use tucked in the back corner. I left them. Everything was as clean and neat as he left his room with the bed made, clothes neatly put away, spare change in a small box, socks all folded, a note by a small utility knife to give to Zac. I returned to the front seat to open the glove compartment. In the end, what was on my lap included a registration, proof of insurance, an oil change receipt from the month before with a big red thank you on it, seventy-four cents in change, sales receipt for a .357 magnum and a box of bullets with one missing.

Before leaving I sat by Lupe's bed. She turned to me and I heard the small rub of her thinning hair on the pillowcase. "I wish I could be as brave as Jody." Where, I wondered, does a griever ever understand the pain of a loved one measured against her own?

Accepting the call is when there is either sustaining resolve to live well or conscious surrender to the forces for healing. I experienced both but respond best to deep surrender. I allow myself to admit emotion or inner conflict I have felt but avoided facing. Once admitted and faced, I gain insight. Sam words this turning point as eliminating distractions and sharpening an outward eye. When he says, "I'm ready for the fight," he knows his goal and method.

When Parrado felt overwhelmed but knew he had to act, he hears an internal voice. "'You are drowning in distances,' it said. 'Cut the mountain down to size.' [A]head of me on the slope was a large rock. I decided I would forget about the summit and make the rock my only goal." Parrado's survival was reduced to walking toward a rock.

The future hero keeps tasks simple. She begins a new hobby, takes a friend to dinner or changes a bedroom to a study. Heroic tasks can appear small but that is their deception. There are no dragons to slay or witches to kill. For me, there was a cake to bake and a car to clean. Resolve lays a future step by step.

Odysseus was on his journey so long his son Telemachos grew to manhood and wished to begin a journey to find his father. He missed Odysseus throughout his boyhood, and his quest is a griever's. Telemachos searches for the Old Man of the Sea who always tells the truth once he has been overcome. He is a threshold guardian as were the guards into the underworld. Like the guards of the underworld, he must be defeated or genuinely charmed before giving access to the next challenge. Facing the threshold guardian tests courage and resolve. Telemachos is found wandering by Eidothea, daughter of the Old Man of the Sea and she asks him, "Are you a fool stranger, or just slack and lazy? Or do you prefer to let things slide, and do you enjoy hardships?" He answers as many people do in conversations with God, "I tell you plainly, divine being, whoever you are, it is no wish of mine that I am stuck here; but I must have offended the deathless gods who rule the broad heavens." When she is satisfied with his sincerity she tells him where to find her father.

Afterwards Telemachos reports: "[T]he Old Man did not forget his arts! First he turned into a bearded lion, then into a serpent, then a leopard, then a great boar; he turned into running water, and a tall tree in full leaf, but we held fast patiently." Grievers also bounce through extremes of emotion or effort as I did with meditation, wine, tap dancing, and astronomy. The phrase "held fast patiently" is the key.

When the battle ended the Old Man saw Telemachos' broken heart and gently said, "My Lord, do not go on weeping so long, since there is no help for it, but lose no time in trying to make your way back to your native land." He then tells him his father is with Calypso and how to get across the fish-giving seas.

Conscious work is an element in all stories of the hero's journey. Traveling heroes come to realize the prize they wish for will not be theirs without effort. Dionysus, a favorite son of Zeus, is the god of cheer and love. Yet, when Dionysus reached manhood he was treated as all others with a message from his father, delivered by Hermês: "My boy, it is time you should earn a place in Olympus. You will not get it without hard work, for the gods have placed hard work in front of all good things." Hard work appears nonnegotiable for the gods and for grievers.

In March 2006, writer Calvin Trillan wrote in *The New Yorker* of his wife's cancer that had been diagnosed years earlier. Struggling to continue after her recent death, he writes, "I know what Alice, the incorrigible and ridiculous optimist, would have said about a deal that allowed her to see her girls grow up: 'Twenty-five years! I'm so lucky!' I try to think of it in those terms, too. Some days I can and some days I can't.'"

It is time to gather wits and experiment with attitudes and beliefs about grieving. How the following issues are handled guides a future. The following seven issues all have potential to encourage recovery or strengthen roadblocks keeping the mourner from happiness and peace.

Symbols, Talismans and Amulets – *Tempered in fire by dwarfs*

Trillan's memories could be a comforting amulet to send him peacefully to the future. The strength and goodwill of the person who died often becomes an inspiration or symbol. Treasured notes, remembered words or worn clothing full of the smell of a loved person can give strength The symbol can represent the life of the past, or a hope and possibility of the future. It is used as a focal point for belief and strength to continue.

The day after the funeral I took down wall photos that included Jody. About a dozen framed prints of family and friends lined a stairway and he was in four. His picture unnerved me, and I easily over-looked the empty spaces for years.

What weakened me, made Mother stronger. The next time I walked into her living room I saw Jody's photo on the small table next to her reading chair. She was never interested in personal photos in her house, instead she prefers artwork and keeps all photos tucked away in albums. Startled, I looked at her. "I need to see him," she answered. The photo was her positive symbol and she needed it as dearly as I couldn't bear it.

Talismans and amulets are reminders of the decision to move forward and can be very powerful in reminding us if we temporarily forget or become confused. They are common to life and not unique to a mournful hero's journey. Wedding rings, lucky numbers, jewelry or any other item a person designates to have special meaning is a talisman. At their best, they provide a centering space for belief and positive action.

My positive symbols and reasons to care were Sam and Zac. Silently, I brushed aside an amulet that could have given me life. The creative and disciplined writing I was enjoying working on when I received the news of his death was instead my payment for real or imagined involvement in his death.

Music provided Styron's Sophie her flickering hope. "[T]he reason she had shut music out during these days of malignant depression was she had found she could not bear the contrast between the abstract yet immeasurable beauty of music and the most touchable dimensions of her own aching despair." Music was a link to life she considered too beautiful to hear during her deepest sadness and she refused it. Mikal Gilmore's doomed family was led by a negative symbol. "[I] grew up in a family where the noose worked as a talisman; it hung over our heads not so much as a deterrent but as a sign of destiny." The surviving sister, Jody, in Harrison's *While They Slept*, found insight and comfort in reading. Realizing how vast the world is and how emotions drive great literature, she was able to confront and in time find, a workable peace.

Talismans invoke strong emotions that comfort heroes through passages and tests or lead them into defeat. Campbell writes: "And so it happens that if anyone—in whatever society—undertakes for himself the perilous journey into the darkness by descending, either intentionally or unintentionally, into the crooked lanes of his own spiritual labyrinth, he soon finds himself in a landscape of symbolical figures."

Campbell writes that the spiritual is an involved, confusing journey, but it is not specifically positive or negative. Talismans act as guides through the labyrinth, reminding the hero of a path. Not haphazardly chosen, they have special meaning and positive ones are often given by a protector or guide. Aeneas tells of his supernatural golden sword. "The goddess who gave birth to me foretold that, if war were at hand, then through the air she would bring Vulcan's weapons to my aid."

The Norse god Odin had the spear named Gungnir, and a magic ring named Draupnir, which were unending sources of power and wealth. In the Norse legend, *Frithiof's Saga*, the questing hero Frithiof tells of his three guiding talismans. Tempered in fire by dwarfs, the magic sword, Angurvadel, was inherited from his father. "Next to the sword most prized was an arm-ring, widely reputed, forged by ... the limping smith Vauland." Last was *Ellida*, the dragon ship given by the sea god. Hollywood screenwriting consultant and hero's journey scholar, Christopher Vogler, cites the light saber talisman Obi Wan gives Luke Skywalker.

Swords were a common talisman in Norse and Celtic mythology with King Arthur's Excaliber being the most famous. Swords were used in battle and warriors needed to believe in their strength, but swords have also historically been used in earth-based ceremonies as a symbol to cut through old, useless or dangerous ideas and habits.

The use of talismans spans the continents in ageless stories. An epic legend from Africa tells of Mwindo who was born laughing from his mother's solar plexus. In one hand was a protective scepter and in the other an adze, making him immediately ready for battle against his father. Mwindo was a mighty warrior born with protective talismans, but he was also known to only fight the worthy battle, spending most of his life dancing with joy and encouraging others to join him.

Later, I copied the Native American use of a medicine bundle where objects are held in a bag. Shamans use them during ceremonies but I only used mine as a focal point. On the lid of a small black lacquered box is a charging warrior in breastplate, shield and metal hat. Behind him flows a red cape and he rides a green horse flying over mountains. There is a locket from Sam engraved on the back with *Love Sam*, a seed pearl and jade bracelet from Zac, a garnet ring from Russia Mother brought me, and a gold charm from my father's time in Saudi Arabia. From Jody are the filigreed gold earrings he gave me on my birthday. Small trinkets from my daughter-in-law and two grandchildren have been added, the people I travel deepest with.

Choose something of inspiration and comfort as a reminder of what has been good in life or is desired in the future. Use it as a motivator to allow or lead the way toward a good future.

Jody's photo comforted Mother for several years, but in time she tucked it away. What had served her well no longer did. Near the same time I re-arranged the photos in the hall, including one of Mother, Jody and me when he was a small boy.

Time Needed for Recovery – *Demeter's wandering*

"And as for you, this is the answer of those who pay court to your mother, a plain answer to you and to all the nation: Send your mother out of the house, tell her to marry whichever her father says, whichever she likes herself ...." The men courting Penelope after Odysseus' long absence demanded her son tell her the time for mourning had passed.

In another tale the young bride, Eurydice, died from a snake bite leaving her minstrel groom, Orpheus, to grieve. After an accepted time young maidens who were enchanted by his beauty and musical ability pursued him, but he was unresponsive. Losing patience with his never-ending grief, they tore him limb from limb, and with his head stuck on his lyre, threw it into the Hebrus River.

When the pall of grief stays too long outcries of surrounding people can be very dramatic. Grief counselors mention two to five years as being common, but that is misleading. If the death is not traumatic and/or a survivor has excellent emotional skills, the grieving process is accomplished much sooner. If the death is traumatic and/or emotional skills are not strong, problems can last a lifetime. As the journey continues, it will be an irony to see that grief quite comfortably settles as a hovering shadow we become accustomed to living under.

Now in his early teenage years, Zac was editor of the school newspaper, was a guest deejay on a local radio station, and he learned tennis. In the summer he demonstrated pioneer equipment at the Utah Heritage State Park to tourists, and we paid him ten dollars for a weekly imaginative story. Under my pressure, he reluctantly took a night class in typing and complained about being the only male and person under thirty who wasn't trying to get out of a dead-end job. It was slightly before computers were widespread, but I imagined he would someday benefit from the secret advantage of typing.

Sam threw himself into the business, routinely working from six a.m. to five p.m., when he left to work on community projects. We were members of the Salt Lake Chamber of Commerce where he served on the board of governors, he worked on political campaigns and was on the board of the American Red Cross. He was given an annual Caesar Chavez Award by the Utah Chapter of La Raza with a reception at a downtown hotel.

Keeping our business successful was a joint effort and I also was involved with the Chamber, the National Association of Women Business Owners and for a short time, the Small Business Administration. There was much to occupy time and provide happiness.

Mother's years with General Motors allowed her a month's vacation plus the week between Christmas and New Year's. Her frugality and determination, the traits that allowed her to buy a house and alway keep us clothed and well-fed, paid for it. She visited Hong Kong, Korea, Rome, Paris, spent time in Australia and New Zealand, January in southern Mexico, an October through the Philippines, Malaysia, Indonesia, Singapore, Burma, Thailand and again to Hong Kong. There was a January in Bogota, Lima, on Lake Titicaca, Easter Island,

and Buenos Aires. Itineraries were so full and varied I would question memory if I hadn't kept them as hope for my future. Mother was finishing her career as a faithful employee in the changing office environment. Older men continued old pre-anti-discrimination ways and younger men hadn't patience for people struggling with the introduction of technology into the business world. And neither had kindness for an aging woman. Mother faced her most difficult working years while grieving her son's death. Time and demand of other duties moved Mother and me along a bumpy road, where appearances can fool people, and we wanted it to fool us as well.

Mother's world travels nourished her in inexplicable ways while Demeter's wanderings left the world in drought. Repeatedly Zeus implored her to return to her life of replenishing earth's harvest, but with her daughter missing she refused.

Five years after Jody's death sharp grief had lifted, but I was now in the midst of accepting our father's death, while waiting for our grandmother's nine months later. When the wrenching pain I felt for my brother did not materialize with either of them, I was baffled. There was love for all three. Why not the same pain?

Like Demeter, I also held pain close until I believed I understood history. I toyed with the idea that I was tired of mourning and had learned how to speed up the process to an incredible few months. That felt ridiculous. In squirmed the memory of realizing my father, whom I adored without reserve, had left. There wasn't a good-bye or an address. The last thing Mother was doing was mourning his absence and Jody was a toddler. With nowhere to let the unexpressed sadness and anger bleed away, I held it inside.

The effort was a shadow and I began feeling different about myself. Childhood wonder, belief in possibilities of dancing in a kitchen lit only by city lights and night sky fell away. Worst of all, using only a child's reasoning, there was loss of belief in worthiness and a right to happiness that sadly slowed the open expression of love to Mother and Jody.

It can take a very long time for deeply buried truths to unearth themselves. It took years until more than a handful of Vietnam veterans began writing war stories. It has taken until recently for many personal stories of WWII to pour out of the aging hearts of the generation that valued stoicism and silence above truth and health.

Unfinished business can also delay recovery. A still grief-stricken mother was reported in the local news even though her daughter disappeared years before. Obscure clues and dead ends hinted she was a victim of serial killer Ted Bundy, so the police were closing the file after his death without ever knowing what happened to her. If. If. If. I'm sure the mother had lived with tracks of "if" sentences across her brain. If I had insisted she not go that day. If she had not talked to a stranger with the trust and enthusiasm she held for life. If someone could only find her bones or see her alive in another city.

Finally, the detail of a memorial service could be relief from grief, not a beginning. I spent my childhood and teenage years secretly grieving my missing father and five years after my brother's death, I at last laid his body to rest. True grief had occurred while he lived.

Watching Grandma Spiking die was witnessing the setting, disappearing sun of her generation. With Jody I mourned his potential, sudden absence, the life he could have lived, and my deeds done and undone. With Grandma I simply missed her personality. She lived eighty years and what is left is the sentimental pleasure of memory.

Every year Grandma Spiking called before the January sun was up and without a hello I would hear *Happy Birthday* sung flat and gravelly, as though she were gargling rocks. In the 1960s she put wheat germ in her cookies and grew sprouts in the basement. She embarrassed Aunt Donna by sending her to school with olive and walnut sandwiches on pumpernickel bread when everyone else ate bologna on white. Jody and I were fed lentil bean burgers on slices of dry, heavy, brown bread and were lectured about the lack of nutritional value in the saving grace of ketchup she allowed us. Vanilla ice cream with homemade plum sauce from a backyard tree was a decadent treat. Then we played gin rummy and she was ruthless; letting children win had not been invented. She expected our attention and phone calls, but they didn't need to be long because she didn't like being interrupted from her book studies. When she was tired of talking, her answers were short and you could feel her unspoken, "Yes, get on with it, I've got things to do." Her history was private and she was never interested in repeating old tales. It was not until months before her death, when I visited her after tap dance lessons, that she talked of her long gone three sisters and six brothers. She glossed over the time she and her sister, Norma, were sent to a relative's farm in Idaho to escape the flu of 1918.

Few people met her standards of being "deep." The world was a serious place with little room for the frivolous. The mold of her face held thought's gravity and when she laughed she seemed embarrassed she had slipped out of character. Her home had a peaceful, near boring serenity that strived for perfection and illumination and felt like a comfortable library furnished with expensive museum pieces.

She believed in reincarnation but her thoughts were rarely spoken outside of her home because of equal fear and disdain for prevalent LDS beliefs. Instead, she quietly met with her "oddball" friends, as she called them, in a house on South Temple that was converted to a meeting place, but is again a private residence.

She befriended a world-wide community of lecturers and authors who visited her when they passed through Salt Lake. Founders of Findhorn in Scotland stayed in her home, she participated in funding their progressive garden and later visited it. Philosopher David Spangler stayed with her when he was a teen-ager, and reportedly so did Edgar Cayce's son and San Francisco's Peace Pilgrim. But she held her life closely and while some of us knew of a few visitors and others knew of more, it took all of us to compile the list. Family reluctance to be open about the self did not start with me. When the last words were spoken at the funeral and the fresh-cut gladiolas died on my grandmother's grave, grief gave its center seat away to a clearer facing of the trials.

Why Me? – *Buddha's mustard seed*

No one believes Superman movies are real, so it was early ricocheting emotions that caused visceral fury when Sam, Zac and I went to the movie. Lois Lane was in a car accident and lapsed into unconsciousness I interpreted as death. Heroically, but appearing too late, Superman flew to her side after wasting time fighting the bad guys. He dramatically held Lois and her eyelids slowly fluttered to a rescued heroine flirt I interpreted as a return to life.

Sam innocently held popcorn and Zac a fizzy drink as I clutched the chair arms to keep from standing up before a packed holiday season blockbuster audience to yell at Superman. I was outraged. Not angry. Not offended. Not sad. Those words are too wimpy for the coursing blood that flooded a salt taste to my mouth and formed words I hysterically pantomimed to release anger's froth.

"Hey, pal, you don't get Lois back if I don't get Jody. You missed your clues, waited too long for the rescue and tough noogies. God gets her or we're duking it out." I'd temporarily lost any appreciation for light entertainment or grace for others if it wasn't there for me, too.

There are a lot of cactus needles in *Why Me?* They hold

bleeding questions, often from a small-hearted, selfish wound. My partial list: Why does someone else have a brother? Why did experience, thinking and events obscure the real him to himself? Why wasn't my family whole and my brother at holiday meal tables? Who else would talk to me when I was alone, old and ugly? And more I've forgotten, but they were important.

Each question was a bewildering combination of rage and sadness that could easily settle to bitterness. I didn't like the feelings, didn't like having to sort through them, their tarnish to my self-image, or how mean-spirited they made me feel. I felt doomed by the easily blamed randomness and unfairness of the universe. I didn't wish tragedy on others, but why me?

I brooded. Why did Jody take dangerous drugs as a teenager? Why did we have to live without a father during childhood? Everyone else at school had one, or so it seemed. Why did we have to live in judgmental Utah, instead of California, land of school bus drivers who talked to you? Memory was questionable, plus I began noticing how many questions centered on me. Every hurt turned and twisted in blame and self-pity. I didn't like the feelings, but grief found me unprepared and unable to sincerely wish others well.

Eventually, the demonizing and malicious inner voices that prompted the questions subsided. My more soothing original inner voices resumed. When thoughts started with "I," it was a familiar resonance of tracking time, noticing everyday surroundings without phantoms and blackness. It was the voice that handled grocery shopping and paying bills.

When thoughts started with "you," a door smoothly oiled with unavoidable honesty opened to a breezeway. The voice alternated between being strident and brutally clear, to a gentle androgynous breath of words through timelessness from something without end.

I was washing dishes and thinking of other things when the new voice said, "Well, Miss Goody Two-Shoes, how do you really feel about other people's happiness when yours is compromised?" Intellectually, I knew other people's lives should be pleasant with all loved ones healthy and near. Still, it was difficult to see others enjoying the company of loved ones when I felt so bereft. I wilted from the question, unable to give an answer.

Another night I sat in the quiet living room with a single lamp lit above my shoulder. A book was face-down on my lap because I couldn't remember what I was reading. I took off my glasses and leaned back on the living room couch. Behind my closed eyes floated the heavy, dark feelings of death and loss that can steal inside as an invisible ghost and live breathing and wasting within. Words floated through me forcing measure, but deep lostness only heard a pebble clink against the sides in darkness. Why, why, why. It wasn't why me or why Jody, it was why. Why did fragile, beautiful life seem to be such an inseparable friend with sadness?

The answering thought was: "You were born and now you live." I opened my eyes and sat up. That voice always jolts me. It is so sure. So soft. It is a ghostly gentle whisper without doubt.

When I was about eight, Mother gave me a necklace with a mustard seed suspended in glass. She told me the story of what it meant, but I forgot until many years later when I read about the wanderings of Buddha. A deeply mourning mother carried the body of her long dead baby to one holy man after another begging it be returned to life. She was referred to Buddha who kindly said if she would bring to him a mustard seed she had obtained from a household where no son or husband or parent or slave has ever died, life would be restored to her son. Encouraged, the mother began her search. Every house gladly agreed to give her a mustard seed but no house could claim it had not encountered death. Eventually, she returned to Buddha. When he asked if she had the mustard seed she replied, "No, my master, but I have found the medicine. I have buried my sorrow in the forest. And now I am ready to follow you in peace."

I am born so I live. I go on in the consciousness I am able to experience. Human beings ask why they suffer. It is such a universal question that there isn't any point asking if it is reasonable or selfish. Suffering seems to be built into us right along with the need to mate and seek shelter. And like mating or seeking shelter, suffering feels individual and personal.

Death is messy and usually unwelcome or unexpected. Whatever circumstance takes the life of a loved one, another person is left to live through grief. Everyone answers their own questions about death or lets them continue unanswered, but what no one decides is whether or not death is inevitable.

The continuum of *Why Me?* swings from believing death is only a result of being alive to believing God specifically selected who died and who would mourn. Some wonder if somehow they deserved this punishment. Rabbi Kushner wonders if apparently unfair deaths aren't also an affront to God and what He would prefer for us.

Mortician Nadle concluded. "Every time I went to work I was reminded that we all die sometime—and that most often that time feels too soon to the people who survive us. In this way, death is neither fair nor unfair; it just is. And no amount of resistance on my part could change that."

Superman's parents named him Kal-El. To save his life on a dying planet his scientist father sent him in a rocket to earth. Found by kindly Kansas farmers, Kal-El was raised as Clark Kent. Kal-El lost his parents and homeland and was raised by strangers in a strange land. He was a youngster with unusual abilities that caused schoolmates to taunt him. He needed to be secretive and hide behind glasses as Clark Kent. It would have been easy for him to feel self-pity and close inward against others.

As an adult, Superman needed to reconcile that he would never be able to return to his home planet of Krypton. Nor would he easily find a woman to accept his two identities and live happily with him. He balanced knowledge of his history and abilities against the derision he received in the office of the *Daily Planet*, and the adoration of a public that really didn't know him. Despite all this, he chose to be a friend and rescuer of people in trouble.

I didn't see it at the time, but the superhero Superman suffered irreplaceable losses, felt alone in the world and still chose to help others. Superman has also traveled grief's hero journey.

In a book I kept from Jody's library, *Journey to Ixtlan*, Don Juan listened to Castaneda talk of his trials in life, "'No matter how much you like to feel sorry for yourself, you have to change that,' he said in a soft tone. 'It doesn't jibe with the life of a warrior.'"

Overcoming vs. Accepting – *Jonah's fear*

Attempting to overcome grief is protective self-defense of a shattered spirit hiding behind shock in a beginning effort to survive. Picking up a fork for a bite of food was an exercise of will. At times, lethargy was so strong I pulled to the side of the road to rest before continuing a drive to the grocery store. Dishes sat in the sink while I gathered energy by sitting in a chair blankly staring at a wall. I would sigh without awareness until both Sam and Zac asked in concerned voices why. In retrospect, I think my body was automatically working to survive by inhaling and exhaling breath when my life force hadn't the energy to assist.

Overcoming is a common first reaction and can feel like the nobler warrior choice. It implies human victory and mastery of an enemy, giving a knock out punch to a cruel opponent. Traveling heroes can believe they are mastering emotions and feelings by overcoming them.

Social historian Studs Terkel recalls his father's death when he was nineteen in the preface of his book, *Will the Circle be Unbroken*, written when he was over seventy. "It was I who found him in bed, his spectacles askew... I was remarkably calm until, seated on the Grand Avenue streetcar the next day, heading nowhere in particular, I surprised myself by breaking into uncontrollable sobs. Embarrassed, seeking to stifle them, blubbering despite myself, I hurried toward the rear of the car, ready to hop off anywhere, just to escape my show of grief." While interviewing for the book, he is told a story of a man having a heart attack on a bus who was in terrible pain, but also embarrassed he was disrupting rides of the other passengers. "The man's embarrassment touched off the memory of that nineteen-year-old boy so uncomfortable at daring to grieve out loud for his father. Everything about this book became, unexpectedly for me, a journey into long-suppressed memories and all sorts of ambivalences in feeling of which I wasn't aware." Mourners can run and hide under stoicism, overcoming and avoidance, but unfaced grief remains.

Prince Hamlet was not able or allowed to grieve his father's murder and was appalled when his mother soon re-married. She said to him, "Do not for ever with thy veiled lids seek for thy noble father in the dust: Thou know'st 'tis coming; all that live must die, passing through nature to eternity." They stand across from one another, not understanding each other as they work to overcome a shock in life, though he does make a judgment that his grief is more profound as he appears to suffer more. He says to his friend, Ophelia, "how cheerfully my mother looks, and my father died within two hours." She answers that it has been four months, not two hours.

Story tellers, psychologists and psychiatrists are aware of the tendency to stall here. When changes in life are too great to absorb, people turn away, shut down, ignore, pretend and can't accept that life is now different. A.H. Maslow, Otto Rank and Sigmund Freud identified the reaction as the Jonah Syndrome. When life changes too rapidly, either through success, a challenge or defeat, some decide it is too much to accept, and as Ernest Becker states, the person experiences "[F]ear of being torn apart, of losing control, of being shattered and disintegrated, even of being killed by the experience. And the result... is what we would expect a weak organism to do: cut back the full intensity of life." The name comes from Jonah 1:3 when God sent Jonah to Nineveh on a quest: "But Jonah rose up to flee unto Tarshish from the presence of the Lord." It is feeling not being up to the task or unable to face it and avoiding what is at hand.

For some the decision to accept, learn and move on is conscious from the start. They expect a brighter day and feel a responsibility to walk on with open eyes and heart. For others, the decision is made in the back room of the brain where desperation forces survival but doesn't give understanding.

Conscious awareness of the decision showed itself to me through Zac. On a spring morning he didn't want to take a test at school. I told him school was unavoidable. After summarily sending him off using the power of parenthood, I sat with a steamy cup of coffee staring out the window where I saw him walking away from me on his way. Inner hums fell to quiet. I saw the lines of his boy shoulders resolved to face the test I had insisted he take.

This was also my choice. School was there to be faced and so was death. Absence of further thought resulted in a new one sneaking in. The bodiless voice presented a thought more directly than words. "Do you understand the difference between overcoming and accepting a death?" The question was unanswered. It's likely I put my head down and cried. At that time it was my routine response when I knew I would have to consider something.

After the initial vulnerability of the first weeks, it felt natural to fall back into childhood habits of overcoming feelings without acceptance. I thought I could use resolve to fight an enemy and push it into a corner of life, refusing to acknowledge it in a world that would not let me express true feeling. Ignore its signs. Pretend the world was fine. Imagine I was okay.

Zac could have played hooky and avoided that test. That small act could have been the first of many, until eventually he dropped out of school and irrevocably changed his life. Both of us made a small and necessary first step of claiming the best for us that day.

I decided to accept death and all its implications for two reasons. First, I didn't have enough energy to spare on anything I didn't need to do, and it used less to accept. Accepting could be defined as giving up in a vanquished defeat. Instead of giving up to an enemy, I believe it as accepting the nature of life.

Second, I wanted long term results. I was in small business and damn it, I understood the concept. Get busy, get ready and go. But underlying it all, I deeply wanted better chances for Zac and less unhappiness for me. To encourage Zac's good future meant I had to be an able parent and quit fighting an enemy I would never defeat. Every day I told myself to hold my shoulders square, face the problem and be as brave as my son.

When I accepted death's no-return-to-the-same-life guarantee, it meant I needed to step aside and admit this soul searing, heartbreaking and socially inappropriate event would always be with me. There plainly is not human victory. There is nothing to overcome because there is nothing we can overcome.

Neeld's grief therapist told her: "You will never be so innocent and trusting. You will never know anyone else who will love you the way Greg did. You may," he said, "meet someone to love and be loved by, but you will then be a different person. You will never be able to repeat what you had with Greg." Incredibly, acceptance frees energy to continue.

Tell Everyone or Tell No One – *Iona's little horse*

"To whom shall I tell my grief?" is the first sentence in the Anton Chekhov story *Grief*.

At four in the afternoon, on the day of Jody's funeral, conversation between all family members ended, as dry as desert sand. Six adults looked out Mother's front window and watched five children pick and eat strawberries. Sam had a tired empty look in his darkened eyes that the afternoon was wearing and he needed to get away. At the same time, Donna, her family and Grandma decided to go, leaving me to spend the night with Mother. As I said good-bye to Sam and Zac I saw a glimmer of the future. I was falling between their ability to resume a normal life and my devastation.

When everyone left, Mother and I changed clothes and went to the kitchen to clean. I saw the *Hi* Jody had written on the freezer door as a teenager. The sharp angular letters were two inches from the handle in green permanent ink and lifted to the right, ending with an exclamation point. The doorbell rang. I didn't recognize the young, muscular man at the door with pain in his eyes it hurt to see when he gave me an envelope.

"Jody never came back for this. It's his. I'm sorry. I tried to do what I could." While Mother was gracious, I stared at his arm. It was strong and young, pulsating. I looked toward his car with a young woman in it. Jody should have had that. The envelope contained a payment Jody never picked up from a job he left a month earlier. Taking shorts out of his drawer, cleaning his glove compartment, cashing his check. None of it should have been ours to do.

We returned to the kitchen, our voices soft murmuring chants chastened from the sincerity in the man's voice. We returned a pan to a neighbor across the street. I noticed the cleomes with their short spiky arms again nodding. All the small red strawberries were gone. The long summer twilight slowly wasted as we sat in the living room watching the light fade behind one another. Yes, we both said, we believed he was now safe. There was life after death, he was without pain. What were we going to do? Why hadn't life been different? Mother didn't want to come home from work and never hear him on the basement stairs again.

Talk trailed through history. Birthdays. The times the three of us made pizza. The clear cold evening we saw the movie *Taras Bulba* with Yul Brynner at the Lyric Theatre. Mother would be stilled by the happy memory and then stab the air with pain-sharpened words. She had to kick him out after high school graduation, she said, he was so rebellious. She had to be strong and teach a lesson. I nodded, wondering if the police might still come for us.

We undressed and slipped into bed on our backs, side-by-side. I had never slept in this bed and had not been under covers with Mother since our last basement apartment twenty-two years earlier. Then, we had shared a bed and I would fall asleep by putting my leg around her waist, securing myself to a remaining parent. She was turned toward the window while Jody slept in a crib next to me.

Now her voice was a tree fallen with only me to hear. "Remember how he only liked macaroni and cheese as a child? It was a Saturday night party when a diced hot dog was added. He was so small when Joe and I separated. Those were such difficult years."

"Yes."

"When I met your father there was such attraction and fun. Everybody always liked Joe. Except my parents. Particularly, Daddy. They didn't think we should marry and they weren't impressed with Joe. They could have afforded a nicer wedding for us. They were busy building the Spiking Motel. They didn't like Joe and didn't give us anything. We got married at the Alpha Delta Pi house. My friends would talk about their gifts from parents of furniture and silver and I wouldn't say anything. After I got married they built that big house by the Salt Lake Country Club on Lynwood, and I knew they didn't want to do the wedding for me.

"When you were born they weren't even very interested. They gave you a dress. For their first grandchild. My friends were getting cribs and dressers. My mother-in-law said, 'Your parents sure favor Donna, don't they?' But, we managed. Joe delivered flowers for Huddart Floral.

"We didn't get invited to the motel's grand opening. There was a big article in the newspaper about it. The flowers from Daddy's shop were planned for weeks. Fancy invitations went out to every friend they had. It was far more important to them than the wedding had been. Joe just shrugged it off but I was very hurt.

"You don't remember Grandma Madsen. She was Mother's mother. She was the only one who ever spoiled me. She would sneak me sugar cubes at the dinner table while Mother warned her and we would both giggle. I was four when Daddy got the call that she had died, and I remember watching him walk over the open ditch that was still on Thirty-third South, and go across the street to get Mother from a neighbor's house.

"Daddy's mother was not so kind. She was a very old woman when you were born. She told me she liked little boys, not little girls. His father died when he was young. She later married again but he died, too, and when you were born her health was failing. She was living a very lonely life, crocheting by the window in a little apartment above where Market Street Restaurant is now on Post Office Place.

"When we moved to Tooele for Joe's first construction job we had a little larger place to live and I asked Joe if Grandma Jenkins could live with us. It is always to his credit that he said yes but before it could be arranged, she died.

"We moved around so much when you were a baby. You wouldn't remember San Francisco, but I do. The job ran out and Joe couldn't find another one. For two weeks we ate nothing but potatoes and beets. We didn't even always have milk for you. I got a secretarial job and the hardest thing I had to do was leave you while I worked. Joe's sister lived in the area and for a few months you lived with her all week and only came home on weekends to live with us in our little apartment by Golden Gate Park.

"The years passed and I just kept hoping things would get better. All I wanted was to be a mother and stay home. I never wanted to be a secretary and leave my children all day. Joe would drink too much and we weren't doing well, but finally the jobs improved some. You must remember Twentynine Palms. We were having real problems but thought having another baby would bring us together so I got pregnant with Jody. You were our little surprise. I was sick through the whole thing and it didn't help the marriage. He was so tiny when he was born early. Do you remember? He was so tiny. Joe's job ran out and rather than be destitute we packed up and went to live with his mother.

"Maybe if Lois had helped me with the drinking and his responsibility to his family it could have been different. But when he would stay out she dismissed it, and I was powerless. Once she bailed him out of jail for being drunk when I thought leaving him there would wake him up. It was then I decided whoever got the next job would determine the fate of our family. If it was Joe I would stay married. If it was me, there would be a divorce."

When we drifted to sleep it may have been from the crushing weight of hearing about those early years. Most of it was new to me, and I realized as she spoke there was no blame, only four stories that didn't intersect often enough.

Therapists believe reminiscing, or as it is also called, sorting, is necessary. Life history needs reviewing, understanding and remembering in a new way. Talk makes that possible. The continuum of a mourner's talking style can vary from a parrot on speed to London's mute and staring palace guards. Some people need a thousand conversations while others find it near unbearable to have words cross their tongue once. The healthy answer is somewhere in between and at a different point for everyone.

Mourners need to consider the results of their talking habits and consciously make a decision. Talk, or a lack of it, is part of an attitude carried throughout the grieving journey, and under the stresses of grief, habits can be exaggerated. There are hazards in talking too much or too little. Whatever the griever decides, the fallout is felt by all members of the household and untold numbers of friends, co-workers and anonymous people in public situations.

The Talker

There are people who easily retell stories. They need to talk about a tragedy and from the beginning they are open about all facts and experiences. They are willing to open the watershed of emotion and let it spill. Everyone knows their pain, emotional fragility and how they think. It feels inclusive to be vicariously huddled in another's story as they unselfconsciously tell sorrows and joys. I'm honored to hear heartfelt feelings and consider it a trust that makes me like him more. Story telling strengthens community when a sympathetic listener realizes the humanity and need of others.

But talkers leave themselves vulnerable to outside opinion. People respond to heartfelt stories, but they can also be questioning, judgmental or unwilling to listen. Job was deeply hurt by the response from his friends when he lost everything. In 19:21-22 he implores, "[H]have pity upon me, O ye my friends; for the hand of God hath touched me. Why do you persecute me as God, and are not satisfied with my flesh?"

In Chekhov's short story the carriage driver is beside himself with grief over the death of his son. Dazed and in shock, he babbles to his customers who repeatedly cut him off because of boredom or fear of his emotion. The story finishes, "Iona's feelings are too much for him, and he tells the little horse the whole story." It may be healthier to talk to a horse than some human beings.

When stories are endlessly repeated, it may be difficult for the listener and less productive for a mourner. Stingo was Sophie's release but it grew heavy for him. "You're just eating your guts out about things that weren't your fault—and it's going to make you ill. Please stop it."

The Stoic

After several of their children died, Robert Frost's wife, Elinor, wrote to a friend, "With Robert I have to keep cheerful, because I mustn't drag him down, but sometimes it seems to me that I cannot go on any longer.... [T]he pathos of it was too terrible. I long to die myself and be relieved of the pain." The talking style of both heartbroken parents left them alone and suffering.

Too soon mourners are expected to be their well-polished selves. We believe in a country of brave puritans, rugged cowboys, intrepid immigrants, and stoic pioneers who buried babies in unmarked graves and immediately continued on covered wagon treks to unknown places.

Grief therapist David Treadway looked back on his childhood and realized the cost of stoicism. "The absence of any intimate connection with either of my parents never even bothered me. I considered our parent-child relationship as normal as freezing weather during New England winters. 'Don't complain about the cold, go skiing' would have been my credo." During a time when only negative memories surfaced, I remembered when Zac was perhaps four. His feelings had been hurt and I got down on my knees to say, "Zac, we cannot cry every time feelings are hurt." I wish I hadn't said that at such an early age.

Shell shock was the term used in WW I for soldiers exhibiting what is now called post traumatic stress syndrome. WW II soldiers were labeled with battle fatigue. Historically, soldiers were expected to discount war's horrors, but Vietnam began to make a difference. A few stories trickled out in the beginning, but most were not written for ten to twenty years. Post traumatic stress syndrome was coined to define what soldiers felt and had been expected to accept without complaint. It has defined trauma for a steady stream of stories from WWII, Vietnam and now Afghanistan and Iraq. By unlocking the vault of stoicism's secrecy that prevents healing, our soldiers have added to the understanding of trauma's power.

In Nadle's introduction she recalls asking friends to read her book draft before printing and a husband said to her, "What have you done to my wife? She wouldn't put those stories down, and she just cried and cried. And she never cries, not when we lost our baby when we were young, not when her mother was killed so many years back. She just closed up, unreachable, and now all of a sudden she's talking about it."

Some events are so horrendous that survivors who loved the

deceased and would talk about a normal death, are overwhelmed in a self-preserving silence. That deserves respect while the person's insides settle and adjust, but silence can be negative in the long run. It is natural to compartmentalize horror to retain sanity, but not dealing with the impact at all encourages it to fester instead of dissolve.

Listeners

Writer Kathryn Harrison is a good observer, listener and supporter for people who have suffered unusual circumstances. She writes: "People who cross the threshold between the known world and that place where the impossible does happen discover the problem of how to convey their experience. Some of us don't talk about murders or intergenerational sex within our families. We find words inadequate, or we lose them entirely. Those of us who insist on speaking what's often called unspeakable discover there's no tone reserved for unnatural disasters, and so we don't use any. We're flat-affect; we report just the facts; this alienates our audience."

Where the beginning mourner is on the continuum of talking and not talking is less important than finally making a conscious decision about what will lead to the best possible recovery. Mother had a good sense of what was best for her. The night of the funeral she sorted and reminisced to someone who loved her and listened. Then she left for the week's river trip and, when she returned she told me she hadn't told anyone. I was surprised she had been able to do that, but I came to believe that week of nature and silence was best.

Overwhelmed by the shocking newness of losing her children, Isadora Duncan could not be comforted. "[E]ven the sound of the human voice had become obnoxious to me." Perhaps a parent's heart can be so stricken that a force demands silence beyond understanding.

It takes time before shock subsides and grievers are able to find words to express their pain to others, though they are not looking for people who talk to them. They are looking for people to listen. The continuum of listeners range from those who salivate while hearing gory insinuating details of scandal to those whose eyes widen and shoulders stiffen as they step back to walk out the nearest door. Finding a good listener can happen as spontaneously as meeting a soulmate on an airplane. It can also be a lonely, tedious task.

Be aware if a person is listening as a friend, tabloid reader or is a nosy gossiper. Be aware if a person is willing to hear heartfelt emotion or wants to say, "Stop!" Be aware if the story is meaningful to the conversation, a bid to outdo another and if the person is ready to hear it. Be aware of the price of not talking if unsaid words are turning your insides into a sad or angry pretzel.

Most listeners want to do what's right and give a story the respect it deserves. They are compassionate to another's suffering, but sometimes it is very difficult to know how to listen or respond. A story can be so painful that some people must step back to protect their emotions. Some mourners are so frank and open that it becomes necessary for the listener to either equally open their heart without boundary or close it like a medieval castle gate. Listeners also deserve respect.

My talking style was quiet, words were painful to say. They were already beating themselves around in my head. It felt redundant and cruel to make others hear them. Just as important was the shame and sadness I could not express or admit to having. "Silence is deadly; it leaves you feeling hopeless, angry and isolated," O'Hara writes from personal as well as professional experience.

It was two years later when Sam and Zac took me to dinner for a birthday. On the drive home I was relaxed from being with comfortable company and having wine. Looking ahead as he drove, Sam talked about his childhood. It was a simple story told with humor of a four-year-old's feelings of displacement when his younger brother was born.

Vulnerable, tired and lost in faded grey memories that deeply hurt, tears fell. Upset, Zac walked away when we got home and I followed Sam to our bedroom. Close by him on the bed, I sobbed about how I had struggled with my brother's birth when I was five. When I blurted, "But I forgave him," there was a tremendous lurch of sound from Sam's chest so strong and unexpected, I was snapped out of my emotion.

I stopped talking because I believed I had gone too far in exposing my feelings. A few days later I asked what the sound from his throat meant. He looked at me and softly said, "I just felt so sad for you." At this far end of stoicism on the continuum it is difficult for people to express care, understanding and love.

Three things very much needed.

Visiting a psychologist or psychiatrist or becoming a member of a support group is often the best choice. They are discreet and can provide a faster path to recovery.

A mourner should observe the continuums of talking and listening. Motivations and ability of both sides are important. What grievers want and need to say should be with a chosen compassionate listener.

Outside Support – *Baba Yaga's question*

I bought the most expensive business suit of my career from the best store in town. Wrapped in plastic, price tag in place, it was prominently placed in the closet as a declarative statement. The next day I decided to visit a psychologist.

Sam was sitting in his office chair the morning I stood above him to tell him. He was accepting, quiet and probably relieved. I said I was allowing myself six visits. Perhaps a stranger would have better perspective and tell me what I wanted and needed to hear so I could put grieving aside. Only vaguely aware of my silly reasoning, I said the returned suit would help pay for the visits.

I felt guilty and weak. Several years had passed and the time for graciously allowed open grieving within a family was more than over. I hadn't been able to pull myself out of the greying, frayed sadness. Life was heavy and moving in ponderous steps I wanted lighter.

Overriding gloom loomed so long I thought it was me. I

didn't know how to kick it out, or even if I had a right to. Maybe I was doomed to suffer until. Until I understood the spiritual reasoning that led to Jody's death. Until I didn't miss him. Until someone said openly, clearly, loudly it wasn't my fault. Until I had suffered as much as my brother so I could say I'd put my time in, too. Until Sam left or I became bedridden with justified illness. Until some horrendous thing happened to prove life had its comeuppance for discounting the suffering of others until they took their own lives. Until I was finally just crazy bored with beating myself up. Murky self-blame and guilt beat sad and angry notes in my head with little relief.

Sam would occasionally listen to something I glossed over, hoping to get feelings out and away while not betraying just how deeply lost I felt. When I did talk with him, I could tell my pain was such a deep hurt that it became his. Talking to him didn't dissolve pain for me. It only gave me another person to exorcise it from.

I tried friends, but widening eyes, slight drop of a mouth and a half step back indicates a person is becoming overwhelmed. Rosencrantz said to Hamlet, "[W]hat is the cause of your distemper? You do surely bar the door upon your own liberty, if you deny your griefs to your friend." Yes, but grievers must discern what friends can handle. Oohs, aahs, head nods and sympathetic tears of friends are comforting in the beginning, but in the long run, those alone seldom have real nutrition to regain strength.

Without mental health insurance, I fell into the rabbit hole of not qualifying for low cost programs, and being unable to pay open market rates for an undetermined time. I hoped six visits would be enough. It was business. If I couldn't get something accomplished for a client in six hours of direct communication, one of us had nothing to gain. I figured the same for a psychologist and me.

My choice was an unintended recommendation of a client and the psychologist's proximity to the office. His office was modest. A woman in the waiting room buried her head in a magazine but seemed not to be looking at it. She was disheveled, unmatched and thrown together. I was called to the man's office. Not much taller than me, he was dressed as casually as his room was arranged. I told him how my brother died and I was not recovering well. I was sad and wanted to get over it. He eyed me like a bug. I sat before him in brown heels, nylons, a brown business skirt, tan business shirt, jacket, brown leather purse, gold earrings, bracelet and necklace. I wore make-up, my hair was well cut and my nails polished. He nodded while we considered each other.

He wanted to hear about that fertile landscape, childhood. After talking about the time of Jody's birth, I told him how I was given the news we were returning to Utah. Against instructions, I stepped off a patio while playing. On the first step I wailed in pain before getting cactus needles in my bare feet. Both parents appeared at the door, Father scooped me up and together they berated me. He returned to the couch and remained behind the newspaper. I was soon on my back on the floor with a foot in Mother's hand. She squinted and aimed the tweezers to pick out the needles while telling me we were moving to live with Grandma Lois in Utah. "And you didn't want to move again?" the psychologist gingerly asked. Defensively, I thought, "I'll run out of time and money talking about such elementary details, and still not have the answers I want."

I loved every move our father's work provided. In Wellton, Arizona I first met the gifts of desert, sun, beauty of sagebrush, cactus and distant mountain. Sometimes there were playmates and sometimes not though my imaginary friend, Henry, was there when children weren't, and we talked with the trees, cactus and sand. We met a desert caretaker with a red hat who Mother couldn't see. He wasn't any taller than me and sometimes popped out from behind a cactus. Henry went with us to Venice and then Twentynine Palms, California, but didn't come to Utah. He told me good-bye before returning to Wellton to work with the desert caretaker. It wasn't until we moved from Grandma's house in Kaysville to the dark basement apartment in Bountiful that I learned moves weren't always good.

The next week he wanted to hear about my marriage and sex life. I avoided sex on the grounds time was ticking away, and I discounted his need to hear. I talked about marriage so I wouldn't appear uncooperative, saying I was the one who handled the money and paid the bills. Again he looked at me. We had not connected. I can only guess I was not like the disheveled, distracted woman in the waiting room and I baffled him. I had some power in my marriage. He could not see how good my mask was or how excellently I compartmentalized.

Intrigued enough, I agreed to being hypnotized because it seemed a direct route. Lying on the couch, I watched the dangling watch he held in front of me and listened to his soft voice. We began talking about the move from California, the stay in Kaysville, Bountiful and then the move to Salt Lake. Half aware I heard myself talk with bits of the scene playing before me. I talked of first and second grade, and a teacher writing on a blackboard at the front of the room. At the sight of the blackboard I sat up without notice, turned and saw his surprise. "Was I hypnotized?"

"Yes."

"How could you tell?"

"I could tell."

He clammed up and I was infuriated. I knew he could tell because my arms were suspended during the time I talked and I felt them come down when I sat up. He ignored my question and refused to give me the barest indication of his method, which I took as an insult to my intelligence and ability to help myself. I had a minor epiphany. No one would address my sadness as directly as me.

Only I could forgive me and anything said by others was inadequate unless it swept through me in clear belief. I was chasing an illusory belief I had in childhood. If my father returned, life would be restored. Now, it was if people would only say the right words life would be restored. This journey was my job and only my job, no one else's. I would have envied the note Duncan received from a friend writing, "Isadora ... I pray you come to me. I will do my best to comfort you."

Scholar Clarissa Pinkola Estés tells the Russian tale of Vasalisa, whose dying mother gives her a doll to use as a talisman for intuition. She tucks the doll in her skirt pocket and becomes friends with it as she learns and grows in a difficult childhood with a distant father, and of course, a cruel stepmother and step-sisters. The doll represents the life source tucked deeply within everyone. Vasalisa is sent to get fire from the fearsome witch Baba Yaga who yelled at the small girl demanding to know what she wanted. Vasalisa trembled and said she had come for fire. "Baba Yaga snapped, 'Well, you useless child ... you let the fire go out. [W]hat makes you think I should give you the flame?' Vasalisa consulted her doll and quickly replied, 'Because I ask.' Baba Yaga purred, 'You're lucky. That's the right answer.'"

Baba Yaga answered in a folk tale. Christ said, ask and you shall receive. Current business sales books teach people to ask for the sale. The beginning hero readies to meet new life by looking at the self, appraising the situation, and being a participant in her recovery.

Asking for help is not always easy. Unfortunately, support groups did not exist when I needed them. There were general ones, but the experience of shame and the response of others who had never dealt with suicide prevented me. Specialized groups came on the scene later when I had come to a peace that didn't need them. I haven't any doubt they serve a tremendous need as people regain their footing. Often the funeral home can suggest one, local community papers carry meeting information, church leaders have contacts, mental health professionals sponsor groups, or a friend who has suffered in the same way may have names.

A support group would have helped me avoid hurting Mother, burdening Sam, and frightening friends. Support groups have unique personalities, just as psychologists and psychiatrists do and if one doesn't fit, look for another. I know years of grief could have been trimmed if I had found people to truly, deeply, openly talk about the messy, awful nightmare from start to finish. Understanding, acceptance and empathy are powerful healers. People with similar experiences can remove any number of awful feelings through discussion. We see in them a reflection of our experience and observe we are human and normal.

Others can point out circumstances and perspectives of family members and friends we know nothing about and who also need understanding. Nadle writes of a young man who was in a psychiatrist led support group after his mother died by suicide. "[H]e'd come to understand that he'd been blaming his father for everything that had happened, when really his parents had issues he knew nothing about and his position didn't require him to judge either of them."

Family and friends didn't hang me out to squirm and suffer alone. Some were too immersed in their own grief. Others could not bear to look at the pain of the situation. Some simply hadn't an interest in hearing what to them sounded like whining. I knew it was difficult for anyone to see how I ached as I muffled myself, leading people to believe my real personality was quieter and more serious than it is.

My marriage was strained in a strange knot of boredom and aggression. We were at a point of needing to settle things or give it enough effort to alleviate pain when it was over. Sam broke the impasse. He started asking who I was and accepting it. Sometimes his questions or observations were silly, tough, insightful or hurtful. We started listening more deeply to each other, both of us armed with years of knowing the other. It took both of us to step out from behind our façades to meet more than half way. Nothing happened overnight or easily, but the effort loosened a knot.

Emotional aftermath can be as fatal as the death itself. Without relief or understanding, the burden can be very heavy within a household. Members of the same family may not see the depth of another's pain. Despondency, anger or a host of other feelings can surface as cover-up. Divorces happen, children run wild or clam up so tight that offered love doesn't reach their un-nurtured souls. It's lovely to say those who share our grief the closest should be our ally and buffer against the storm, but they are also sufferers, often deeply wounded ones. Mistakenly, one can be seen as uncaring while another appears melodramatic or weak. Others are genuinely rapid in working through grief to a true, peaceful acceptance and they can become confused or angry when another can't. Impartial outside ears can counteract tension and misunderstandings.

The grieving hero needs a support group, social worker, psychologist, psychiatrist or a friend who will sincerely be the listening ears and watching face. Isadora Duncan visited her friend, and later wrote that the friend said, "'Tell me about Deirdre and Patrick,' and made me repeat to her all their little sayings and ways, and show her their photos, which she kissed and cried over. She never said, 'Cease to grieve,' but she grieved with me, and, for the first time since their death, I felt I was not alone."

Revenge vs Justice – *Hamlet's choice*

People want justice for the death of a loved one when it was because of a foolish driver, cruel, sadistic or careless person, painful random disease or failure of so-called good equipment. Every day there are deaths that require something be done to right a wrong. Imaginations run wild as grievers mentally replay what should happen to the person, faulty equipment manufacturer, or impersonal disease that caused an unnecessary death.

Bereaved people focus on injustices to help them regain control and "make things right." Delivering justice maintains order, prevents chaos, has improved society and protected others. Candy Lightner, the inspiring force behind MADD, changed society's views and saved lives. The Amber Alert was started after Amber Hagerman was randomly abducted and murdered. The community effort of her hometown of Arlington, Texas began after it was ripped to the core by witnessing the media frenzy and family suffering that made everyone feel vulnerable.

Disease also stirs the spirit to find cures and fight corporations, health standards and governments. The successful Susan G. Koman Race for the Cure was started by her sister, Nancy G. Brinker, who promised to work to save others after Susan's death from breast cancer. Started in 1982, the foundation has donated over one billion dollars to research, education and health services. Unnecessary deaths have inspired survivors to fight corporations for higher safety standards in industries ranging from automobiles to fire-resistant clothing.

Revenge and justice both rise from tumultuous emotions: The death was wrong, cruel and/or needless. Like any emotion-filled argument, justice and revenge create its own energy that builds to a pitch. Admit the feeling, feel it deeply, let nothing stand in the way. Cry, scream while passionately banging a hammer, cutting firewood, digging a new garden or hitting balls. Eventually, the body tires of peak emotions; often long before the heart is ready. During a lull of spent emotions, when a person feels drained and empty, is a time to closely look at this continuum.

What is felt in grief's beginning isn't important. What is important is what ends up being the griever's overriding attitude and desired end result. Is the goal to improve the world, reset society's parameters of behavior and make a positive difference for others who follow, or is it to strike back with equal or greater force of pain and suffering?

The need for justice can be so overwhelming that all sense

of what we do to ourselves and those around us is forgotten as we work to right the wrong. Hamlet stood at the door of decision in Act I, Scene V when his father's ghost talks to him, "If thou didst ever thy dear father love—Revenge his foul and most unnatural murder." The scene ends with Hamlet's resolve to take revenge and he answers, "Rest, rest perturbed spirit. O cursed spite, That ever I was born to set it right!"

Throughout the play, Hamlet becomes increasingly distraught and vengeful until his choices take him to the black backwaters of destruction. While talking with the new king and his friend Laertes, he says, "Then Hamlet does it not: Hamlet denies it. Who does it then? His madness. If it be so, Hamlet is of the faction that is wronged; His madness is poor Hamlet's enemy." He is so distraught he talks of himself in the third person, thus moving blame of his action outside of himself. He sees himself as a victim of grief and madness. Mental health, commonsense, love for others, law, personal safety and health are compromised.

Hamlet was propelled to revenge, as was Aeneas when he sees the bodies of his soldiers and family in Troy after losing the battle. He vows, "[A]nd it will be a joy to fill my soul with vengeful fire, to satisfy the ashes of my people." Summoned to her son's side because his raging emotions reach heaven, Aeneas' long dead mother pleads, "My son, what bitterness has kindled this fanatic anger? Why this madness?" She successfully convinces him to leave the destruction behind and lead the remaining soldiers to a new home.

King Arthur's nephew, Sir Gawain, was consumed by revenge when he followed Sir Lancelot to France and challenged him to fight to the death. Sir Gawain's last words were, "I am about to die; and I would make it known that my death was of my own seeking, that I was moved by the spirit of revenge and spite to provoke you to battle." A consuming quest for justice and revenge can be every bit as devastating to the griever as the death of the beloved.

Traumatic griefs often require survivors to sort through justice and revenge, wondering how a murderer, driver, negligent caretaker, etc., or situation such as faulty equipment, disease, etc., should be held responsible. Grief's target can be a person, situation, disease, corporation, or the self. The rest of a griever's life can be spent making someone or something pay for a real or imagined part played in the death.

Grievers can be convinced the justice system doesn't work. Quirks of law and rules of evidence can seem irrelevant or shallow. Perhaps the police could have done a better job, the defense lawyer was sneaky and unethical, or the accused bought their way out of courtrooms. There are thousands of tragedies where justice does not satisfy a griever.

Justice and revenge were sacred duties to the Norsemen, though their god of justice, Forseti, was described as wise and gentle as he held court in the hall of Glitnir. Forseti's father was Odin's favorite son, Balder, who was accidentally killed by the blind god Hodr. Odin sought revenge through another son, Vali, whose only purpose in being born was to kill Hodr. The grace of Forseti's life is instead of dwelling in revenge, he reconciled enemies to bring peace.

The Norse warrior woman, Brunhilde, was in a magical sleep until kissed by the hero Sigurd. They should have lived happily ever after, but Sigurd was tricked into betraying Brunhilde. She was then tricked into arranging Sigurd's murder as vengeance. Brunhilde changed herself from a victim to a perpetrator. When she discovered the truth of Sigurd being tricked, she took her own life. Brunhilde made a decision for revenge as did Sir Gawain at the hand of Sir Lancelot. Some people run headlong and alone into their own ruin while others prefer company. Distraught people who fatally challenge police to end their lives are often deeply suffering from earlier unsettled hurts.

At the Gate of Trials – *Kali's invitation*

The griever stands at the gate of trials with consciousness, a style of grieving and a degree of acceptance. There have been attempts to recover in ways thought to be appropriate or expected, but still grief remains.

In this land of everything happening at once and in no particular order, I found myself out of the horror of the underworld, standing wobbly kneed, staring at problems. Sam and Zac were symbols of respect for the life I needed to live. I accepted that recovery would take time and forever be in degrees, which was fine because I thought total recovery would mean Jody's life meant little and wasn't worth remembering. I also knew my recovery was still too close to a mental self-destruction. I believed the why me issue was an immature view that assumed unhappy events should only touch others. I knew overcoming was impossible, only accepting would grant some peace. Talking and outside support had lost some importance, but I wanted acceptance and the company of other people. I didn't like the body feeling of revenge and didn't feel capable of understanding justice.

Standing at the gate of trials is a time of conscious attention to facing the trials. It is Harry Potter no longer afraid of learning the power and potential of his wizardry. It is Superman accepting his situation and still working as a positive force. It is Dorothy, the Tin Man, Scarecrow and Lion the night before they set off to kill the Wicked Witch.

Interfaith minister Judy Wolf writes in her book, *Spiritual Life Rafts*, that she spent several years caring for her son's every daily need after he was hit by a car. When he passed away, she came to this gate and wrote, "yet with brokenness comes possibility, an invitation to heal, to become a changed person, to transcend the sadness. Do I become bitter or better?"

The griever has been in the dark underworld chambers and emerged forever changed. But whether new consciousness and sight of death touches her with wisdom and growth or shackles her in grief's pathos is still to be tested.

It is time to face societal and personal stumbling blocks that hinder recovery. It is daunting, perhaps overwhelming, when the hero realizes all the areas of life that have changed. The hero, Hercules, was sent to kill the monster, Hydra. When Hercules struck with his club, Hydra instantly grew new heads. He tried again and again, only to see more and more heads grow. At last Hercules tried a new method and burned them off, and they did not return. Clubbing monsters and handling grief in the same old way does not work. When there is no creativity, new life is denied.

Kali, a goddess of Hindu tradition is described by Campbell as a cosmic power. "[T]he harmonization of all the pairs of opposites, combining wonderfully the terror of absolute destruction with an impersonal yet motherly reassurance. As change, the river of time, the fluidity of life, the goddess at once creates, preserves and destroys."

Kali does not menacingly grow when attacked like Hydra. Instead, she invites grievers to transformation. Kali confronts grievers who sit too long in the unchanged bedroom that has become a shrine, or refuse to acknowledge how grief has changed them. Glorify the past. Deny the importance of the past. Both responses miss the potential of Kali's message of destruction, preserving and creating. Her dance entices us to not be afraid of following her.

My less dramatic experience with Kali and Hydra was the realization that simply ignoring my responsibility of participation in recovery does not remove it. Pretending I could keep a problem to myself and expect the rest of life to not be effected didn't work. Pretending life was normal because my daily routines hadn't changed didn't work. I had to participate, probe and look at each issue until it was healed. And, like Hydra, if problems were not faced and openly admitted, more heads grew and snaked their way into other parts of life and relationships. The potential hero slowly learns through trials that new ways, better approaches and more thoughtful thinking are what work.

If Kali's invitation is frightening, the mental picture of a gentle sleeping princess can be imagined. Years can pass recovering too slowly or not at all if we are in a mental sleep, until eventually, there is an awakening by a kiss from a deeper, stronger part of the self. Revitalized, it is now time to face trials and learn to live again.

The kiss I received came as a three hundred page catalog. Seeming to come out of nowhere, Sam and I got a large job that required endless keystrokes, dozens of page layouts and six months of work. As pages came in we re-arranged our schedules to keep pace. Days still required regular work for long-time clients, so I began staying late. My work day started at 11:00 am, and at 5:00 I took over from the typesetter and stayed, sometimes until 11:00 pm. Only on Friday did I leave early, at 8:00. In the beginning I was irritated by the time it took, but soon I was grateful. For the first time I could be alone without tears dripping down my face. The routine click of the keys and attention to details insulated me from realizing I was alone. Only twice, when I was very tired from the work and long hours, did tears blur the screen.

Curser move by curser move I did the work. When I would

leave the quiet building late at night, I felt satisfied my work had value. Others depended on it. My days were filled with the same expectation, but the routine of life before the death was discounted. I needed this sliver of newness. It angered me when Sam suggested I take an evening off. Did he think I was unable to carry my load? Itty-bitty as my effort was, it was the first time in two years I didn't feel like a weak-willed, compliant blob.

The catalog meant a good chunk of extra money and from the beginning Sam had several ideas where it should be spent. I only wanted to have it, not use it, not squander anything or take a reward. The idea of spending it felt painful. If it was safely in a bank I could point to a job completed with evident payment. The money was not to be enjoyed, it was to be held as evidence of my value.

Sam wanted a week-long Caribbean cruise. I suggested Mazatlan as a compromise. No, he finally declared, the three of us were going to visit the historic, exotic and intriguing Caribbean. A week before leaving, I was weak with nervousness and fear. Would this go through? Did I deserve it? Could there be pleasure? Zac and I went on a Sunday walk and I felt weak enough to embarrass him by sitting on a stranger's front lawn to recover before walking on. My eye twitched, and body muscles ached and jerked. I couldn't concentrate. What was wrong? I had always been the one who wanted travel, not Sam. I felt disbelief, guilt, anticipation, fright, pleasure, joy, hope, fear.

I wondered why I hadn't felt this way when we went to

Mexico after Sam's mother died, "Because," the voice whispered, "you expected no pleasure. It was too soon. Too soon after Jody's death and too soon after Lupe's. You were cradling Sam as well as yourself. It wasn't a reward for work accomplished. It was a drastic step to see if you could still breathe. Now you're going for pleasure. For yourself. You worked for it."

    I stared at the miles below passing in miniature scale as we flew across the country. In the Dominican Republic I saw a young, shoeless boy of about seven holding his morning catch of colorful fish over his back while he walked alone, smiling and confident. He didn't lose a footfall to beg from our passing jeep. Miles before and after him, other young boys would leap from the forest to run with arms outstretched for loose change thrown toward them. Their faces were drawn, hypnotized in belief the money thrown on the whim of people born to more was their fate. There was no hope or animation in their faces like in the little fisherman's. What made the difference? What made the other boys persist in an exhausting and usually fruitless run after jeeps that never stopped to offer solace, never cared or understood the lost looks in their faces?

    In bright Haitian sunlight fears lurked in quiet streets at noon. Passengers were told to hire tour guides and travel in packs. The French iron grill above gates was whimsy against fading green and pink colonial buildings masking danger. Eyes in the market looked through us or at us in anger. As our ship pulled away I wondered if filigreed iron gates enclosed their lives until the next ship harbored. I wondered why the dappling sun reflecting from the sea to the rooftops did not bleach and cleanse the danger they held for each other.

Energy over-rode fear in Puerto Rico's daylight while a million people bustled to earn a living. They jostled one another on streets, honked car horns, took children to school and noisily chatted in cafes until sunset, when they disappeared in their homes as hostages. Traveling by bus through the deserted night streets was like entering a child's dream of darkness immediately after school where everyone vanishes and I am alone. As we sailed away, sipping fruity drinks and listening to the band play for our personal party, the city's twinkling lights were an illusion through the hauntingly quiet streets left to the few who use them at night.

Walking the ship's deck, exploring in mad, excited dashes each unique island, all three of us felt the largesse of the world and potential of lives so different than ours. Exotic foods cooked in open air pots in front yards and oversized perfumed flowers made our sedate mountain flowers seem puny and stingy. We were among smooth, black-skinned, beautiful people who smiled, ignored and disliked us as we walked their streets.

"What was it, Jody?" I thought on that trip, "You didn't realize how big the world is, how many possibilities are outside of our valley, how many ways of life exist? Did you think there was only the way you had grown up and since you could not make it work, no matter how hard you tried, you thought you were a failure? Just because you didn't fit where you grew up you thought you could not move?

"Now that you see from an endless horizon of space do you ache for what could have been? Do you see the masses of unhappy people, working every day for just enough to eat? Do you see the life you lived was a grain of sand? Do you see the people you could have met, who need your love and will never have it? Do you see a life's work that wasn't where you were, but now will never be found? Or was your purpose in life to know how easy it is to drive one's self crazy, to experience the drama, the pathos of ending your life? Perhaps Mother and I are ghostly secondary walk-ons to your drama. Are we playing our roles well?"

Traveling is a Pandora's box of possibility. Before a trip I study the itinerary, and imagine what it holds. During my travels the Pandora's box always opens, and out flies adventure, learning, fabrics, new food, faces, sex, quiet, noise, trees, rocks, water, life I have never seen in that way. Then while coming home, I realize they are gone to me and all I am left to hold is memory.

When Pandora opens the box, all problems fly out to cause heartache and misery in an innocent world. The only thing left she could keep was hope. Perhaps that was the very slowest to leave because it is the last thing people have, a frail persistent butterfly that does not rely on planning, knowledge, birthright, circumstance or work.

There are terrible things that happen without apparent human choice or desire, but life is also full of choices. It is a choice to die or stagnate at this gate along the path of the lower branches. Mentally and/or physically. Many have.

Stranded in desolate mountains, his life in peril, Parrado stood with his mother and sister's bodies only yards away. His hope, his symbol, was the devastation his father would be suffering, and he vowed, "[I] will come home. I will not let the bond between us be broken. I promise you, I will not die here! I will not die here!"

The Fourth Challenge

Society's Trials

Society is operating as it always has, but now the griever has an altered view. He might assign new meaning to beliefs he didn't expect to ever question. Society's trials center on standards, reactions and expectations in daily life. News reports, surveys, scientific studies, friends, psychologists, psychiatrists, judges, and juries broadcast their opinions and decisions on the behavior of everyone involved, reinforcing collective beliefs, while the personal experience of grief can seem planets away.

Watching Others Take Risks – *Icarus' flight*

A friend was in a motorcycle accident on I-80 outside Wendover, Nevada. He was life-flighted to a hospital and months passed while he hovered between life and death in a deeply drugged existence. He has a lot of friends who watched and waited with his wife and family until he regained consciousness. Newly aware of what happened to him and who we were, he looked into each of our faces as if for the first time. "So beautiful," he declared each of us with a voice so sincere it felt as a benediction. Survivors who return from the edge of death are full of new awareness and appreciation. Always a gregarious, cheerful and grateful person, my friend became more so. On the other hand, everyone around him reconsidered their relationship with motorcycles. His motorcycle friends had one more reason to drive defensively. The rest of us settled at degrees of awareness, respect, gratitude, alarm, fear and loathing.

Icarus and his father, Daedalus, were imprisoned by King Minos in a Greek myth. To save his son and himself, Daedalus took a calculated, but risky chance. Methodically, he constructed delicate wings of collected feathers and wax so he and his son could leap to safety. After careful testing and instruction, the loving father began his flight with Icarus closely following. Countless works of art portray the moment Daedalus looks back to realize his son was flying against his instructions, toward the sun's heat. The delicate wings melted and Icarus fell to his death in the blue sea. In another myth Phaeton, Apollo's son, rode his father's chariot toward the sun against Apollo's instructions, and also fell to his death.

Icarus and Phaeton did not follow instructions. Daedalus believed he needed to take the risk, Apollo was convinced to allow the risk. My friend wanted the risk. Tom Shaw's son, Seth, also chose the risk when he took up mountain climbing. Initially upset with his son's mountain climbing, Shaw eventually came to terms saying, "It was just something he had to do, which I could not relate to in the slightest." Seth died during a climb in 2000.

Extreme skiing was the subject of the 2007 documentary, *Steep*. A local reviewer wrote: "This documentary about big-mountain extreme skiing can be captured best by the line 'The closer you come to dying, the more alive you feel,' uttered memorably by its main subject, ski legend Doug Coombs, who died skiing in the French Alps."

Grievers know the world is unreliable, capricious or dangerous. Life is fragile and people are forever in danger. They reassess the risks of everyday living. Car accidents give new awareness to driving. An airplane crash can traumatize survivors about flying. Diseases are silent, invisible invaders.

Experience can turn survivors into skittish observers. They might decide people shouldn't have, be around or even look at guns because they are unpredictably dangerous. Perhaps no one should be allowed to drive until they're twenty-five, mountain climbing should be illegal and why are ATVs allowed? Germs are marching armies to be constantly fought. Plus, if God wanted people to fly, we'd have wings. Daedalus and Apollo know what can happen.

I know it isn't funny when someone laughs and says, "It was so embarrassing, I could just kill myself." I look closely at the talker and strain to listen with a third ear. How serious are they? Meanwhile, the old mental film replays of Jody buying a .357 magnum and a box of bullets on a beautiful August morning. I see his chest spraying blood, heart and bits of muscle all over a picnic ground. The memory doesn't always replay now, but there is a momentary zap I push myself from.

New mourners live in the cracks below normal living. They can't separate trauma of what has happened from the casual way people live day to day. When lost in the crack it is easy to believe you have new information on how the world works and it can feel like a duty to yell warnings. "Don't speed!" "Don't have guns!" "Don't climb mountains!" "Don't fly!" "Don't smoke." "Don't take drugs." "Remember your insulin." Survivors want to grab strangers and dear ones to save them from themselves and each other. It's difficult to understand the casual expectation people have of living another day.

In the beginning, when Mother and I needed to fill time we didn't want, we sometimes went to a movie. We picked them carefully to avoid any replay of not only gunfire, but almost any other re-enactment of death. We couldn't separate grief from entertainment. Before I was ready, I tried a mainstream movie with Sam and Zac where blood was as present as the leading man. I had to leave and wait in the lobby.

I knew where Jody bought the .357 magnum since the local store's name was on the sales receipt I found in the car. I never shopped there again. Not because they sold guns, but because I knew where Jody bought his. I might walk his footsteps away from the cashier and out the front door. In my reasoning, the steps might tell the universe I accept the situation, and will continue life untouched.

But, I knew I must adjust and regain perspective if I wanted to be healthy. I made myself listen to and read the positions of the NRA. I forced myself to stand in front of the gun display in K-Mart and stare at handguns as shoppers walked by and salesmen eyed me. I wanted release from the grip of that .357 magnum.

I didn't like guns before and don't love them now, but I comprehend the reasons some people are attached to them. If Jody had died in a car accident I wouldn't give up driving. I doubt Parrado wants to rid the earth of mountains or airplanes. I understand, too, why some people dive into working with charities and non-profits that deal with the reason for death.

Time lessens the sensitivity to society's indifference to risk taking. Slowly, a more normal perception re-emerges. Fear of guns, automobiles, dangerous sports, planes or the inevitability of germs and genetics subsides but doesn't disappear.

In time there is acceptance that people will recklessly drive cars, misuse guns and people who swim well will drown. There is realization free and brave spirits who willingly try what most won't are the people who lead into new territories. They push the limits of sports, endurance and science. There are body and mind pleasures that sports and thrill-seeking give their devotees. They earn the pleasures and should have them.

Witnesses may have wondered if they should interfere when Layton Kor announced, before attempting Yosemite's Steck-Slathé, "I want to see if I'm afraid to die." On the other hand, society is impatient with frightened people who refuse risk. This is a continuum the loved one staked a place on. Both extremes of the brave and the frightened have the right to live at their point in the continuum.

I had a small surgery and when I came out of anesthesia there was a day of return to that crack under normal living of unprotected emotion and awareness of fragility. Television commercials were achingly poignant and filled with life's potential. I sniffled as I watched men mow lawns and mothers and children smile at each other over pudding. People are beautiful. The effort to live well through simple acts is tender. Life is fragile. I try to remember this.

But like the Greek hero Daedalus who worked to save his son only to lose him, the best, most sincere efforts to protect, educate, warn, and prevent do not always succeed. The forces of chance, nature, physics and human personality are not to be controlled.

Edward Abby wrote in *Desert Solitaire*, "A venturesome minority will always be eager to set off on their own, and no obstacles should be placed in their path; let them take risks, for Godsake, let them get lost, sunburnt, stranded, drowned, eaten by bears, buried alive under avalanches—that is the right and privilege of any free American." He can call it a right and privilege. I will add people's actions and decisions are not decided by those who love them.

Reaction of Others – *But, you must know, your father lost a father.*

News of Jody's death was on radio and television the day it

happened and had press coverage the next morning. Utah experiences over three hundred suicides a year so it wasn't how he died but where. It happened in a picnic area in the middle of the day on an otherwise slow news day.

At first I didn't notice a thin support because I was busy hibernating into invisibility, afraid and too fragile. The horror I saw in people's eyes and heard in awkward phrases at the funeral was enough. I'm also sure the haunted looks of shock Mother and I wore warned people to be careful. Feelings of responsibility were laying fast deep roots into shame, and feeling that way, I was not anxious to be around others.

Sudden, unnatural deaths can cast implicating shadows on surviving mourners that keep them from the company of others. Endlessly they recall the lost moment when a child disappears in a swimming pool, or the fatal decision to give car keys to a teenager. It would be difficult to mentally process the results of requesting a spouse climb a ladder to put up holiday lights, or remember the shrug of hopeless disgust when a loved one took a fatal dose of a drug there was argument about for years. Agreeing an abusive partner could be given one more chance would be a regret.

Survivors easily imagine others hold them responsible whether they do or not, and the surrounding feelings can keep them isolated and afraid of people's responses. For several weeks I avoided social activities though I returned to work, where people seemed either unknowing or uneasy.

A few times I felt myself losing breath as though I were

drowning when people said benign phrases that left pinholes imagination could twist to believe they held me as responsible as I held myself. The internal voices were so loud I routinely said, "What?" to people because their voices were drowned out by internal ones. Much of my depleted energy went to conscious effort to not publicly cry or scream in fear of my own vaporing existence that floated before me as a ghost.

"An odd byproduct of my loss is that I'm aware of being an embarrassment to everyone I meet. At work, at the club, in the street, I see people, as they approach me, trying to make up their minds whether they'll 'say something about it' or not. I hate it if they do, and if they don't." C.S. Lewis' wife was expected to die, but he felt society's discomfort.

Lewis and I were around people whose words were spare, but others viciously attack. There certainly is enough volatile emotion after dramatic deaths for ammunition, but whichever way angry or hurt words fly, it isn't helpful. Job's friends in the Old Testament were kind enough to visit, but unfortunately it deteriorated into accusations, hurt and anger.

When Grandma Spiking began facing a slow winding down of life, it seemed she was upset that after a life of faithfully serving her spiritual beliefs and being a good independent citizen she was suffering age's indifferent indignity. I didn't learn whether she was angrier with the slow loss of body control, death in any form, or that she was in a nursing home. She had spent time living in both daughters' houses in the last years, but at the end she was cared for by strangers, and when I visited she sat staring out a window with arms folded in what seemed to be angry prayer. Only a strident "humph" or a weary nod acknowledged my visit.

When she died people were somber but always empathetic. I was sorry to lose what my grandmother added to life, but incredibly light-headed with relief I did not feel responsible or judged. Her death was the accepted life's path and didn't cast shadows. Still, there are people who act like any mourner has a communicable disease. Years later, when I felt familiar with the social awkwardness of death, I listed possible reasons why talking wasn't easier.

1. People who are uncomfortable or unfamiliar with death suffer their own shock and grief, and are unable to offer condolence. They can be so unaccustomed to death that they need reassurance.

2. Perhaps those with a similar event in their history had not forgiven themselves of something, so how could they be kind to me? Their avoidance was based on a fear for themselves more than knowledge of me.

3. They truly believed I held responsibility and were communicating that belief. Many do blame surrounding family members for suicides, parents for accidental deaths of children or any driver involved in a car accident. Society's judgment can be so brutal it can result in people moving to different neighborhoods, cities or states, vowing never to reveal their full history.

4. Perhaps they also felt a twinge of guilt or responsibility about something in their relationship with Jody. For that, I

have compassion.

5. They hadn't any idea of the ocean-sized need I had of their understanding or how I was interpreting their actions. Therefore, I reasoned, they were innocent of any purposeful intention and I needed to get over my self-consciousness that assumed their belief.

6. Some believe mourning is a waste of time and avoidable. They may see any death unemotionally. Hamlet's step-father, the King, said to him, "Tis sweet and commendable in your nature, Hamlet, To give these mourning duties to your father: But, you must know, your father lost a father; [T]o persever in obstinate condolement is a course of impious stubbornness; 'tis unmanly grief ...."

7. Something else, and did it matter?

As I wrote this list I worked on not being hurt, angered or vindictive of anyone's response. Later I also believed that everyone's feelings of understanding and forgiveness, or the lack of it, is their responsibility, and has nothing to do with me.

Separate from judgement or social awkwardness, the value of openly acknowledging the death with one to three sentences is important. This is helpful for a new mourner to hear for two reasons. If she is still in shock it reinforces the truth she barely comprehends. Just as important, it lets the mourner know there is awareness and there isn't an obligation to deliver the news, so at the next meeting there aren't any questions on how the now dead beloved is doing. My mother agonized numerous times when she didn't know if a casual acquaintance "knew."

She didn't want to bring it up if they did, and yet she dreadfully feared the next time she saw the person he would ask how her son was doing.

Acknowledgement also tells the mourner there is care and acceptance for her as a human being. When the people we live and work with accept the situation as openly and factually as a divorce, it removes uncertainty and gives acceptance. Even when this is done, emerging heroes eventually face a realization: Kind words from others is sweet, but heroes nourish themselves.

Society has made tentative steps in accepting death and making it easier for everyone to openly acknowledge it. Still, talking to the newly bereaved can appear frightening and a loser's gamble to people who want to say the right thing. The short, but not always simple, answer is that people need reassurance and words from others at the time of death to welcome them back into the fold.

As time continues we meet new people who do not know our past. Some deaths and family circumstances always remain difficult to talk about, so choices are made about what to tell people we want close. Painful as it was to tell people of his brother's life and death, Mikel Gilmore felt it was important. "I also met women who, when they learned who my brother was, would never see me again, never take my calls again. I also got letters from people who thought I should have been shot alongside my brother." In time I became immune to those who judge. I believe they don't know what they are doing and even if they do, their opinion no longer matters.

Deflecting Conversations – *Gilgamesh's question*

"Do you have brothers or sisters?" A new acquaintance with blue, brown or hazel eyes would be open and friendly as I stuttered a no. Lying was painful, so the next time I said yes and mumbled, "A brother." Interested eyes watched for an explanation of the brother's whereabouts. Knowing I couldn't answer, I changed the subject. I'd told the truth and not denied his existence. At first I was capable of nothing more. Usually the conversation awkwardly continued, but people felt rebuffed. New acquaintances present a problem until a griever is re-oriented in how to participate in social conversation with people who do not need or want to hear about a tragedy.

"Yes, but he passed away," I said as I held my wine glass at another event and felt victorious I was so smooth. Human beings are curious creatures, so again I was confronted with a tilted head waiting for a response. "Uhh," my voice cracked, "he did it. Four months ago." She walked away.

"'Why do you draw back like that?' He asked." Gilgamesh saw fear in a new friend's eyes as she looked at him. Mourners shouldn't be blunt with strangers, but in the beginning we are awkward at diverting conversations. My sympathies are with the struggling griever. The person who unwittingly asked the question is, in my opinion, obligated to stanch the wound. A simple, "I'm sure it was awful. I hope it gets easier for you," is enough. It's unlikely mourners will plunge into a full story in an awkward social setting. It is more likely they will take a deep breath, blink their eyes and change the conversation.

Without a lump in the throat and still smiling, I later said, "I had a brother, but he took his own life. Years ago and it was awful." Then I continued on another subject so the listener wasn't put on the spot, "You said you have a brother. What's his name?" The answer was usually so quick that I wondered if commas existed in speech. A cocked head and lifted eyebrow with a look of sincere interest has persuaded me to say more, but only if the circumstance is right. Everyone is entitled to the secrets of their lives. If and when I decide a person will listen with a caring attitude and the situation is comfortable, I am no longer afraid or unable to talk, but there is also no obligation.

Candy Lightner writes, "Before Cari died, I had three children. Now what do I say? For a while, I said I had two children. Then I got irritated and said I had three. Now I explain, when there is a need for more conversation, that one is dead." What listeners don't realize is how painful it is to deny the existence of someone we love very much, yet we know they don't want to hear any pain or anger in a voice.

There isn't an easy or right answer. It was important for me to be as truthful as possible, but if another chose to deflect the conversation or avoid an answer, I support their right. I know how difficult it is to know what to say, especially in the beginning when it is perhaps impossible to feel pleasure for another's fortune of having a spouse, child, parent, dear friend or sibling. When Terkel's wife died, he expressed feeling blue to a friend, and the reply was, "For chrissake, you've had sixty great years with her!" Our fast paced society expects drive-up and drive-by mourning.

Blossoms of the Lower Branches

For a long time I glided and glossed over subjects I wished to avoid. I was good at turning conversation away from unwelcome questions. It became easier to listen to people talk of their families and few returned the interest. Most of us are far more interested in talking about ourselves, so I let them. They often get so wrapped up in meandering stories they never ask me anything. If they say, "My brother's a chemical engineer," I'll counter with, "What does a chemical engineer do?" They seldom ask if I have a brother.

Being comfortable with the continuing lives of friends was slower. One would say something as simple as, "I'm going to my brother's for dinner," and I felt sad for an hour. In time I smiled at the news but said nothing. In more time I learned to say, "Does he do the cooking?" Later I learned to enjoy hearing the answer.

It became an advantage to hear others talk. I compared life experiences and gained perspective. The stories didn't end like mine, but the relationships I heard about were often littered with disagreements, and more than one was estranged. The value of hearing helped me more fully accept that the cause of Jody's death was not as simple as saying his childhood was flawed and his sister a screw-up. My ruined childhood memories that lived in shadows very slowly regained a little color from the conversations, and I became more aware of the world's need for happiness. It didn't happen with the first story, but slowly, as a scab on the knee, the pain healed with new skin underneath until I was pleased for others.

Mourners have blind spots. How many healthy, happy people want to spend five minutes with a morose friend who endlessly says things like, "[F]or there is nothing either good or bad, but thinking makes it so," as Hamlet did? The abyss of a deep griever is disorienting and frightening. Hamlet would have done well to carefully write his thoughts for private reflection or hire the company of a philosophy student caught up in the same issues.

Guiding conversation to a gracious end and not swerving from the truth of our life is a private and worthy victory. The ability to make the asker of a small and friendly social question comfortable and without regret is earned mental recovery. At first it didn't feel like a victory or recovery. Having to talk of my brother as a dead person was one more piece of his existence floating away. Much further down the road of the hero's journey through these lower branches, I realized that was impossible. He is forever an indelible part of my history.

Talking with Mother was a different story. In the early years we would find ourselves with throbbing throats and red eyes trying not to cry while wounding ourselves time and again with what could have been, should have been and never would be. At some point I suggested we try not to bring up Jody's name. I could no longer bear her many sentences that started, "When Jody was here." When Jody was here we would play cards and he always won. When Jody was here I could blame my messiness on him. When Jody was here I didn't have to chop my own wood.

Mentioning her son, my brother, needed a "was" and I would never be enough. I could not refill either of our hearts. I survived to forever be only half of what Mother and I knew was possible. We were depleted by his absence, realizing the richness he took with him. There is no keeping a father who needs to leave or being enough for a mother left behind.

I hope it was the right time to suggest we slow down on our talk of Jody. It may have been too soon for what she needed but I felt crushed by the conversations. What a terrible position I put her in. Unable to talk freely with the living child about the dead one. We have never stopped talking about him, but it is less often.

Mother would not accompany Grandma Spiking to a fiftieth wedding anniversary party for friends from years ago. She shuddered at the possible question, "How are your children, Gloria?" I went instead because fewer people would ask me questions. In fact, nobody did; they smiled at me and asked Grandma about her children.

Reassessment of Value – *Salt Woman's lament*

The Zuni Indians in the Southwest were said to annually visit Salt Woman to gather her life sustaining mineral. They stayed for days in her lake home, walking barefoot in the soft sand to gather salt and offering thanks. She was always happy to see them, but as years passed the respect and kindness people showed her became irregular and then disappeared entirely. They came to expect the life-sustaining salt as a right and didn't stay to visit. Sadly, she caused the lake to dry, leaving sharp salt rocks to cut their feet. In time they covered their feet and approached her dry lake bed with renewed appreciation, "Salt Mother, we are glad that you have come to this house, we are glad of your flesh."

In grief many things are reassessed along a continuum of value. Everyone has a system of valuing things, people, and religion. We learn value from parents, teachers, friends, strangers, school, churches and experiences of every sort. On my last birthday before his death, Jody gave me a red rose and filigreed gold earrings. Fresh flowers are always wonderful in cold January. I wore the earrings and appreciated he had taken the time to choose them.

It is easy to treat gifts, whether a red rose or salt, as expected or normal. Until, of course, the person who gives them is gone. On the way to Jody's funeral I stopped at a florist and bought a single red rose. The smell was overwhelming in the car, so I parked on a busy street, got out of the car with the rose, marched to a curb, yanked the rose out by its skinny green neck with thorns, and threw the wax paper with baby breath and ribbon away. The sweet rose breath reminded me of Mother's garden in our childhood home by the cemetery. I remembered the full heaving red peonies Jody and I picked and placed in mason jars with water to sell on Memorial Day. We stood on the curb and hawked the flowers for twenty-five cents to the somber people driving to the cemetery. Alone in the room with him in his casket, I tucked it to his side. I wore the earrings before he died, but afterward I tucked them in the black lacquered box with the charging warrior on the lid.

Cherished items don't need to be gifts. Mourners keep bathrobes steeped in the smell of a loved one. They will not part with a broken toy or a lock of hair. Tool sets never again used are also never sold. All of it is valuing an object that didn't have the same value when the person still lived. We are creatures that hold symbols as if they contain a fragment of the lost life. They can comfort or sustain in mysterious ways. Or, they can be on the other end of the continuum where monument building to a past that cannot be retrieved cripples ability to face the future.

"Come visit us in Birmingham, Zac. I've got a few weeks before returning to Balikpapan. You've never seen the south," my father said during his annual visit to Salt Lake. Zac's eyes lit up and he looked expectantly at Sam and me. Jealousy, then fear, hurt, and last, recognition, drained through me, but I said nothing as I nodded agreement that he should go.

Zac chose the clothes he wanted to take while I watched, sitting on his bed helping arrange his suitcase. It was easy to encourage him to fly away and see the world. I wanted him familiar with it. When he was a baby I knew he needed to go away to college, and live as I had only dreamed. I was jealous that the man who was at the center of my childhood's inner life and left me to fend alone, now so easily would take my son into the world and still leave me behind. But I recognized he was the symbol of a larger world outside of Utah that perhaps could now nourish Zac. My father was offering possibility. I knew when he left I would still be here.

I didn't know this man. I knew his ghost in my mind, but not him. Would my son be safe? Yes, I thought as fear dissolved, he would be safe. With jealousy, hurt and fear explained, it was easier to recognize my father's value in molding potential.

This was an internal re-valuing, but there were external ones. When Sam and I bought the home we were living in we expected to be there until Zac finished school. We had improved it and been comfortable in the fifty-year-old red brick home in the settled Sugarhouse neighborhood. We didn't need to move, but we both felt itchy to go. Habit played a part. I had never lived in a house over five years and it felt like a train schedule was ticking with a new experience ahead. Slowly, I also realized I needed a new nest, an airy, breezy one where I could nurture and be nurtured without history.

Sam's reasons were less clear. I knew he wanted something more urban, matching his love of Porsches and his style of dress. It seemed he also wanted to escape something and little could be agreed on. Sometimes we looked at houses, other times we drove from condominium to condominium. We became impatient with the search and with each other's priorities.

Over six months passed and I wondered if we would move at all. Sam read the ad for one more condominium and I reluctantly agreed to look at it. The building was halfway between the city and university and was almost completed. Looking urbane for Salt Lake, it viewed the valley and promised drenching sunshine and spectacular sunsets. By the end of the second visit days later, I understood how much he wanted this small beautiful space that rose above surrounding houses to face the city. His face sparked happiness I hadn't seen for a long time as I signed an offer for a penthouse with one thousand square feet. From the date of signing until we lived there a few months, I had endless dreams of not having room to keep a broom and giving away cooking pots.

The marriage of King Arthur and Guinevere started happily, but after years of Arthur focusing on the Round Table and kingly duties, both realized there were problems. He asks her what is between them and she answers, "Perhaps your high hopes have come between us ... you are trapped in the meshes of a task no man can fulfill." From Guinevere's view, it was Arthur who changed and emotionally left, but Arthur sees the changes in Guinevere.

The deepest values and loyalties are tested by grief and families, friendships and lives can be torn apart. Stripped of innocence, grievers are not guaranteed to have wisdom, insight or compassion in its place.

The heart can be very divided. I held Sam, Zac and Mother more closely, but my ability to show that in a healthy way was disrupted. I didn't express it well or from a happy heart, though I signed the condominium offer to pay for what I believed I had taken from him.

Zac needed me to mentally return. I held and kissed him, fearful of his disappearance, and then forgot to fix breakfast. Sam needed the return of his wife and a more interested business partner. I was physically there, but without an abiding heart. Mother still needed help surviving the greatest loss of her life. There in degrees for each of them, I failed as often as I succeeded.

Zac was moving through his high school years. Disappointed in the academic attention and challenges he received in public high school, we moved him to Rowland Hall, a good, local, private school where he would graduate with fifty students. Momentum toward adulthood began with choices and responsibilities he accepted. I pointed out (or maybe he did) a beginning speech class being offered at the University of Utah the summer before he started Rowland Hall. The professor wanted an interview with the fifteen-year-old to be sure a stage mother wasn't pushing him so I was dismissed before a private interview. He felt more comfortable in the speech class than the earlier type class. He studied journalism at Northwestern University the next summer and was later an intern in Senator Orrin Hatch's Washington D.C. office through the Congressional Hispanic Caucus. Close-up views of journalism and politics caused him to abandon both as possible futures. He lettered in tennis while wearing shoes out every third game. He showed an interest in statistics when he and Sam attended Jazz games. While fans screamed he calmly worked individual stats, beating the release of half-time statistics by the league. Sam would get the photocopied results and Zac compared his numbers that were seldom at odds. In high school he calculated them for the school athletic teams.

Zac and Sam's value was in my heart. Reassessment of the

rose and earrings was sentimental and symbolic. Weighing my father's invitation to visit Birmingham was a realization of history's weight and value. Spontaneously asking a jeweler about a moonstone ring was how I grasped at self-worth. My father and Chamsie had given me the ring from Singapore several years earlier. I was in the store for other business when I asked the jeweler about the ring's value. He peered at it and before he answered I blurted that my father had given it to me. I'm not sure if I saw a reflection in his eyes and demeanor, or I imagined it, but he seemed reluctant to say as he gave a gracious answer without a cost.

When I returned to the car I sat staring at my ring. Moonstones are not expensive and the diamonds, should they be real, are so small a person who needs reading glasses wouldn't see them. Still, it was a ring I loved.

When Gordon Livingston learned he was adopted as a baby he asked his father what he had paid for him. He and I were both interested in our value to a parent and reading his story reminded me of the jeweler and my embarrassment. I wasn't asking the jeweler how much my father spent, I was declaring my father took the time to buy me something beautiful. That ring with a moonstone and small diamonds once sparkled from a fine jewelry cabinet where my father picked it out of many. Maybe, I thought, Chamsie had picked it up as a present to easily bring back. I knew he hated shopping.

The task at this way-station is to pay attention to new value. An emerging hero looks about and with Salt Woman, asks what is worth keeping, what is not, and are there things we need to appreciate.

Grievers often re-appraise circumstances and interests. Knowing it will never be the same and realizing priorities have changed, marriages and careers dissolve or become something else. Hobbies are taken up or set aside, as are politics, social issues or work with non-profits. Many begin quests of travel, education or studies of religion and spirituality. Art is often turned to as comfort and tribute to a lost loved one.

Greek Apollo solemnly turned his regrets and grief to music after accidentally killing his friend Hyacinthus. "Thine is the suffering, mine the crime. Would that I could die for thee! But since that may not be, thou shalt live with me in memory and in song. My lyre shall celebrate thee, my song shall tell thy fate, and thou shalt become a flower inscribed with my regrets." Art, new interests in work or charity can become a griever's solace and gift to others.

The Fifth Challenge

Inner Trials

Confused and wishing answers, the Norse god Odin hung himself by his ankle for nine nights from Yggdrasil, the cosmic tree that supported earth. *The Poetic Edda* from 1200 AD reads, "Myself an offering to myself: bound to the tree that no man knows whither the roots of it run." He reflected deeply and was rewarded with insight and the gift of the runes, an alphabet of divination and communication.

Buddha spent years seeking enlightenment, but it was not until he spent time under the bodhi tree in deep reflection that he received it and "the significance of all things made itself apparent."

King Arthur gazed in a fire and reflected. "If fame fell away like ash, what was it that made a man a man." He wanted eternal answers to understand life. Heroes are led to their experience through the same emotions grievers feel; an internal lostness and loneliness. Life can be full of activities and responsibilities, but without peace.

Neeld notes loneliness is a feeling of being without, but solitude is companionship of the self while exploring ideas. Lightner writes of learning the difference between isolation and solitude. She says isolation is feeling alone while with people, but experiencing solitude leads to calm and an inner strength. Both are expressing a need to feel peace. Isolation and loneliness are felt as emotional emptiness. Odin and Buddha were led to the nourishing experience of solitude, while King Arthur struggled in a demanding human world.

After Neeld's husband died and Lightner's daughter was killed, each bravely faced life and attempted to go on. It worked for a time, but peace remained elusive. Prodded by therapists, friends, or serendipitous self-discovery, they experienced healing with solitude.

Mental peace and strength to face inner issues is found in many places. Traditional stories tell of nature, the presence of great teachers or religion. Humans are resourceful and the gifts of self-inquiry appear everywhere. Harrison describes Jody's place of safety for solitude after the murder of her parents and sister. While adapting to a new guardian and school, she was generously given the use of a red Audi she came to refer to as her "Audi-womb." The car nurtured reflection, self-esteem and triggered metamorphosis.

Facing inner issues is finding time to sit restfully, ponder and become comfortable without distractions. I sat with eyes closed and listened to sounds, not caring if I was successful. The word meditation felt like too much work, so I told myself I would just sit and let my brain drain. Only after several tries did unfiltered thoughts flow. Tears fell, I let them, and then they stopped. I wrote some of the thoughts down to release pent-up feelings, and that alone was helpful. Over time writing and solitude helped me piece together ideas and emotions. Solitude encourages internal issues to surface to be settled more peacefully.

Changed Memory – *Mimir's well*

Five months after her mother's death, writer Toby Talbot wrote: "But in the throes of tears, memories inevitably get foreshortened. Reduced to freeze shots of her in the hospital, in the coffin. Then again, silently, incredulously, I have to begin from the beginning and repeat: She's dead." Memory can be deranged and short-circuited in unexpected ways.

My childhood memories felt gone except for a few stark awful moments. It was as though someone had stuck a siphon in my ear and withdrawn memory of my first twenty-one years, leaving a few craggy-edged air pockets haunted by laughing demons. I was tormented that I had been so blind as to believe childhood's rawness could be escaped or redefined. The bits I did remember were twisted pieces of the unhappiest moments looked at through a carnival mirror.

Mother was throwing my toy china in the kitchen in Santa Monica while Father and I watched. Chips and shards of blue and white porcelain shattered and fell by the wall. My father's face when two policemen appeared at the door of the basement apartment in Bountiful, Utah where Mother had moved Jody and me from Grandma Lois'. Nameless' smirking face as I chewed toast with strawberry jam. Jody's eyes as he said goodbye when I left my wedding as Sam's bride, when he told me he was lonely in the last year of his life, and the last time I saw him.

I mentally replayed events soon after Jody's death. While at Grandma Spiking's, the telephone rang and she picked it up. We heard Mother's shrill cry that staked my heart and still echoes. My father's last words before he returned to Indonesia were, "I can see you'll be fine."

Sips with mythical heroes at the River Lethe would have been comforting. In Greek and Roman mythology, soon-to-be-born souls drink from the river to forget so memory does not interfere with human life. In *The Purgatorio*, Dante writes, "[S]o may High Grace soon wash away the scum that clogs your consciousness, that memory's stream may flow without a stain in joys to come." A River Lethe would be comforting.

The River Lethe guarantees forgetfulness before birth, and Mimir's Well gives full memory. Odin visited Mimir's Well, and asked its guardian, Mimir, if he could drink. So valuable is the gift of true and long memory, that Odin was asked to pay with one of his eyes by giving it to the well. The remaining eye represents the sun, while the eye that rests at the bottom of the well represents the moon with memory, wisdom and truth.

Seventeen years after his brother's execution, Mikal Gilmore recalled his mother at that time, "I suspect that by this time the chain of all the disappointments and deaths had made her crazy, and she felt driven to reexamine each link in her mind, looking for the key to where everything had gone wrong.... [A]s my mother replayed her past, she began telling remarkably different stories about her youth than she had told before."

Hope for the future rests heavily on interpretation of the past. What was quirky or forgettable the day before a death can suddenly be ominous, but redefinition is natural throughout life. Twenty-year-olds often have clear ideas about their history and future. So do thirty, forty, fifty, sixty, seventy and eighty-year-olds. Transformation and movement through life from age twenty to eighty happens so slowly it isn't always noticed how life plays with memory. A dull glow on a childhood memory can change to nostalgia and affection until it becomes unrecognizable by earlier definitions.

When Jody was seven I held a birthday party for him. I gave him invitations to take to school, planned the games, wrapped two prizes, baked and frosted a cake. The oven rack was uneven, making the cake higher on one side than the other, so I suggested to the disappointed Jody that we create a winter scene of figures playing on a sloping snowy mountain. He settled for the idea and I was relieved it tasted fine. The six boys came after school and we had most of the mess cleared before Mother came home from work.

I hadn't thought of the party for a very long time and when it re-surfaced I was puzzled. Did Mother not want to give a party? Why wasn't it moved to a Saturday? Was she unable because of work? I remembered it as being my idea, but was it? Details of my life had slipped away and their re-appearance was spotty and riddled with questions. Maybe forgetting is a helpful survival tool. I wanted the party as a memory of kindness to a brother now gone.

In Treadway's book, over fifteen years had passed since his mother's death. He compares his wife's easy, happy memories of childhood with his own. "I have only a handful of memories of my childhood tucked away in my mind like some faded black and white pictures discarded in a drawer. I don't look at them very often."

C.S. Lewis was seized with fear that memory of his wife would dull. "[L]ike small flakes that come when it is going to snow all night ... the real shape will be quite hidden in the end." Elie Wiesel waited ten years to gain perspective before writing his memoir, *And the World Kept Silent*, though experiences remained vivid and horror filled. In an interview he explained, "It had to be something so austere, so sober. Pure as a police report." The clipped language counterpoints the tender, loving prose by Lewis, but both are efforts to arrange memories, compose their story in a way they could live with it and continue on. I also know that Wiesel, Gilmore, Lewis and I experienced, felt and learned more than is expressed well or openly on a page.

For a short time I believed my brother, parents and I were innocent. I now believe we were neither innocent nor guilty, but rather flawed human beings working within our understanding. There were errors and graces on all sides. Life is full of decisions and circumstances and one person seldom has all the facts at the time of a decision. Whatever the reason for a person's death, there will likely be people left behind who wish a memory was different. It is a griever's challenge to make peace with decisions and memories.

Urging memory to return and reorganizing it was important. I lost time staring into space contemplating what I remembered. Walking a grocery aisle and seeing young brothers and sisters interacting jogged memories. I compared reactions and tried to calculate results. Seeing the backs of young men with similar builds and hair to Jody would cause a wave of sadness and I would sit on a public bench, or pull to the curb in the car, and sit thinking what the memories of that hair meant. Remembering him standing in the kitchen with a long time high school girl friend, hearing him talk of a date in college, seeing him eye a woman walking down the street, all echoed lost possibilities and hope, becoming sharp burrs of pain.

I turned to scrapbooks and looked through them with a rising poisonous mix of anger, regret, self-pity and sadness. I didn't know the inner lives of the people I had known since childhood, and part of me didn't want to. At times I didn't want to know them at all.

I came across two saved letters. The summer I was sixteen I visited Donna and her family temporarily living in Birch Bay, Washington and Jody stayed at Grandma's while Mother traveled with Nameless. His excitement and cheer at everyday events in the first letter was a two-pronged fork of gladness he was a happy child and sadness that happiness was not to stay his.

Dear Beckie, If you think I'm going to fill up this paper your crazy. I am sure having trouble watching Where the action is, Grandma wants to watch password, but is working out. Monday I was downtown and I saw a man in a complete yellow suit and yellow shoes and tie! I was home and two phone calls came for you and one for Mom. Say hi to everybody even the cat. Love ya, Jody. P.S. Don't forget to tell us when you'll be back. Grandma sends her love. Mother gave me $5!

The second was written three years before his death.

Dear Beckie, Tonight I was rummaging through all my possessions to get them in order and I came across all the lovely letters you have written me in the days gone by. They made me realize how much you, Sam and Zac have tried to reach me with your generous love. Now is the time for me to return your love the best I can. As I read your letters there were too many that said you came by but I wasn't there or for me to call or come by. I must say I was selfish and isolated during that time and I want dearly our family to be close. We have grown apart during the past years but surely we can find things to share in our lives for the joy of being brother and sister we should be grateful forever. I start a different shift at work Tuesday from 3:00 to 11:30 for school and will be busy the first of the week, but will call Thursday or Friday. My love to Sam and Zac, love always, Jody

Jody and I went to movies when Mother gave me my allowance of thirty-five cents. He was still young enough to hold two of my fingers instead of my ten-year-old hand, while I paid a nickel on the bus and twenty-five cents for the Jerry Lewis and Dean Martin movie. It was special when Mother gave us extra for foil-wrapped Flicks chocolates. I parceled every other one to each of us. The hot dogs we fried and ate in the kitchen. The oranges I peeled, dividing the segments to share while we watched *Gunsmoke, Pallidin* and then *Perry Mason* as we waited for Mother to come home from a date. Memories fluttered to the surface with a deeper sheen, leaving me as the sole storyteller with only my heart to hear.

I can also hear the lighthearted tap of Mother's high heels on the school's wooden floor as she walked to the closed door of my classroom. When she opened it my whole class and the teacher turned to see the beautiful woman in a slim lavender skirt and matching vest with a silken blouse. Our mother. The only one who came to class who was glamorous and unmarried. And then the three of us are at the kitchen table on a Sunday morning, still in nightwear with uncombed hair, Jody is talking and Mother is giving him a steaming soft waffle.

My now grown son lives two states away and I think of him daily. Perhaps it was practice with these memories that made it possible to hold his face and voice in thought. Backward glimpses have a fringing patina of appreciation and melancholy. Science says other memories exist, but I no longer look for them.

Imagine Death – *The River Styx*

Athena implored Zeus to release Odysseus from his wandering journey and allow him to go home. Zeus replied it was not he who kept Odysseus away, but Poseidon who, "kept the man wandering about, although he does not kill him outright." During the darkest part of mourning, grievers also wonder why they, too, have not died with the loved one.

Grievers sail with Odysseus to the River Styx, where he saw the souls of the dead: "young men and brides, old men who had suffered much, and tender maidens to whom sorrow was a new thing; others killed in battle, warriors clad in bloodstained armour." Intellectually, everyone knows birth guarantees death, but now its infinite, indiscriminate power is realized.

In shock, it is not uncommon for family members to drive directly to the morgue or scene of the accident to see the loved one as soon as they hear the news. "Permission was finally granted for me to see Timothy on the condition that I 'didn't do anything silly.' I desperately needed to hold him, to look at him, to see his wounds. These instincts don't die when your child dies. We are tearful and sympathize when an animal refuses to leave its dead offspring, nuzzling him and willing him to live again. That is exactly what a mother's human instinct tells her to do. If a mother is not able to examine, hold and nuzzle her dead child, she is being denied motherhood in its extreme."

This brave and spontaneous act of running to the rescue was reported by a mother to grief therapist Kenneth J. Doka, Ph.D., in the book he edited, *Living with Grief After Sudden Loss, Suicide, Homicide, Accident, Heart Attack, Stroke.* She describes the experience as a last chance to be protective and a valiant last stand between the survivor and the inevitability of death. It also gives undeniable proof of death to the survivor.

Many people who want to know details contact police, medical examiners, witnesses, or anyone with first hand information. Stories are endless and endlessly sad as mourners rush to both deny and verify the truth. Seeing and hearing details is not for everyone, but the urge needs respect when it exists. With or without details, a griever can resonate with the victim's experience until it feels as her own. I thought of contacting the medical examiner but have felt peaceful not doing so. I know how he died. I saw his body. The facts I was told verify my vision when Mother gave me the news. My imagination sees enough details. I prefer other memories.

Two challenges are at this difficult inner passage. First, the griever must handle her pain about how the death occurred, the pain suffered by the loved one, and perhaps the indignity of what happened to the body in an accident or murder.

The second challenge is the wholly consuming physical and mental imagining of our own death. During our father's first visit, he shuddered and his face paled as he said, "I could never do that." His brown eyes widened and then fell distant for a fleeting moment as he imagined death. Months later I woke from a nightmare heavy with images of Mother grieving from the suicides of both her children. I felt dangerously close to slipping into my brother's emotions as though they were mine.

Elie Wiesel said, "After the war, there was a point I felt I could have slid into death. I was sick. It was a strange moment.

I felt on the edge. I was seeing the land of the dead, and I was no longer alive. It was strong, dark, powerful. I knew I was dying, and if I had not resisted, I would have died. The resistance itself was a conscious decision."

A military wife was composed and stoic when her husband died in a routine flight. She described the first hours to therapist Doka. "Yet, I was serene, my heart protecting my head from news it could not possibly comprehend." Her composure continued through the funeral. Six months later she fell so far into despair that "I begged for my own life to end. I was paralyzed by fear, overcome with pain and lost in a monochromatic world." She saved herself through a conscious decision to gather with other women who were widowed by the same event. Together they visited the crash site to laugh and cry over grief and its cruel jokes no one else understood.

My conscious awareness came on a workday morning while I crossed a street after a client visit. I was in clear view in the crosswalk of an intersection when I saw a car driving toward me and not slowing down. I took another two steps and still the car didn't slow. Did I want to live? I would not be leaving guilt with my family if I died this way. I stopped and the car brushed by so closely the wind swept my hair, blouse and skirt.

Wanting to die can be a subconscious desire a griever gravitates toward. Sophie's twisted grief propelled her to sensuous and tumultuous passions in death with a lover. "How strange it was that she should not fear death, if he was truly going to force death upon her, but that she should fear simply death taking him and him alone, leaving her behind." Unhealthy choices of lovers, poor driving habits, dangerous use of alcohol or drugs can all be harbingers of death wishes deeply hidden in a griever.

In Styx's underworld Odysseus meets his mother whom he did not know had died while he was gone. He asks how she died and she replies, "The Archeress did not shoot me in my own house with those gentle shafts that never miss; it was no disease that made me pine away: but I missed you so much, and your clever wit and your gay merry ways, and life was sweet no longer, so I died."

She didn't value her husband, daughter-in-law or grandson who could still hold future pleasures and joys. First deaths can lead to a second. Studies show deaths of close family members can appear to contribute to another family member's death.

Halcyon's story shows how one death can lead to another. After Morpheus confirmed her fears in a dream that her husband, King Ceyx, was dead she pitifully mourned. While crying at the seashore where she last saw him, his body washed ashore. Her anguish was so great that when she leaned to kiss him she died.

Some survivors become deeply involved in imagining death. The circumstance that so abruptly ended a loved one's life plants itself in the mind with recurring nightmares and daytime memory flashes. During the grieving process death scenes are lived and relived. Severed attachments and all their vulnerabilities can ferment in unhealthy, frightful ways.

Mourners may feel guilty or anxious picturing themselves or their loved one dying. Repeated replaying is not healthy, but visualizing or imagining is a common process. In professional grief therapy survivors are encouraged to re-live the experience for better understanding and acceptance. Sorting, reviewing, visualization or reminiscing are used to dissolve fear and horror. Psychotherapy recognizes the continuum of extreme avoidance and countless repeats.

People who watch the slow grinding of time and pain as it robs someone of life do not need imagination to make death excruciatingly real. As Sam, Zac and I watched Lupe, she changed from an energetic, large and clear-browed woman to a frail, small person with pain and anxiety on her face. Seeing a loved one die of multiple sclerosis, Alzheimer's, Parkinson's, AIDS or any other slow taker of life doesn't need imagination to make death vividly real.

Odysseus' mother slipped away by clinging to her son's disappearance and imagined death. When Odysseus went to hold her in sorrow and love she was a ghost without substance who assures him her soul survives, but he must go because he does not belong there. Her last sentence should be remembered, because it will make more sense as the hero's journey ends. "Make haste back to the light: but do not forget all of this ...."

Personal Responsibility — *The three-headed dragon with the killer tail*

"Maman died today," is the first sentence of French Nobel

Prize winner Albert Camus' novel, *The Stranger*. In the second paragraph the protagonist says, "I asked my boss for two days off and there was no way he was going to refuse with an excuse like that. But he wasn't too happy about it. I even said, 'It's not my fault. He didn't say anything. Then I thought I shouldn't have said that. After all, I didn't have anything to apologize for." Camus describes a common immediate experience of personal responsibility. Work is neglected, plans are disrupted, all because someone died. Some people understand, but others don't. An employer's aggravation at being inconvenienced can be felt over the phone.

A current popular belief is to "own" responsibility and display personal power. Everyone is a master of destiny, and if we aren't, it's a personal failing. Society has a high standard when measuring responsibility.

The people of myths and legends did not take mastering destiny for granted. Bravery, a sense of destiny, desire and hope filled their lives, but they believed in limits and superior powers that could capriciously withhold success. No one made it beyond what fate decreed. Both the Greek and Norse traditions portrayed fate as three women spinners who endlessly spun the threads of past, present and future. The Greek Clotho, Lachesis and Atropos measured each baby's destiny at birth.

Norse mythology called sisters Urd, Verdandi and Skuld the Three Fates. The Norse believed the yarn was weaved "in the inevitable drift of events." It was also believed the Fates warn "[O]f future evil, to bid them make good use of the present and to teach them wholesome lessons from the past."

When the Irish cyclops, Balor, was told his grandson would kill him he attempted to prevent it by imprisoning his daughter in a tower. Still, she was visited by Cian and gave birth to the sun god, Lugh, who killed his grandfather with a slingshot, leaving fate the winner. Ancient people did not believe they were in total control, nor did they believe they could escape fate, yet their stories were often in the tradition of the classic hero's journey. They had respect for fate and destiny that did not rule out responsibility, choice and effort.

Responsibility of Participation – The first head

It is only the beloved who pulled the trigger, drove too fast, got drunk or drugged, had the heart attack, crashed the snowmobile, or returned to a dangerous spouse. Insurance and medical people, witnesses, and police confirm this. But participation in another's life arouses feelings of responsibility. Grievers may question their decisions of buying the car, discounting warning signs, recklessly racing with the snowmobile, or initially liking a spouse.

Lord Raglan, a scholar of the hero, concedes on the first page of *The Hero*, that all events are judged, fairly or not, more by consequence than effort. Aeneas was not a hero when he lost Troy, only Odysseus was the hero. It was Virgil's book, *The Aeneid*, that followed Aeneas' travels and adventures after the loss of Troy to the founding of Rome that made him a hero. That is what makes Virgil's hero journey of Aeneas a parallel for the griever. It is not about what happened before the death, it is how life continues to be lived. The hero's journey is not about the life before the inciting event, or call, that makes a hero, it is the subsequent life that transforms him to a hero.

We are told not to be enablers by encouraging another's bad habits, but anyone close to a person caught in excessive or careless behavior knows how difficult it is to control others. Grievers are often powerless or ineffective witnesses. Self-destructive souls caught in addictions and repeating patterns can be very difficult to watch, and impossible to control.

Other times a routine act of life turns fatal. A bike ride ends in an accident, food becomes lodged in the throat, or a child slips in a pool or wanders off. Grieving survivors review the "what ifs," trying to work out their responsibility.

Responsibility can be imagined from a tangled knot of many threads. Oscar Hijuelos, 1990 Pulitzer Prize winner for *The Mambo King Plays Songs of Love,* recalled he felt responsible for his father's unhappiness because of a childhood illness he suffered. Later he heard that after arriving in New York as an immigrant from Cuba, his father invited his brother to follow. In the course of preparing for the trip his brother was in an accident. After weeks of suffering he died, leaving Hijuelos' father feeling responsible though he was thousands of miles away. This new information caused Hijuelos to reassess his illness in his father's unhappiness.

In the continuing story of Demeter, the wandering, grieving mother is unaware Zeus agreed to their daughter's disappearance. She also does not know Persephone's abductor, Hades, knowingly enticed her to eat a handful of pomegranate seeds. Once nourished by food of the underworld, Persephone is changed from an abducted goddess to queen of the underworld.

Rain was falling at an angle in unusual, long, hard drops I associated with summer thunderstorms instead of winter. I watched as I cleaned a pomegranate and heard the football game on television mixed with Zac and Sam's voices. It was only three months since Jody's death and the first Christmas without him was nearing. The rain pelted the small, green leaves of a pyracantha waving stiffly above the neighbor's fence. Pelting rain and thoughts of Persephone's pomegranates turned the memories.

Jody and I were waiting in a neighbor's car with her children while she ran into the store during a rainstorm to buy Mrs. Paul's fish sticks. Five-year-old Jody was playing with the other children, his voice charged and happy as they ran small cars over each other's bodies. Older and uninterested, I sat by the window and stared at a tree reaching high above telephone poles. Bright leaves slightly bounced from heavy rain. The strong, rutted trunk was blackish-brown. I turned to look at Jody who was so happy, and without remembering why, I began to love rain's promise of life and nourishment, though it gave only on its terms.

At the kitchen sink while cleaning a pomegranate for my son, the rain and nearby thunder shook deeply embedded childhood memory. I slowly peeled and cleaned the kernels from the membrane separating cells of fruit. My fingers became flooded with the seeds' blood-red droplets. Mother bought one pomegranate every fall for Jody and me to share. Being the oldest I was in charge of getting the bowl and arranging napkins across our fronts so the red juice wouldn't stain clothes. Mother gave me the knife and said be careful.

I broke off chunks, handed my brother one and together we carefully separated jewel seeds and membrane. He ate them as fast as I freed them and I told him not to because I wanted some, too. When enough were in the bowl, we bit the surprising fruit of sweet juice before the hard, bitter seeds. He smiled with red smears around his mouth and told me to hurry.

Before the time Jody and I were teenagers we stopped the annual pomegranate ritual, and now Zac had decided he wanted me to do the peeling alone. Peeling pomegranates in the deep fall, watching rain or going outside and jumping in puddles were all happy memories with my son, but they were plotted and practiced from life with my brother.

The rain outside the window now was a relentless pounding as I cleaned my hands of juice and the sink of bitter rind before taking the prize of pomegranate seeds to my son. My son, the loved boy child of sprinkled freckles and dark beauty. It was with another loved boy child of sun-lightened hair and blond beauty where I first practiced the responsibility and guilt of being a mother.

Responsibility of Ignoring – The second head
Poet Robert Frost and his wife regretted delaying calling a doc-

tor for a young child who died from the flu. Family members don't always know what they are looking at, for a second, a day or a lifetime. Responsibility of ignoring a symptom, action or person is self-defined. Others realize the impossibility of foreseeing every action's result. Especially when previous experience tells us the situation is normal, nothing to be alarmed about.

Nadle tells the story of a father who, she was told, was dismissive of his young daughter. She was hit by a car, and after her funeral he went to Nadle's office looking disheveled and dirty. "I've been at Merrie's grave all night. I tried to dig her up with my bare hands. Too many rocks.... He looked toward the room where Merrie had been viewed. Can I go sit in there? I won't stay long. I just want to be alone for a few minutes where I saw her for the last time."

I don't have a defense for discounting Jody's warning sign behavior; except to say I don't expect anyone to always have perfect comportment of manner and dress. Neither Mother nor I were trained or aware enough to know early signs.

Responsibility of Surviving – The third head

Wiesel said in an interview, "There is no need of guilt in the survivor: why my little sister and Buna Rabbi died and not I. The guilt is irrational." People often feel survivor's guilt. Parents, passengers in cars, co-workers, or any event where another died can be haunted by questions.

Still on the mountaintop with no rescue in sight, Parrado experienced guilt. He writes of two people who lived through the crash and died days later in an avalanche. "Why them and not me? Was I stronger? Smarter? Better prepared? The answer was clear: Daniel and Liliana wanted to live as much as I did, they were just as strong and they fought just as hard to survive, but their fate was decided by a simple stroke of bad luck—they chose their spots to sleep that night, and that decision killed them....The arbitrariness of all these deaths outraged me, but it frightened me, too, because if death here was so senseless and random, nothing, no amount of courage or planning or determination, could protect me from it."

To me, this lack of power touches deeply at the heart of this issue: We grieve for our power and place in the world because without doubt we now know we are not the lone master of our destiny. We stand with the Greeks and Norse wondering at the power of fate's weaving.

Years later in a letter to my brother, I wrote as though he would respond:

I will tell you a reason I was distant. I believed my life was finally "coming together," and I wanted to encourage it, savor it, as though any distraction would steal it away. My marriage was feeling more comfortable, my son was well, I had a new home, the business was starting to succeed, there was a social life, time finally seemed available to be creative with writing. The psychic ground my life was founded on was very tenuous. Underneath my unsure steps was earthquake country, and I did not want to change a step that would jeopardize my neatly arranged life.

You were a threat. You were the link that tied me to having to turn and face the frightful rumblings under my feet. You were the symbol I ignored, convincing myself it was imagination. When you died self-delusion could not be sustained. Yet, for months, maybe the first years after, the shock was so great I didn't really know what hit me.

Last spring on his short visit Father said, "Jody must have felt it was hard to live up to you. You were always so perfect." Not me, I was just gutless. A quiet child can harbor deeply. His words stuck hard. Me, the lucky one. The one alive because I got advantages that from his years of absence made me look perfect. Memories of both parents, an unspoken affinity with Mother because we were the same sex, the ability to be quiet when you raged may be why I live. Now I live as this lucky perfect only child who feels a psychic arm torn off.

I was the surviving child with complicity who could never fill the hole in our mother's or my heart.

The Killer Tail

One or any combination of the three heads of responsibility leaves the mourner vulnerable to the ever-waiting, twitching tail that strikes hard. The privilege of being involved in another's life turns to a warped, perhaps unconscious conclusion of being powerful or aware enough to have changed the situation to prevent death.

Loved ones review what was done or what could have been done, what foods could have been avoided, what driving lesson was overlooked, what moment of inattention was responsible for lives ended. Perhaps an action could have been different.

That doesn't guarantee a different result. More important, it diminishes the loved one's ability to control his destiny, choice, or power to face his life and death.

Many grievers need relief from whatever their hearts hold as their responsibility. There are no guaranteed phrases of etiquette. I will always be grateful to the few who leaned my way, perhaps touched my hand and said, "It was awful and it wasn't your fault. You did what you could." I still wrestle with my involvement, but they helped to make my struggle to understand the twists and tricks memory and life played easier.

The hero facing the three-headed dragon with the killer tail is reviewing the dilemma of personal responsibility vs. the responsibility of others vs. randomness vs. fate. Conrad Anker was on a climb on Mt. Everest in 1999 with friends and professionals who died. When asked during a radio interview about his feelings of guilt and responsibility, he answered that instead of that he asked, "What is the gift?" That is closer to the Norse spinners of fate who were to teach "the wholesome lessons of the past."

Genetics – *Trickster's primal creativity and pathological destructiveness*

Genetics is a teasing games player quietly planning our ruin while we do everything in human power to be aware and responsible of good health and safety. "Trickster, [is] a figure who, at one and the same time, represents primal creativity and pathological destructiveness, childish innocence and self-absorption." Abrahams defines trickster in *African Folktales* as a rascal who repeatedly teaches that all is not as it seems. Trickster is a universal figure recognized as Loki in Norse legends, Hermes and Cupid in Greek and Coyote or Raccoon in Native American.

Trickster snickers when we feel confident of escaping a family's heritage of high blood pressure because we eat broccoli or Alzheimer's because we do crossword puzzles. Laying in wait, Trickster lets some people who eat broccoli and do crossword puzzles die peacefully in sleep at age one-hundred-one. And then, whack, when it's least expected, a young, outdoorsy cousin who nibbled on cranberries and drank six vegetables a day dies from a stroke, or a doctor verifies the onset of early Alzheimer's in the brain of the family's rocket scientist. Reliable enough to gain trust, trickster cruelly claims its victims. Genetics tricks with the disadvantages we can do nothing about except take the help we are offered.

Science is making very provocative genetic advances. Over the last years pre-disposition has become popular when referring to a person's chance of heart disease, diabetes, Parkinson's, some cancers and mental illness. Everyone can look to their own uterus or sperm sac and feel fear for their children.

Yet, humans often rationalize and dismiss the power of genetics. Anthropologist Geoffrey Gorer who specialized in grief and mourning rituals realized his naiveté after his brother was diagnosed with terminal cancer. "[I] had unconsciously thought that I would take the burden of our cancerous heredity away from the others." He believed that because he more closely resembled his father's family in looks, he would inherit their likelihood for cancer, leaving his brother healthy because he resembled their mother.

In 2004, the Center for Disease Control reported heart disease as the number one cause of death. Cancer was second, diabetes was six and suicide, eleven. They are all linked to genetic predisposition, the environment and personal habits. At the same time, science declares families hold genetic potential of great athletic ability, scholastic brilliance or exquisite beauty.

Imagine if science gave the power to choose genetic makeup. What would people do? Could we choose only what we consider good attributes? Would beauty still be considered an attribute if everyone was beautiful? Would standards climb still higher? What would it mean if most people were predisposed to be outstanding athletes? Would enough parents choose a contemplative child? Would ordering ala carte or du jour make any difference? Or would we end up regretting deliberate choices gone wrong?

It would be exciting to choose genes for a gifted athlete mixed with intelligence and a humble independent spirit. The choice suggests a healthy future of a strong person capable of long practices who pushes to break records, earn endorsements and create a charitable foundation. How will parents cope when instead they produce a brash bully too powerful and confident in abilities she only uses selfishly? The same attributes of superior athletic ability, intelligence and independent spirit also describe assassins and confidence schemers. Not every beauty has a happy life. Not every brilliant mind improves the world in positive ways. Not every athlete is a gentle giant who humbly earns gold medals.

Whatever dreaded illnesses are in a family history young people traditionally believe they will beat the odds. I looked at Zac and knew my father's side held the possibilities of a robust pioneer health well into the eighties, or dementia and alcoholism. Mother's provided business acumen, heart problems and schizophrenia.

Alongside genetics there are the very real forces of environment, nutrition, nurturing and the belief that each person is a distinct personality of personal making. Mikal Gilmore left his unhappy family behind and pieced together a life by becoming a successful journalist after Gary was executed. After talking with a third brother he writes of their childhoods: "I suspect what Frank means is that he simply shut down emotionally, though the psychic costs must have proved enormous. Gary, however, couldn't shut down: The outrage and unfairness of being beat that way became a sticking point in his heart. It was as if, for the rest of his life, he would be reenacting the drama of his father's punishments with every authority figure he encountered." Three brothers had three different responses to genetics and a difficult home life.

Wayne, Mother's younger brother, whose black and white photo reminds me of James Dean, could be our trickster. Long since dead, Wayne was forgotten and shrouded in mystery I never unravelled. When he was on leave from the Navy, he let Jody and me climb on him like a pony and he bucked us off on Grandma's living room carpet. He had an older girlfriend named Jewel whom Grandma didn't like. She pinched up her nostrils and folded her arms when Jewel visited. Wayne was diagnosed by the U.S. Navy as schizophrenic, and was put in the care of the VA Hospital where he received shock treatments. Honorably discharged, he moved to Los Angeles where he was shot by a new girlfriend.

Mother, Grandma, Donna, Jody and I, his whole family, drove through the night to Los Angeles. We stayed in his apartment and I remember lying awake in the quiet with Jody beside me, watching shifting lights on the ceiling from passing cars on the nearby freeway. After business and arrangements were completed we visited Disneyland, our one childhood visit.

Wayne fell away from conversation. Unfortunately, too, so did any understanding of warning signs that might have helped Jody. Later, I learned of the whispered innuendos of suicide of Grandma Spiking's nephew years before, leaving me to wonder about the lines between nature and nurture.

Advertising executive, Bruce Bendinger, reflected to Studs Terkel, "We live in a world where you've got to keep updating the software. I think we're finding out that a lot of what we thought were defects of character, it's really that you got yourself dealt a little bit of a strange hand in terms of your body chemistry...a problem in your brain that doesn't have anything to do with you having a bad attitude, or how Mom and Dad raised you."

Epigenetics is a branch of genetics exploring how nutrition, exposure to toxins and a mother's touch can change inherited characteristics. Scientists seem as full of questions as any griever over the roles of nature and nurture.

When Jody told me he heard voices, it wasn't the screaming clue it should have been. I've always heard them, too. I considered myself and my family as slightly off-center thinkers and I had some evidence to back me up. Jody's thinking was beyond normal, but I knew society acknowledges the "small voice within."

Jody was a young man with common reasons to be confused. He had grown up without a father or any positive male companionship, felt alone, was facing an insecure and frightful first year out of college and had used a menu of hallucinogenic drugs that may have re-arranged his chemistry. A level of distress was expected. Mother's concern and reports of his behavior became more alarming, but I remained protected. He was rational around me, and I forced myself to believe he was okay for too long. I did help him make the first of two appointments to a mental health professional, but it was too little too late.

It is embarrassing to admit I found relief in knowing people die of preventable diabetes, heart problems or inherited cancer. Grief reasoned it doesn't take any more will or intelligence to change poor eating and exercise habits than it would have for my family to deal more directly with my brother's problems. It was an immature way of equalizing odds and allowing acceptance, if not self-forgiveness.

With genetics the hero battles issues of physical inheritance vs. ever changing environment vs. medicine vs. personal levels of risk vs. a trickster's dose of the absurd and unknown. It is grim humor that Shakespeare first introduces two clowns in Hamlet to bury Ophelia after she drowns herself in the throes of grief.

I entertained the idea that several generations of hit-and-miss polygamy on both sides resulted in Jody's tormented death. He was the end of generations made weak by inbreeding without a good shot of outside blood to lessen the chances of madness. Perhaps three generations on both sides undiluted by anyone beyond the Salt Flats to the west and the Rockies to the east were responsible. But they did a beautiful job on his curly, thick hair the color of sandstone, the cornflower blue of his eyes, the black of his eyelashes and the strength and physical health of the body that held his unhappy soul.

Family Damage – *Halcyon's loss*

Lord Raglan lists twenty-two events in the lives of mythical and religious heroes. One is an effort by an enemy to kill the future hero at birth. Another is not being raised by the natural parents. In the Bible Pharaoh tries to kill his grandson, Moses, so Moses is sent away and brought up elsewhere. The Greek Dionysus was raised by nymphs, and the Irish sun god, Lugh, was raised by a foster father. The planet Krypton would have killed the future Superman in a natural disaster if he hadn't been sent to earth to be raised by Kansas farmers. Harry Potter is an orphan being raised by an aunt and uncle. Before the story begins, future heros suffer trauma and loss with a damaged family.

Similarly, the griever often struggles to heal problems that existed previous to the death, besides those that emerge because of it.

Previous Family Damage

Poet Robert Frost had a tragic list of loss in adulthood after a difficult childhood. His father was erratic and violent, his mother dangerously over-protective, and his sister, who spent time in a mental institution wrote, "I am very peculiar and did not start right. If I ever was well and natural it was before I can remember." Frost's string of losses throughout adulthood include the death of a three-year-old son to the flu, an infant at three days of age, a son to suicide and a favored adult daughter from a short illness. Another daughter, Irma, suffered from mental illness and spent her last years confined in an institution.

Biographer Jeffrey Myers writes that Frost was never able to openly talk about the deaths or to successfully settle them. When his wife Elinor died in March 1938, it "[C]hanged the course of his life and the development of his poetry. His fierce quarrel with Lesley *(a remaining daughter)* alienated him from the closest member of his family. He was also debilitated by illness and depression. He began to drink heavily, use foul language, and by his own admission was "crazy" for the next six months." Lesley and Frost reconciled, but were never close. Far too much happened to damage both of them and each carried anger.

Frost's family may be unusual in the number of traumatic deaths, but his life shows unsettled problems from the past add to the potential for new problems among still living family members. If there wasn't time or inclination to mend family hurts before death, they complicate the grieving process. Unsettled past sorrows can be the largest reason for difficult grief.

Four females surrounded Jody, along with Nameless, our thief and enforcer. The female bonds were ragged and broken in far too many places that didn't always feel safe or reliable. This is only my view and may not be theirs at all. Still, the comfort of my childhood family was their familiarity, smiles, phrases, and turns of shoulders that resembled mine.

They talked of each other in sentences laced with black comedy, concern, confusion, affection, judgment and hurt. Grandma did not approve of Mother's divorce and held her accountable for the problems in her life as well as the fatherless lives of her children. Mother did not feel accepted by her mother, nor appreciated by the world at large for her ahead-of-her-time adventuresome, challenging spirit fettered with responsibility in a chauvinist society. Donna felt abandoned by her father's death when she was eleven and was baffled by Utah society which did not accept her as the good, rule-abiding person of gentle spirit that she is.

I hold myself to two sentences. I was the youngest female who, at age seven, became self-enclosed, sad and fearful, sure I had been torn from the life I wanted to lead to live one of recompense for unknown crimes. Mother dealt with a child who unconsciously harbored belief the joy of early years would never return to save her from desertion, lost love and lack of adventure. Jody was a bright, cheerful ray of sunshine happy to get up in the morning, caught in a naïve web of an indifferent society and broken family of flawed human love. Our father was rooted in pragmatism and was a popular, jovial, person who grew best into himself with age and being away from home.

A few years before Jody's death, Mother left Nameless and began traveling. Grandma was frail but her life appeared safe, independent, routine and filled with the studies she enjoyed. Donna was a married housewife with four children living an hour's drive away. I was married, a mother and business owner. Four different trajectories that seldom converged with Jody as a lone traveler between each female, joining for holidays and living with Mother as he finished college. On the side, seen only by Jody and me, were our father's annual visits.

Current Family Damage

Struggling with one's own grief it is easy to ignore or discount it in others. Irish writer Maeve Brennan wrote a short story of a husband and wife whose three-day-old baby died. The husband tried unsuccessfully to console the wife, but she deliberately turned away from him and Brennan writes, "He could not understand her. It was his loss as much as hers, but she behaved as though it had to do only with her."

Grief can subside only to make us aware of the hurt and anger created since the death. Candy Lightner plunged into organizing MADD within the week after her daughter's death. By her account that meant she neglected the necessary work of facing her grief as well as the needs of her two remaining children. "Much later on, Serena and Travis told me how much they resented my involvement. They were right: I did put MADD first, and I shouldn't have, although I didn't realize it at the time. I was so obsessed that, in many ways, I did not permit life to go on outside of MADD." Eventually, she faced the needs of her children and healed the relationships.

Nan Watkins and her husband of over twenty years suffered after the unexpected death of a grown son. "Every minute I was afraid my daughter would die, and I lost all desire to live myself. Then gradually, but also rather quickly, the rest of the family I had worked so hard to build fell apart. The cord that once had bound my husband and me to each other grew taut, then snapped. Our daughter, stunned and confused, went her own, tentative way." When she found herself alone she began a physical and mental journey through Zurich, Katmandu, the Himalayas, India and Singapore before returning home.

The Damage to Others

It can be startling to return from grief and assess the cost paid by focusing on the lost loved one. Ceyx lost his brother and followed his grief by setting sail to the Greek Oracle. His wife, Halcyon also had reason to mourn because she lost her husband to his grief. Too late, Ceyx realized the cost of his grief. In the terrible storm he perishes with "no name but hers on his lips."

In the flood of released emotions I reasoned that a confession to Mother in adult words about Nameless would break a barrier to bring us closer. I let myself believe if I couched my words in sentences containing, "I was afraid to talk because you were the remaining parent I didn't want to lose," or "I barely had words for it myself," she would see the vulnerable, naïve child I was, and we would cry together as we rode off into the sunset in fuzzy mother and daughter love. I practiced, "At first, I wanted Nameless to like me, and it took a long time to realize he wouldn't and what that meant." I figured blaming him made my confession a shoe-in. Instead, memory is fragmented, but ended in her screaming and me knowing I had touched her grief too closely and sent us spiraling backward.

For a time we stiffly talked, she stayed hurt and I refused to filter every word, or squelch emotions. One event was a birthday party in early summer. Mother, Donna and her now-grown daughter, Jennifer, and I were at a restaurant. Conversation was a relaxed mixture of female seriousness and cheer as we talked family gossip and history. We were seated on a patio with pink sunlight lengthening through the trees and often wriggled from uncomfortable iron-backed chairs. Perhaps we were talking about camping. Donna had wearied of it through years of planning, packing, unpacking, and cooking meals without benefit of kitchen for at least six people. Jennifer was a backpacker and avid camper through western backcountry.

Retirement had at last come for Mother, and in her fully equipped Chevrolet van with kitchen, bed and bath she spent months at a time driving to Nova Scotia, Key West or Alaska.

I may have started, "Remember, Donna, when you, Mother, Jody and I went to Wyoming and you and Mother put up the tent? It stunk so of oil."

"I remember Gloria getting upset we couldn't get it up."

"We got it up once I made you sit at the side and just help me. And Rebecca never did like camping."

"I didn't really know what it was. That was close to the only time I ever went. You camped with Nameless."

She squirmed at the name. "I should never have stayed with him so long."

"I didn't like him."

"Why didn't you say anything?"

"I'd already lost one parent. I didn't want to make you choose."

By now she had heard it, I had said it several times, and we had both settled in our stage lines we refused to edit. Her lower lip became prominent as I remembered in childhood when she was angry. "Later I realized I should have said something. It kept us apart but I don't know if I even really realized it at the time." I was talking faster.

"Don't torture me with him."

"I know I never said anything. I was afraid." The words were between us too long. I mixed apologizing with explaining but knew it would never be enough or entirely forgotten. I wanted to stab a Nameless doll with kitchen knives, hoping wherever he was he'd plop over in bloody pain. Not die. He should suffer first.

Sam could take anything I said about Nameless, but it didn't unravel a childhood knot with the woman who helped me tie it. Eventually we stopped repeating the lines and stepped back still holding our beliefs. Nameless was a barrier between us I resented and I know he was why I did not see her with more nuance and forgiveness. Family relationships are often exceedingly knotted, and healing family hurts is sometimes more productive with the ear of a friend, support group or professional.

Mother reacted emotionally and to the point of what I said, while Stingo listened heartfully to Sophie's retelling of deepest hurts and memories and decided peanuts should be talked about. "For during the two hours or so following her story I don't think I had been able to say more than three or four words to her.... But peanuts allowed me at last to breach our silence.... 'The peanut's not a nut,' I explained, 'but a pea ....'" He sincerely wanted to help, and he believed distraction was the answer.

Weaknesses in relationships become magnified. Hurts can go so deep they never heal. A few families are especially hit by tragedy and never respond to the needs of its members. It becomes unhealthy to stay with a forever sad or battling family. Grievers need to piece together a new life and it isn't always possible staying in the family rubble. Mikal Gilmore left his grieving family after Gary's execution. "But the truth is, I did not feel lost in the world when I lost my family. If anything, I felt relief: I was no longer tied to the wreckage that had been my family's spirit, and whatever undoing might come in my life, at least now it would be my own. I would no longer have to sit around and dread the next kindred disaster."

A week before Jody's college graduation I was planting summer flowers during a long sunset and thinking of him, imagining partial credit for his success. The graduation was a brilliant June morning. I arrived near the end of the ceremony and waited outside, wondering if I should go in. Of the dozens of doors out of the building, he suddenly emerged directly in front of me, throwing the door open. His eyes were shining, purposeful. The flowing black robes and eyes gave a bearing of a great hunting bird just before flight. Words seemed blocked in his mind as a foreign language. With difficulty he began talking.

From the demeanor of a stalking bird, he spiraled down within seconds to the weariness and unhappy complexities of a confused young man. His eyes lost fire, the shoulders slumped, the walk slowed. No, no, no, I told myself, it is just the long ceremony, the distraction of the day, not anything odd in his manner. We began taking pictures and huddling in our small family group—him, Mother, Grandma Spiking, and me. His gaze wandered to other family groups with dozens of fawning babies, wives and husbands, always with more. I pointed to smaller groups like us.

Mother had an evening party for family and his friends.

When he introduced me to a female friend she exclaimed, "I didn't know Jody had a sister!" She was astounded and the hurt I felt was quickly replaced with recognition.

Two years earlier I was with a friend of several years. When I mentioned Jody, she stopped short. "I didn't know you had a brother. I thought you were an only child." My revelation was as startling as her words to me. She had a right to expect this simple information, our conversations had room for it long before, but I talked obliquely about myself and less about childhood.

Some people reveal themselves as clear, shining suns with nothing to hide and everything to like. Forever questioning likability or worthiness, I revealed parts specifically requested as though people were sergeants and further elucidation was burdensome, dangerous or unnecessary. For the first time it occurred to me that was now counter-productive. Silence was protective during childhood as an outsider among Mormons, but now, it was distancing.

Sadness and Anger – *Vasalisa's corn and poppy seeds*

So many emotions and thoughts collide into such a dizzying confusion that finally the emerging hero can collapse into what could be depression. That was my catch-all word, though at first I didn't use it. "I'm sad," I said, because I had a prejudice against depression and people who dwelled in it. When the feeling didn't go away and time passed, I was beaten enough to self-diagnose and use the word. Immediately, I felt like an attending nurse put her hand on my forehead and murmured,

"Take a nap." Nothing was demanded of me. I sunk into it, comforted depression never required anything except to be blue. The emotion was sincere to grief's sorrow, plus tribute to the amount of devastation I thought I had endured, but as it languished it facilitated a refusal and/or inability to continue recovering.

Finally, I could not justify my inertia. When colliding emotions made everything look still and grey, I sighed and thought, "This is stupid. Think it out." Soon after I began my search for a psychologist and returned the business suit to justify the cost.

Kübler-Ross describes anger and depression separately, sorting them into manageable parts. I found unraveling these two forces closer to a task Pinkola-Estes describes in the Russian tale of Vasalisa. The witch Baba Yaga requires the searching and grieving daughter to separate mildewed corn from good corn and poppy seeds from dirt. "Observing the power of the unconscious and how it works even when the ego is not aware .... More learning about life (corn) and death (poppy seeds)." Separating feelings and beliefs of life and death was Vasalisa's and my task to learn discernment in judgment and distinctions.

Sadness

In the first months the times of sadness were like bursting bubbles a person might have watching a sad movie, or a momentary frustration that flares when a car cuts too close in traffic. Here and gone. Strong, but short. Over time it changed to strong and encompassing, until I felt engulfed. Grieving was the story while sadness was the tone of daily life. Sadness couldn't be picked out and examined alone. It was far easier to emotionally look the other way and believe all collecting emotions were one with only sorrow causing it.

When life had wonderful days of celebration like Zac's graduation from middle school, the next day would be grey and I would be overcome with weariness. When I sat on a stranger's lawn the week before leaving for the Caribbean, it was for the same reason. I would be overcome by the generosity and beauty of life and feel so ill-prepared to receive it that I would need to suffer with a wave of great weariness that would slow every movement and feeling until I could not think. The mental work of keeping everything at bay and unexamined was exceedingly tiring. Several times I pulled to the side of the road to rest because I felt so detached and emotionally embattled I wasn't sure I could turn the steering wheel or step on the brake.

"And no one ever told me about the laziness of grief. Except at my job ... I loathe the slightest effort. Not only writing but even reading a letter is too much," wrote C.S. Lewis.

Timeless, immortal and stronger than me, weariness was attached to accepting death's severe reality. I looked at walls believing I could see space between the paint molecules flashing as their own universe. Seeing my son walk from the car to a soccer practice could bend my body forward and heave my head and belly, leaving me dizzy. I couldn't discern perspective of everyday life from glimpses of cosmic. Scaring myself, I focused on laundry, taking Zac to the library, watching television or having one more glass of wine to urge sleep to overtake.

Joan Dideon writes of the waves in *The Year of Magical Thinking*. "Grief is different. Grief has no distance. Grief comes in waves, paroxysms, sudden apprehensions that weaken the knees and blind the eyes and obliterate the dailiness of life. Virtually everyone who has ever experienced grief mentions this phenomenon of 'waves'." It is a time impossible to comprehend.

Tears were a large part of sadness, and I came to think they did two things. Tears let out pent-up emotion that needed to flow and they were physical evidence, like a nose that needs blowing, that something practical needed to be done. Freya, the Norse goddess of love, lust and fertility constantly cried through her quest to find her dead husband. Goddesses have special tears and Freya's turned to gold when they fell on stone, and to amber when they fell into water. Grief's tears express love and care, becoming emotional gold to be felt, not held back.

Anger

A widow told Neeld after she visited New Orleans, "All I could see was couples. Couples laughing. Couples with their arms around each other…. At that moment I hated Joe more than anything else in the world. I hated him; I hated being one-half of a couple." Also a widow, Neeld remembered going to her husband's study and pulling a kite off the wall. "I made balls of the crushed paper, scattering them all over the room. I cracked the sticks until they were hardly larger than match stems. I knew Greg had loved that kite, and could hardly believe I was destroying it."

Grief therapist Sanders mentions six types of grief angers: confrontive, displaced, ambivalent, internalized, helpless and appropriate. Mine was closest to internalized and I did not allow full realization for years.

Anger grew as I wondered if I should have stayed living in Mother's house longer to be helpful to Jody. That I had married and become a mother when work was left unfinished with Jody anchored sadness and guilt. Finally, the decisive voice whispered, "But it was normal for you to want to grow up and leave home." I listened and wrote to Jody. *"What makes you think, Jody, you can just dissociate yourself from the world's problems? For all my complaining of our childhood circumstances, I also know you were raised better than that. Plenty have had to put up with a lot worse. To many we'd sound like whimpering weaklings. They didn't do what you did. They are lawyers, chefs, teachers and forest rangers, all like you could have been. They grew up, fell in love and are raising children, having money problems, fights with wives they love and they'll die from normal things like cancer, diabetes and heart attacks. Isn't it about time you and I got over it? Mother did a better job than a lot and we know it. Isn't it about time we had a good laugh about childhood and pat each other on the back that we've done so well? Shouldn't we dwell on the good times? Because they were there, you know."*

More memories surfaced. There was the Easter egg hunt Mother created when we lived on N Street. For over an hour we searched in the moist earth among crocuses and grape hyacinths for chocolate bunnies, sugar chicks and eggs we colored the day before. There was his high school graduation and the South American themed birthday party Mother prepared for him where nobody could name a single dish on the table. Jody hadn't held up his end of the bargain. Initially anger felt like revenge, but when time was right it felt clean and energetic.

On a spring day I waited in a restaurant for a friend. I was by a large steamy window watching full bellied grey clouds through moisture dripping from the warmth of people inside. I watched the beaded stream and felt sensual and full of possibility. I felt slick under lingerie, protected and fighting in my heeled black boots. My nail polish shimmered against the votive candlelight on the table, and the voices around rose like sentries sent to remind me of life. I wanted Sam, a bottle of wine and to lie on a mountain peak or a desert floor open to the sky. When my friend arrived I turned my attention to her, but as I took the first bite of clams and linguini languor spread through me like the sweet feeling of wine dripping in my blood. I felt soully, deeply fed and realized what I hadn't missed. After three years taste was again in food.

The passing of time was distancing the horror. I had cried an obligatory river and self-destructed with enough wine and sadness. My brain and body were finally saying, "Enough." It wasn't the first time I tried to turn myself around and put misery behind, and it wasn't the last, but it was the first time there was internal agreement. Anger at last was allowed and accepted.

Brunhilde and Hamlet followed anger to the point of murder, while Halcyon and Freya forever cried. Both ends of the continuum are visited through grief and both ends can lead to self-destruction or renewal.

Anger and Sadness

Anger and sadness are convoluted caves where there is not a prescribed or easy way out. Every story is different in timing, intensity and justification as anger and sadness fight, kick and scream at our innards until they are given their due. Candy Lightner called her doctor because of unexplained weepiness. He attributed it to grieving for her daughter and she replied that was five years ago. He answered, "You dealt with your anger, now you have to deal with your pain." So she suffered through upcoming holidays as though the death occurred the week before.

When Jody and I sold flowers from the garden on Memorial Day it had the singular meaning of taking flowers to the cemetery and was unattached to a weekend. We were like a child's lemonade stand with our drooping peonies, yard cut lilacs and roses next to the dozens of florists lining N Street. The first year Grandma Spiking stopped to buy flowers from us, but she didn't come the second year and I asked why she didn't take flowers to Grandpa's grave. I was eleven and still felt the loss of my father, but I had come to wonder if that was a failing. I wanted to know if she missed Grandpa. She paused from her reading, lifted her head and seemed to focus where the end of that day was to meet the evening before answering, "It holds them to earth, our sadness, the flowers, and we must let them go." I asked about Grandpa, but she answered by including her parents, almost a dozen brothers and sisters and two sons.

In emotion's convolutions, I reasoned in some backward, inside out way that refusal to acknowledge the deeper reasons for grief meant I could stand up to it. The violence of Jody's death cemented the need I had of retaining the illusion for a longer time that my human judgment had power. I was fighting a battle with a formidable enemy: myself. I convinced myself I was honoring Jody and the good that was in our relationship. For a time that was true, but now I knew what I really had to heal was contained in these sentences:

Mother's, Jody's and my life had lost potential with his death. There was no time to undo misunderstandings or share happiness. My life history and assumptions were in chaos. My life and other loved ones were as vulnerable to death. Remembering this as I sorted mental corn and poppy seeds helped me cross the point of realizing it was my grief of life that needed healing, and that had little to do with the lives my mother, father and brother had lived.

Compensation -- *The armless maiden's baby*

When Zac was in high school I began having dreams of a baby. At first it was a sleeping infant appearing from nowhere that I would be alternately confused, angry or indifferent toward. Later, it could be twins, a checkerboard baby of black and white, only black, only white. It might be swaddled in blankets or a young, hungry waif. It innocently looked at me or stood patiently between Sam and me, but I was the only one who saw it, and it seemed to need me for its care though I did nothing to help or hurt it. The dreams happened so often I became curious and started thinking about what caused them.

The obvious answer was my son was growing and soon leaving. I missed him before he left and was mourning the passage of motherhood with a child under the same roof. I began to understand women who purposely had children when others were almost grown. I was going to miss my son's close company and though I accepted it was inevitable and right that he leave, I never looked forward to it.

Later, I read the folktale of *The Armless Maiden*. Africa, Asia, and Europe all have variations of the story and through this story I began to understand the dreams in a new way. Often the maiden is armless, but sometimes she is only handless. It is an angry father or brother who does the chopping because she refuses something or he is making payment to the devil. She flees to a forest and barely survives with the help of animals. Hungry and struggling to eat corn or pears she stands on her toes to reach, she is rescued by a prince, king or the prince's mother. The armless maiden marries the prince or king and they begin life together.

Pinkola-Estes and others interpret the armless maiden's brutal father or brother as the masculine ego part of anyone that demands life be lived its way with material rewards and comforts. The maiden represents the creative, intuitive part of the self that threatens the masculine ego, so the father mutilates her to get what he needs. The creative, intuitive self becomes armless and loses its unique way of handling survival and living. Pinkola-Estés calls it "The Bargain Without Knowing" and it represents something given up.

I was meditatively watching stars, moon and a couple of racing satellites on a summer night with a glass of wine beside me. The view from the condominium eighth floor window was mesmerizing. "God isn't punishing you," came the clear inner ghost voice that has served as my provocateur, guide and fairy godmother. Scholars might call it a guiding supernatural aid.

No, I admitted, after not touching the wine while I thought this out. Negativity in my life seemed human created. Beginning at 8:30 p.m., I drank too many evenings toward sleep, didn't feel creative in a life's work, and was often sad. I knew the choices were mine, I wasn't being punished. I had evidence of Sam, Zac, friends, profitable work and good health. I lived in a beautiful care-free condominium.

Life supporting positive habits and decisions can crumble in the face of devastation, and time is spent punishing the self to buy a way back into our own good graces. Human beings seem to have an innate sense of fairness. People know what a reasonably split last piece of cake is, what earning twice the money for the same job means, and which child in a family is the one always picked on. There is often an effort to even the score.

I remembered the flitting thought of asking Jody to meet me for lunch the day of his death, but instead I chose to spend a quiet hour writing. I couldn't forget I was wading through notes from interviews for an article when Mother and Grandma Spiking arrived at my door. I began realizing the ways I had secured my weak position in developing who I was, and what I wanted, by living in the protection of not facing myself.

I felt armless and was so accustomed to it, it was unnoticeable. The forest where I wandered was about searching for peace by snuffing my desires and undeveloped talent. Sam and Zac were the mythological princes of my subconscious who appeared to save me from doom. I did find satisfaction and love in caring for and being with them, and used it as an excuse.

The story continues. The husband is called away, leaving the armless maiden alone. She discovers she is pregnant and a happy message of the news is sent. But a mythological trickster scrambles the message and the husband becomes confused. His messages, too, are interrupted before they arrive. The healthy and beautiful baby is born and news is received the husband is on his way intent on murdering his wife and child. The baby is strapped to the maiden's back, and for their safety they are sent back to the forest where she first wandered.

Most versions of the story call the birth of the baby a renewed realization in the psyche of inner need and potential power. Jung writes, "As a plant produces its flower, so the psyche creates its symbols. Every dream is evidence of this process." The second time of living in the forest is one of deep learning and regaining the lost self. Sometimes silver hands are fashioned for her by kindly helpers. Other times, through the good works, dedication and love she shows her baby and herself, her limbs re-grow until they are again healthy and perfect. The entrance of the baby into my dreams was the slow movement from subconscious to conscious that it was time to return to my forest of creativity and self.

My career was profitable and good. I didn't try to leave working with Sam though that had been my original plan. I had agreed to help get the business started, but I never felt it was a good fit for me. It no longer mattered because I could do it well enough and there were parts of it I did enjoy, plus, like Thumbelina, I could not leave where I was told I was needed. The dreams became more frequent when Zac was accepted as an undergraduate at Harvard.

My subconscious continued pushing the idea I had sacrificed enough and it was time to change, but I stifled it. The baby dreams continued until a beautiful black baby was sitting in slowly rising water screaming in fear, its large tear-filled eyes overwhelmed and afraid to drown. I felt the child was mine though I did not recognize it at all. The people I was with casually turned away, expecting me to follow. Finally, I said, "If it is mine, I must claim it," and I turned to pick it up. In nights that followed the baby alternated between black and white and I offered it meat, a hug, shelter and then began following the child along paths, up mountains and into caves.

Emboldened, I told Sam I wanted to move. The condominium was beautiful, but I felt cramped and I used it as my crowbar. We tried twice to sell but the housing market was not good.

On a Saturday morning when I sat on the bed after making it, I felt a strange weakness. A subtle inch toward death. Other times I sat on a chair or stood at the kitchen sink feeling an internal sway that felt like something was so deeply wrong that if I didn't move the condominium would kill me. I was weakening inside like I had never before felt.

I knew if I didn't push that inch toward death back and away, it would take another and another until I died. I decided to hold the baby and return to the forest. I became insistent on moving, even if we couldn't sell and had to rent. I pushed borders and planned a twelve day trip to France and Spain. Slowly, my arms returned.

The condominium sold, we found a good house and I turned a bedroom into a study and library though I had nothing to study. I haphazardly became more appraising of books I read, but my efforts went into letters to Zac. Curious, I began noticing artists who sat in hot booths in summer heat at festivals hoping people would buy their art.

The story of the armless maiden finishes when the husband returns home to learn the truth of his bride. She was not faithless, the child was healthy and she ran to the forest for protection from him. Now, he must follow her. The masculine worldly strength in all of us must go to the forest to make peace with the inner feminine self. Some believe when he comes to the forest to propose the second time, it is a marriage of equals with respect and appreciation for both sides of the self. It is ying and yang, the two sides of life that now live happily ever after.

In *The Lion King* the cub, Simba, suffers greatly believing he has caused his father's death. Once settled in the magical forest with new friends, Timon and Pumbaa, he believes he has made a new permanent life. Instead of a baby in his dream, Simba is visited by his childhood friend Nala. Nala reminds him of his greatness and that he should be leader of Pridelands. Though groups of lions are called prides, it is still meaningful screenwriters Irene Meechie and Jonathan Roberts named the uncle and Simba's nemesis, Scar. Simba must confront the scars of his own psyche to claim his inheritance.

Dorothy also can be reworded as an armless maiden. Understood as a story of one person's quest to confront her fears, she discovers after many trials she always had a heart, brains and courage. Finally she confronts Oz, the part of the ego that holds her back and demands what is rightfully hers—the right to go home.

Heroes in grief live less cinematic lives, but the story is similar. Grief expert Elizabeth Harper Neeld felt destroyed when her husband died suddenly from a heart attack while on a run. She thought, "If trying to be a good person ... if taking risks and making the changes required for two adults who have fallen in love to create a life together... if feeling a deep desire to make a contribution to others ... if none of these things finally matter because you come face-to-face with the truth: Things happen in life that destroy everything you've worked for, and you can do nothing about this—so what is the use of anything?" Like me, she was her own cruel accuser, and she began living a dangerous, self-destructive life-style.

Years later on a trip to Greece she was shown a forest planted by her host on property the family owned for generations. It triggered a sleeping sense of self. "I didn't quite know what it was that had touched me so, but it had something to do with making a contribution that will live on after you, something about looking out at life instead of always obsessively peering inward. I knew the experience had made an opening in my thinking, because for the first time since Greg's death I found myself considering the idea that there might be projects worth doing in life, commitments worth making."

Some people are observant enough that all they need is to have the caretaker of a forest show it to them. Eventually, all grievers should be ready to reclaim any lost parts of the self.

Apotheosis and Boon

Sighting the First Blossoms

A day comes when the emerging hero realizes grief's urgency has subsided. There is relief the pain has dulled and sadness the loved one no longer feels real like they once did. This passage marks the beginning of the last phase of the hero's journey. Apotheosis is illumination or new understanding. Boon is the benefit of the illumination or understanding of the changes made in life. It is the metaphorical first sighting and appreciation of the blossoms of the lower branches. The higher ones belong to heroes who are applauded and appreciated by everyone, the top athletes, movie heroes and world peacemakers. Grief's new hero is in the shadows of the lower branches where finally there is a shy or reluctant glance at the blossoms and unexpectedly, there is realization of what they now hold for him.

Hero scholars define apotheosis as elevation to a divine status through illumination. Knowledge and understanding merge duality into wholeness. Campbell explains Buddha, "[H]is god-like being is a pattern of the divine state to which the human hero attains who has gone beyond the last terrors of ignorance." Leeming writes of mythical and religious completion, "He is taken out of the cycle of life and given a permanent status in recognition of his divine divinity—his real self." It is the ascending to heaven completed by Dionysus, Jesus and Abraham.

The grief hero quietly reaches this point with tentative hope or faith a good future awaits. He understands Pearson's description. "We can respect the process and honor ourselves as evolving beings, rather than fearing there is something wrong with us for our discontent."

C.S. Lewis describes this new time. "Today I have been revisiting old haunts, taking one of the long rambles that made me happy in my bachelor days. And this time the face of nature was not emptied of its beauty and the world did not look ... like a mean street." He wrestled mightily with his ideas of God and grief, but now he has regained some peace and writes, "There was no sudden, striking or emotional transition. Like the warming of a room or the coming of daylight. When you first notice them they have already been going on for some time."

Dorothy has an apotheosis when she and her traveling companions return from melting the Wicked Witch, and Oz admits he cannot keep his promises. Pressured, Oz gives encouraging symbols to the Tin Man, Scarecrow and Lion, but there is nothing for Dorothy. She is ready to go home and live as a renewed person, but she discovers no one can do it for her.

Some would-be grief heroes stop here and the story is never

a completed journey. Entangled in grief and bitterness, life is seen as a crueler and sadder place than previously realized. He gives in, gives up and forever stays rooted here, believing life is good for some but has less hope for himself. Here the griever dwells and festers in angers or hurts, holding others, or himself, responsible for a bitter or broken heart he cannot mend.

Grief can worm deeply into our psyche by endlessly listening to tear-soaked or angry lists of grievances. It never lifts a finger or an eyebrow to disagree about any charge yelled at it. Feel mistreated, victimized or picked-on and the universe will never disagree. It didn't when Hamlet made a decision to kill his father's murderer. "Now might I do it pat, now he is praying; And now I'll do't; and so he goes to heaven; And so am I reveng'd." Hamlet's grief poisoned the lives of everyone around him, ending in one of Shakespeare's most tragic plays.

Others are so weary they rest. King Muchukunda of Hindu tradition was a great defending warrior of the gods. Extremely tired after a significant and lengthy battle, he was granted his wish of undisturbed and endless sleep. For eons he slept hidden deep within a mountain. Grievers, too, become so weary they remove themselves from the heartaches and dramas of life. They ask for little—just a simple life of routine without hope, anticipation or new love.

Confirming life goes on, grievers see changes time has made on their faces the loved one wouldn't recognize. This gentler, calmer place could be mistaken as the end of the journey. Without notice the griever slips into a secure and dependent relationship with grief. Since life's happiest days are history, invitations are declined without desire to enjoy new people and experiences. There is quiet resolve, weary acceptance and a carry-on attitude.

Norse woman Freya, gentle and forever saddened, spent the rest of her days crying for her dead husband and at the end of each day dividing the dead of that day's battle with Odin. Odin took his to live as victorious warriors in Valhalla to enjoy company, eat the always renewing boar of life, and rest before rejoining the next day's battle. Freya took hers to her palace and spent nights crying over the destruction.

On a brilliant June Sunday afternoon I pushed a lurking illumination into conscious acceptance. I knew deep grief was behind me and I needed to get on with things. Five years had passed. I also knew there would be no forgetting and that memories would remain. I had long ago completed the wine class and then astronomy, improved meditation, regained interest in food and handled life well enough. The wave movement was carrying me up the spiral of recovery but I needed another body effort to convince the mind and settle the heart. I left Sam and Zac home to watch basketball playoffs and went to the garden nursery to buy a linden tree.

The sapling with a trunk only as thick as a thumb flapped out the window of my car as I drove to the cemetery. I hadn't told Sam and Zac where I was going because Sam would have insisted on planting it. Quietly, he would have humored me, wondering if the grieving would ever end. It was me who had to lower the shovel and split the grass. I had to do the digging, deeper and wider, a few feet up from the casket until the gangly young roots of new life had a chance to survive. I had to loosen the tight hold of earth until the tree would be free to wriggle into place and grow with vigor into the future.

It replaced a linden tree that was in the front of the house Mother bought on 1300 West. She had it removed because she thought it too messy and she had other plans for her ever-changing yard. I held it affectionately as a slow growing, perfectly cone-shaped, graceful marker of the years I lived there.

Finished, I stood back to look. It was as frail and unsure as the legs of a newborn foal and invisible against the towering pines in the surrounding blocks. I stood with eyes closed and tried to conjure up my brother like Dorothy before the gates of Emerald City. "Jody, Jody," I pretended, trying to make a solemn moment lighter. When an attendant came I sounded sincere and worthy of his audience in my pretend hope for spirit communion. I heard, "No, there is no time here for silly air-breathers who should be paying attention elsewhere. Please state your message and we'll place it in his box." Even in imagination the voice returns me to the present.

So, I turned to face the clear blue sky where I stood and thought fervent words for both of us. I talked about how life had moved along and wished him well, wherever he was, before walking away. That would have been the easy Hollywood end. I would walk to the car surrounded by cleansing, forgiving sunlight, symbolically reunited with the California sun of childhood memories, but my life never was Hollywood.

Father was spending his annual time in the states away from Balikpapen, Borneo, where work continued on the fertilizer plant. He and Chamsie had visited us in May and then continued to California to see his brother and his family. When they returned to their stateside home in Alabama, he had surgery and was recuperating before returning to Borneo.

Mother was preparing for a trip to England and Ireland in July. We did some shopping and lunches in happy preparation. Our chatter was light, with only a few sentences prefaced with, "Before Jody left …," that now acknowledged our mutual empathy without early horror.

Three weeks after planting the tree, in the grey shadows of an early July morning, the day Mother was to leave, I was roused from deep sleep to an awareness of voices, flying light bodies, and urgency beyond my dream when the telephone rang. Chamsie's mother told Sam my father had died. Sam roused Zac and the three of us lay on the bed, hugged and tearfully talked about our father and grandfather.

Mother was bustling about watering houseplants when I arrived to take her to the airport at 10:00 a.m. She was excited and talking faster than usual with a spring in her step she didn't often have. When I kissed her good-bye in front of the airport she disappeared without a glance back, and I stared after the strangers behind her.

Two people who were passionate enough to marry, whose lives created two more, who still had the power to sting me to the core, had no involvement with each other. I don't know why I didn't tell her. Maybe her excitement for the trip was rare enough to be appreciated and respected. Joy was not often in her life. Perhaps I wanted to savor the memory of my father to myself. I didn't need her questions, opinions, concern or indifference.

There was something else, too. Staring after Mother at the airport, I realized it did not matter what either of my parents or brother did or didn't do. I loved them differently and they loved what frail human parts of me they knew. What was I going to do with that? The emerging hero will sigh, straighten her shoulders and begin the next part of the hero's journey where innocence is gone, the fight is over, knowledge is gained and life calls.

Unlike classic heroes, human heroes stumble through scattered lessons with flawed reasoning. As Campbell points out, "The boon bestowed on the worshiper is always scaled to his stature and to the nature of his dominant desire: the boon is simply a symbol of life energy stepped down to the requirements of a certain specific case." The hero's challenge now is to step forward, look about, see and claim the boon.

Rebecca Guevara

The Choice to Return

After years of trials Odysseus is tenderly placed by King Alcinoö's sailors on his home shores while he sleeps. Upon waking, he asks Athena where he is and she replies it is his home, Ithaca. He pretends he has only heard of Ithaca and begins a long, untrue tale. She listens, smiles, realizes he is afraid and replies, "Irrepressible! Ever lasting schemer! Indefatigable fabulist! Even in your own country you wouldn't desist from your tales and your historiological inventions ...."

She is a true friend who sees his confusion but does not allow it to get in the way. She disguises him as an old man to travel about his home country, discover what has changed and make things right. The emerging hero has been so busy with grief perhaps she also has not noticed the distance traveled or how much the geography of home shores have changed.

Some have fallen by the wayside with Hamlet and Sophie. Others are resting with Hindu King Muchukunda. Emerging heroes continuing on will look around with Odysseus and assess the landscape.

Neeld writes, "While it is true that we must be left alone to make our own way, at some point we need to listen to—and actually hear—either our own wisdom or the wisdom of someone around us, wisdom that urges us to do something about the quality of our lives."

If we don't take control ourselves, a messenger may come as a spouse, child or friend who out of exasperation and spent patience rightfully declares, as Athena implied, "Is this how you're going to spend the rest of life?" Or like Lewis, the returned sunlight has been making days less grey for some time and now it is finally noticed.

This is the griever's climactic moment before rebirth that is described in scholarly studies of mythology, religion and hero journeys. It is a last passage in the journey before returning home. The task is to eliminate any bad grieving habits. They may be self-protective, comforting and positive in their infant state, but now they are not. It is a strong emerging hero who now assesses the self, makes adjustments and finishes the journey.

Becoming genuinely involved in new activities or interests is a step, but before I could do that, I stood at this passage and worked to be rid of behavior I knew no longer served me well. It wasn't because I understood the hero's journey. I'd not heard of it when I came to this point. Instead, it was that I had experienced a few seductive habits and seen them in others and I knew they weren't productive or attractive.

The following subjects are the seductive habits I knew I needed to break. *Visiting the Grave* is about whether I wanted Jody's life and death to overtake mine. I saw that possibility becoming far more important in defining me than was healthy. Was sadness, regrets suicide leaves behind, and angers that were never resolvable the real me? *The Martyr* is about sacrifice, compensation, and redemption as weapons that tried to look sweet, self-deprecating and humble when they weren't.

Allowing Happiness is about encouraging growth and inviting new pleasures. It includes the evening wine that led me to sleep. It was a necessary friend in the beginning, but what about now? Yes, it was soothing and it held up its end of the bargain, but it was also demanding and its deadening qualities were in the way.

Humor and an ability to laugh at oneself should be returning now, so imagine the fall into seductive habits as a love trap, because it is lost love that got the hero to this point. Imagine meeting someone with whom you are sure a friendship wouldn't work. Perhaps it was an irritating speech habit, brusque manner or way the clothes were worn that was unappealing. Given a choice there wouldn't be a second meeting, but she is in the social network of friends or you work together and contact is unavoidable.

Slowly something happens and ideas shift. Perhaps she defends us or makes us comfortable. On another occasion she is gentle and genuinely funny. Without warning Cupid sends an arrow or we're visited by Dionysus, the god of friendship.

Grudgingly we admit that not only is she acceptable despite a habit or two, she is desirable.

Like this person, grief that was initially distasteful becomes comfortable and idiosyncrasies are discounted. When we first discover we have to live with grief, interact with and sit at the emotional table with it, no one is happy. We kick and scream, yell at God, shake our fist and whatever else feels good to show anger and sorrow.

It is a surprise the grief that initially destroyed turns out to have a few charms. Or if not charms, it has seductive habits that cause would-be heroes to stumble. Endlessly patient and listening in its cold cruel way, grief slowly, amazingly, feels natural. Like an established friend or lover, we rely on its support and comfort. But some friends and lovers do not continue to sustain us. A few become abusive, sometimes using clever psychological twists.

At first the griever may not be aware of abuse as she accepts a diminished life. Momentary spurts of believing in recovery may result in a gasp for fresh air, but grief lunges and yells it is the keeper of memory and respect for the dead. Even with realization of the trap, it is difficult to see a way out and it takes strength to try.

The hero is violently thrown into chaos, visits the underworld, travels through tasks and emerges with information, knowledge, and potential power. The question is: emerges as what?

Visiting the Grave – *My friend becomes a part of me!*

Remember the days we played in the city cemetery by our house on N Street? Our grandfather and relatives we never knew were buried there though we seldom walked by them. Oh, Jody, that cemetery seems a symbol of our childhoods. It was our park and we chased each other through it, jumping over headstones and hiding behind them. In winter we tramped soft snow into child steps earlier crossed with deer hooves. Your boots were buckled black high tops and mine dirty cream white, topped with mashed fur. Mother bought them for us at Karl's Shoes in the basement of the building on the northwest corner of Second South and State.

The open letter remembered quiet winter Saturdays when Mother read by the fire, and Jody and I ran under rolling winter clouds nearly reaching down to join us. When we returned home, unwrapped scarves and took off boots and gloves, I once got a camera. His golden boy face gleams, contorting as he stuck his tongue out. I made a childhood treat of hot gelatin fashioned like tea and took the shaking china teacups with steaming sugary red cherry drink to the dining room table. Scattered papers, pencils and crayons were in disarray as he scrawled the drawings of a four year old and I "wrote" a story.

Mother planned a 4th of July trip to Zion National Park when Jody was five and I was ten. On Friday she rushed home from work, threw the prepared fried chicken and potato salad on ice, directed us to the backseat of the maroon Mercury and off we drove to Grandma's for Donna. Before we were around

Blossoms of the Lower Branches

the Point of the Mountain, twenty miles from home, Mother started feeling ill. Hoping she would feel better in the morning, we drove as planned to a canyon and looked for a place to pull over. Jody nestled with Mother in the back or it may be his feet I remember met mine in the front seat. I'm sure I was scrunched in the car by the steering wheel and heard Mother leave the car several times to retch into the trees.

Too sick to continue the next day and as the only driver, Mother headed home, once pulling over on the highway where cars sped north and south. She stepped to the shoulder to spew a vivid egg yolk yellow. Once home, she went to bed and I packed the chicken and potato salad in a sack. Jody and I walked to the cemetery and sat on a bench to eat and talk about what the canyon, we never did go see, would have looked like.

On a day when the ground was soft from melted snowflakes, and leaf buds were fat brown bulges on branched silhouettes against grey sky, Jody and I walked along a high crest where the valley can be seen. Not very far from where he is buried. We spotted a paper atop a low gravestone held by a rock. On the envelope the name of the two-year-old girl lying beneath us in the sodden earth was scrawled in large, very slanted, unsteady script. Jody was surprised I pried into the letter and began walking away, glancing over his shoulder. I was too curious to put it down, too compelled to feel his dignity. It was a single page, written from the mother to her dead child. "I miss you. Life has not been the same since you went to heaven. Daddy sometimes is angry and leaves the house for a time but it is because he is sad."

I replaced the letter in the envelope and returned it to its resting place under the rock. Studying the early spring sky I wondered if the girl knew of the parents' unhappiness and did she care for them? I ran to catch up with Jody.

The grieving mother wanted comfort and communication with her child, so she unburdened her heart in the physical act of letter writing and placing it by her daughter's body. Visiting the grave is done in many ways for many reasons and doesn't have to involve physical visits at all. Studs Turkel wrote of his wife, "[S]he did live to the ripe old age of eighty-seven, but it doesn't cut the mustard, Charlie. I still see that girl in the maroon smock who liked yellow daisies. Each week, there is a fresh bunch of yellow daisies near the windowsill. On the sill is the urn with her ashes. On occasion, either indignant about something or somewhat enthused, I mumble toward it: "Whaddya think of that, kid?" Her way of seeing things had always been so clear eyed ...." Terkel was comforted with ashes in his home, but not everyone would be.

Visiting the grave has two continuums. One is the number of visits and one is what is gained or lost from them. At its best, mental or physical visits are a place where life questions and emotions are released. It is a place to look around, gather thoughts and meditate or pray to gain equilibrium. It can be at a cemetery, in the marble halls of a mausoleum, or while sitting in the untouched bedroom of the beloved that is still dusted with care.

Frithiof, the conquering Norse hero is asked to be king, but he declines in favor of the rightful heir. Grateful, the people agree to give him Ingeborg, the woman he has always loved. He greatly desired her, but as a man of high Norse honor, he travels to the mound of his dead father to ask permission. It is the fates of Norse mythology he wishes to please by asking the merciful god, Balder, permission to marry. He implores Balder, and is given a sign to rebuild a temple he had caused to be destroyed as atonement before marrying Ingeborg. It is often permission to carry on and enjoy life that is the purpose for returning to the gravesite.

Elizabeth Kübler-Ross and David Kessler state, "Some people go back in their minds or hearts or even to their loved one's grave and ask for permission to continue with life." Loyalty to the lost loved one can be very deep and graveside communion has given that release.

Some grievers visit as a duty or remembrance. It is the primary reason for Memorial Day that floods cemeteries with flowers, plastic windmills and gently swaying balloons. Aeneas visited his father's grave. "I should fulfill, as due, my yearly vows, the solemn funeral observances, and heap the shrines with gifts." As time distances, visits restate love and remembered affection.

My first visit was three months after the death. I wrote, *"We needed to know if the marker was right. It was. A grey cool November day. Workmen in the next two blocks arranging for new funerals. He felt discarnate. Two places at once. In the sky* and in the ground. Very confusing, but also a security in quiet's aloofness. The valley below visible beyond the trees, homes hugging a ledge above. His name on a stone so remote and cold from the brother I picked up at the airport last Christmas, the Jody who came to see me days before his death in August. Somehow, I feel whenever I, or anyone else close to him genuinely needs him, he will be there. I told Sam about my feelings, but he didn't say much. I would like to tell our parents, but I don't know what."

In night's darkness cemeteries have another face. Teenagers often thrill their macabre side by visiting them. A favorite of local teenagers was a small monument in the south end where trees planted in the 1800s had matured to give full cover to the narrow lanes. An urn was inside the five foot marker, and at night it was imagined the legendary ghost face of Emo appeared. The group I traveled with in my early teens enjoyed scattering in all directions from the night security guard who had a BB gun he was reported to use on kids like us.

On the north side of the cemetery, Eleventh Avenue winds between a mountainside and a sandstone fence. On a summer night I left my friend at her home after visiting a bar, and struck with a wave of grief, I drove to the familiar cemetery. I pulled to the side of the road by the wall, got out and looked. Here the lawn was open as a golf course, next were neat rows of short, white stones where soldiers lie before my brother's block. Tall pines stood like a black arrowhead fence and beyond, the city lights sparkled. I sat on the low wall, lifted my bare leg and sandaled heel over and stood in the cemetery. I brushed the back of my skirt, tightly held my car keys and walked down to my brother. As during day visits, I stood in front of his stone and looked east to the university. After only seconds I felt a swooping of distraught, angry, lost and cruel faces around me shouting in a chorus, "What is *she* doing here?" There was pain in my lower abdomen so severe I began doubling over before walking back to the car. I sat inside with doors locked and the pain gone. I steadied myself before driving home with tears falling to my skirt.

Motivation needs to be understood. Visits can give comforting communion that is peaceful and helps acceptance, or they can establish an attachment that compromises mental health and adapting to changes. The first years I visited Jody's grave about six times a year. It was equally comforting and upsetting. Graveyards encourage peace and inner quiet from torment. But I also looked down at the engraved stone with my brother's name, birth and death date and felt suffocated imagining him frozen in winter, sweating in summer, and breathing always against the casket and dirt as his body disintegrated in thin peeling sheets of skin, muscle, then crumbling bone.

Hindu goddess Kali, wearing a garland of human skulls and a girdle of human arms, promises transformation from death with her shocking images and dance. Her lord Shiva smeared his body with ashes and danced in cremation grounds. Together they represent fearless change and life's renewal as they play with our serious images.

Mourning the death of a childhood friend, Dionysus visited where his friend was buried. From the burial spot grew an unusual plant, "with leaves curling like a boy's hair, and clusters of grapes blushing like the boy's cheeks." From these grapes Dionysus made the first wine. He declares figs, olives and bread are good, but of wine he gushed, "You run through all my veins like my blood, and my friend becomes a part of me! You shall give joy to the feast ... those who mourn will forget their sorrow." After reading this version of wine's history, I more clearly understood the tradition of turning to wine as comfort. Time spent in wine's soft embrace can feel like a lost loved one still runs through the veins like blood. It is the attraction of visiting the grave through wine beyond the time it serves the griever well.

At my insistence, Sam and I drew up papers for Zac's care and handling of our estate. I added cremation for me because I didn't want them to feel the anguish I felt at Jody's grave. Now I know both of them well enough to realize what was true for me would not hold for them. Visits or lack of them and what they mean is as personal and idiosyncratic as a favorite chocolate filling. Mother has never visited, and that is best.

Places related to the death can also have their haunts of visiting the grave. The tract homes built in the forties and fifties south of our high school, in the Glendale neighborhood, had mature trees lining the streets in front of small frame or brick homes. Some were in disrepair, but many were meticulously cared for behind four-foot chain link fence. I didn't know many people who lived there, though I sat in classrooms with the area's teenagers at West High School. I was a transplanted student and being quiet didn't help in the fifteen hundred student body.

Meeting people and having lots of friends was Jody's area, so he was familiar with Glendale's variety store where he bought the gun. When Zac was little I shopped the store several times to buy lipstick and clothes for him because it offered discount prices, but since finding the gun receipt from the store I had not driven down the street. But the situation changed, and again I drove to the store through the neighborhood of minimum wage workers and immigrants from around the globe. A friend had now married a man who owned the store and turned it into a cheery ethnic grocery with fruits, vegetables and canned goods then not found anywhere else in the city.

I visited a metaphorical grave to support my friend and wish her success by walking through the aisles that now held bottled molés and prickly pears. I pushed my cart, stopping for bright fresh chiles, avocados, onions, and tortillas. Where I picked up cheese was the place of the gun cabinet. I hope I didn't retrace my brother's last steps out the door, but now I knew life relentlessly moves on without respect or care to those who do not acknowledge it.

Treadway recalls his first visit to his mother's grave many years after her death. The plan was to bury her wedding ring under a miniature rose he plants. It is before Mother's Day and the helpful floral employee warns him there could be a killing frost. He writes: "'Well, that's a good tip. I'll take them.' 'Do you want a card? We have quite a selection of Mother's Day cards.' 'No thanks, I don't need a card. The flowers will say it all.'" Uncomfortable through the visit while recalling the tragic events of her death, he writes: "I fumble for the ring in my pocket. Burying the damn thing is definitely melodramatic, but I know I don't want to take it home. I drop it into the little hole." In the crazy meeting of strange convergences, take the humor, peace, horror and sweet memories to the gravesite in body or mind and learn to dance away into new life with Kali.

The pull to graves and scenes of fatal accidents is very strong. After all Parrado experienced on the high desolate peaks of the Andes, he has returned several times with fellow survivors and his father. "My father's face was pale, and tears wet his cheeks as we shared this sad reunion, but I felt no pain or grief. I felt tranquility in that place. There was no more fear there, or suffering, or struggle. The dead were at peace. The pure, perfect stillness of the mountains had returned." Then, after the comforting visit, the traveler turns his back, takes Kali's hand, and returns to life still to be lived.

The Martyr – *Phaeton's sisters*

It's easy to slip from being a sincere griever to a martyr. The distance from genuine grieving to continuing to grieve because of a principle is an inch. A time came when I knew I had walked the inch and was falling in the rabbit hole, and like Alice in *Alice in Wonderland*, I looked. "There were doors all round the hall, but they were all locked, and when Alice had been all the way down one side and up the other, trying every door, she walked sadly down the middle, wondering how she was ever to get out again." Many doors with roomfuls of problems behind them have been opened until at the natural end of grief, the rooms no longer serve the same purpose and awareness of the change can be baffling.

Death creates a void by explosion that leaves parts of life shaken bare of meaning. Grievers busy themselves by cleaning the debris and re-arranging thoughts and emotions. It is the hero's journey, but the rooms can change from a hero's trials to personal showrooms of suffering. Time passes, honest emotions are experienced, life re-patterns, and another void hits. Instead of an explosion, this one is created by the slow leak of urgent grief until we are spent and empty.

Telemachos' search for Odysseus began as a healthy quest of a son for his father, but time wore on and his men suffered. He was helplessly continuing when Eidothea, the daughter of the Old Man of the Sea, appeared. She was plain-spoken at an intersection of decision. "Here you are all this long time stuck in this island, and you cannot find any way out, while the heart of your men is fainting!"

When Sam's mother died, I knew I needed to fully listen to him without my sorrow. He talked about her death alongside the beauty of trees, the warmth of sun, a friend's laugh. Who needs forty hours of work a week? Or a car payment? Why bother with talking about politics when life was really only the joy in our son's eyes? Sam complained of body aches I connected with Lupe's death. Most of it I considered necessary to say and feel, but then he came home with the blazing eyes I saw in Jody when he stepped out of the stadium on his graduation.

"I'm not afraid of death, Beckie. Death sounds nice to me." I made a doctor's appointment for him the next day. I felt needed by his mourning, and when he recovered, I believed in small measure I was vindicated. He talked with his doctor, passed all the tests and we were both relieved, but I knew he was still suffering.

Zac, Sam and I were each grieving in different ways and for different reasons for Lupe and Jody. Sam began consciously working harder and joined activities. Zac soothed his father by attending basketball games and watching television. He calmed me with afternoons at the theatre and reading together in front of the fire. Sam and I thought we were helping Zac, but I know his presence helped us. He was not left to bring himself up and he never disappeared into the night with dangerous friends, but this was a difficult chasm for a young person to navigate.

In a dream I had at the time, Mother, Grandma, Zac and I wandered across a mountain like an abandoned herd, spotting small blazes of fires we tried to kick out with dirt while looking around for help to extinguish them. There were many fires and we walked until we approached a town and wondered why everyone was so nonchalant. Feelings of helplessness support the slow move to martyrdom.

Seeds of martyrdom innocently sprout in healthy grief when

emotions are large. If there is a lack of support or not enough talking to others with healthy feedback, grievers easily default to relying on their vulnerable reasoning. An old note of mine read: *In order to keep Sam and Zac in my life I could not let them know the depth of my self-questioning and self-loathing. Perhaps they would not want me when they realized the extent of my guilt and despair. So I made small whispered covenants over my emptying wine glass. I would give my life to Sam and Zac. Everything they wanted. There would be nothing I wanted that was not first for them. Temporarily satisfied I had appeased any power that would take them away, I drank the last of the wine, checked on Zac, and kissed him on his beautiful hair before going to be with Sam.*

A mother in Judy Wolf's book relates, "[I] made the unwelcome discovery that I was a "grief junkie," a sympathy gatherer, telling and retelling my story of James so that my experience of life and others' experience of me revolved around that event. And I'm a little ashamed to admit that I think sometimes I liked that, I liked the drama and the shock-value, and the way people reacted to me when I told them." A benefit may have been new sympathizers who unwittingly helped keep grief alive.

Carol A. Pearson believes: "Martyrs can hide behind this mask of being good and unselfish as a way to avoid taking their journey, finding out who they are, or taking a stand." I would rephrase only a few words for the griever. Martyrs can hide behind the mask of grieving and show of undying love as a way to avoid finishing their journey.

Like Joan of Arc, they may be willing to give anything for a cause, but it can slip into the style Anzia Yerzierska writes about after overhearing a conversation at her mother's funeral. "Such a good mother, such a virtuous wife... never did she allow herself a bite to eat but left-overs, never a dress but the rags her daughters had thrown away." Seldom pretty, martyrdom has a long continuum.

Siduri fell in love with grief's first hero, Gilgamesh, and tried to help him through it. Unwilling to return to the pleasures of love and life, Gilgamesh refuses her and she accuses him of being blind with rage and loving himself for it. After slamming the door on him, he screams, "'I am not blind with self-love but with loss!' He felt his head split with the pain of making himself heard by her, by all the world." After a time, it becomes difficult for others to see the sincerity or use of raw emotions that should have been left behind. Eventually, it is best to review personal motivation and the cost of active grief.

When time distances death's immediate pain, life takes on the flavor of the Jewish phrase, "and yet, and yet." The situation is good and yet (it is not) and it is bad and yet (it is not). There may not be a full engagement of life, but there is definite improvement from the first weeks, months or years.

Eventually, it's decision time. The mother in Wolf's book realized, "Don't get me wrong. The story is true, of course; it did happen. James' suicide changed me at depth; I will never be the same person I was before his death. But this loss, however tragic and life altering, is not who I am, and at that time, it started to become who I was."

Orpheus' father, Apollo, gave him a lyre he played so well people cried from the musical beauty. When Orpheus' beloved wife, Eurydice, accidentally died he was so stricken that he visited the underworld and played his music to beg she be returned to life with him. Enchanted by his music, the underworld overlords granted his request as long as he did not look behind him to see her until they were safely back to earth life. He promised, but of course, at the last second he did look back and lost her forever. He lamented while other lovely and worthy maidens pursued him and patiently waited, but his grief went on too long. Orpheus fell into martyrdom and the maidens became so angry with his refusal to live they tore him limb from limb and threw the pieces and his head on the lyre in the river Hebrus. Eternally, Orpheus is a martyr to grief.

"You are such a good griever," the inner voice whispered one quiet evening. It was weary, bored and did not soften. I waited for more so I could defend, retaliate or use self-empathetic tears, but nothing followed. I was like Phaeton's sisters in Ovid's *Metamorphoses*. "Four times had the moon rounded her crescent horns into a full circle: the sisters, as was their habit – for constant practice had made it a habit ...."

"So, are you going to waste it?" was the voice's next indictment. I knew what it meant. "Can't you be just a little gentler? After all, I've gone through a lot," I answered. It wasn't without regret that I hadn't written a creative sentence in years while putting aside hope and effort to further any writing skill.

I defensively argued but lost the round when I compared how I was handling another semi-conclusion I was trying to learn from the death. When it came to Sam, Zac and Mother I believed life should be enjoyed far more than suffered or endured. I wanted their happiness so I reminded myself perhaps childhood was a bit much for an immature girl who didn't always see the happiness presenting itself, but that didn't mean as an adult it couldn't be chosen. I'd never considered this view. Jody's death slowly revealed the choice. I remembered what gave me real, spontaneous, uncontrived pleasure. Writing.

Writing was a slow go with halting starts and stops. I felt punished for success and failure. It was difficult to believe I might be a successful and worthy writer. Scary ideas given the light of day for the first time can quickly retreat to darkness until another part of us begs it to be revived and re-considered. My desires were popping up in the night dreams of the handless maiden's baby needing my care. I had slipped from missing Jody to missing my inner life, which I had killed in recompense. I was sacrificing myself to the principle of guilt. It was time to step away from martyrdom.

Thumbelina said she could not leave the field mouse who had been kind to her. It took another year of captivity and fear of having to marry the mole that finally broke her of the martyr's bond. When the grateful bird returned and again asked her to join him, she accepted. Only by freeing herself did Thumbelina finally meet her love and prince, the Flower Angel.

At times I viewed leaving grief as a duty like dusting. I got more action with, "So who are you choosing here, dead Jody or living Zac?" This is what Eidothea was telling Telemachos. He was stuck on an island, without direction, while his men were fainting from need. Was he going to waste his life over a missing, probably dead father he'd never met, or take care of his men, whom he was charged with leading?

The end of consuming grief should give good self-sustaining conclusions. There are remaining loved ones who need us or new ones waiting to be found. Talents exist to be improved and enjoyed. New pleasures can be enjoyed and there is goodness in the world that wants to be added to and enjoyed. If there is a belief the loved one should have been able to live a fulfilled life, shouldn't the survivor?

Lands lay fallow, seeds were diseased, seasons passed, and still the grieving wandering Demeter did not attend to earth as she endlessly searched for Persephone. Finally, a nymph lifted her head and implored, "Great mother of the corn crops, you who have sought your daughter throughout the whole world, enough of unending toil, enough of violent rage against the faithful earth! No blame attaches to the earth: if it gaped open to receive that robber, it did so reluctantly." Demeter was told of Zeus' part and enraged, she flew to confront him. Martyrdom was turned to action and she demanded her daughter's return. Unable to fully grant her wish because Persephone was the residing queen of the underworld, the chastised god who made his deals without regard for others, worked a compromise. When Persephone returns to visit her mother, the earth warms with spring and then summer. When she is with her husband the seasons are fall and winter. Demeter is a symbol of the always revolving seasons of life. She brings fruitfulness in summers and self-reflection in the winters of emotional life.

Allowing Happiness – *And so I kept my grief*

After losing a daughter seven years earlier, a mother told writer Judith Viorst, "I'm proud of myself when I can say her name without a tremor. [But,] I'm horrified when I can say her name without a tremor." Allowing happiness requires grievers settle conflicted emotions.

A trickster must oversee this passage. In an African tale, spider trickster Ananse trapped Leopard in a hole. Cruelly, he then lured Leopard to the edge of freedom before slashing his paws. Wiley tricksters Cupid and Coyote also invite grievers with hollow promises until they are strong enough to push them aside.

Like the mother who talked to Viorst, I was pleased when I again fully enjoyed light reading, being able to hear stories of another's brother, or anything without the background of Jody. Ananse was pulling me out of the hole, and then, when I neared the top, there were twinges of abandonment. If I let grief go, wouldn't Jody irretrievably disappear as though he never existed? Unconsciously, I thought grief kept him mine. Ananse easily dropped me into the hole again.

In *Hannah Coulter*, Wendell Berry's widowed protagonist says, "My grief was the last meaning of his life in this world.

And so I kept my grief. For a long time I couldn't give it up." I knew people worked their way through grief but I didn't understand how. I vowed to smile more and "pretend." After an exhausting day of that, I sat down with grief's trickster who leaned close, patted my hand and whispered, "I know you want to be strong. I love you so I will support you."

But that was a lie because grief knew my secrets and it reminded me of all that was lost. I whispered that perhaps it was my duty to carry it on my back forever. Grief nodded in agreement. C.S. Lewis recognized this. "Part of every misery is, so to speak, the misery's shadow or reflection: the fact that you don't merely suffer but have to keep on thinking about the fact that you suffer. I not only live each endless day in grief, but live each day thinking about living each day in grief."

Psychiatrist Gordon Livingston treated many people who continued being without energy or appetite and were unable to sleep. To break the spell he "[R]edirect[ed] people's attention to the possibility that there might be advantages to their being depressed." For some it is being a martyr, and for others it can be fear of allowing happiness.

"I imagined I must have been a good person to be so sensitive and sad. I was very good at feeling bad," wrote author and teacher Stephen Levine in *Unattended Sorrow*. Later, he realized what was driving that. "Then, rereading my journal, I realized what delusional thinking that was. Just another way for me not to deal with my grief, nor to get on with it."

A good ending of a hero's grief journey will not allow the bad habits of grief to continue, though how to lose them is not always clear. Livingston suggests to his patients. "All significant accomplishments require taking risks .... Happiness is the ultimate risk." Trickster is forcing a choice: be its victim or get out of the trap.

As with all seductive habits, a few would-be heroes are left behind. Not because they are weak, since most people visit here, but because they don't leave. The flamboyant, gifted Isadora Duncan never improved in her mother's grief. After drinking too much at an afternoon party she carelessly wore a long scarf that got caught in the wheels of the convertible she was in and caused her horrific death.

Gilgamesh asked an old man if he knew of Enkidu. The man, "[S]hrugged and shook his head, then turned away, as if to say it is impossible to keep the names of friends whom we have lost. Gilgamesh said nothing more to force his sorrow on another." At last, he was recovering.

Parrado thought deeply about all that had gone wrong to diminish the potential of his life. "I began to understand my ordeal in the Andes was not an interruption of my true destiny, or a perversion of what my life was supposed to be. It simply was my life, and the future that lay ahead of me was the only future available to me."

Emanuel Swedenborg, who lived from 1688 to 1772, was a pioneer in what he called influx and correspondence. They were a precursor of Emmet Fox and Ernest Holmes' mental equivalent, or the now popular law of attraction that proposes the ability to hold thoughts and urge the universe, God, to respond. In *Science of Mind* Holmes writes about the mental equivalent. "[C]reative Consciousness, which is receptive, neutral, impersonal, always receiving the impress of our thought and which has no alternative other than to operate directly upon it, thus creating the things which we think."

A motivation to allow happiness was realizing grief could be a habit like trusty brown shoes that won't wear out. It kidnapped my personality, and as with any abusing trickster, I was the one who needed to stand up and leave. So, I slowly stepped away from the trickster who knew my fears too well and genuinely turned to the possibility of a happier life. Occasionally grief revisits, but now I affectionately pat its familiar cheek and thank it for teaching me so much. Then I stand up, walk away and do something that makes me happy. I refuse to mess up more than I already have from its rough lessons.

REBECCA GUEVARA

RETURN TO LIFE

The Blossom's Fruit

Simpleton was the youngest of three sons in the Brothers Grimm story of *The Golden Goose*. The father sent the oldest out with food and wine to cut wood and bring it back. When the son refused to share his meal with the tree's keeper, he was injured and returned home. The same happened to the second son, so the father was not expecting success when he sent Simpleton, but he broke the habits of his older brothers and shared his meal. As a reward, the tree's keeper gave him a golden goose. On the way home, he met a young woman who wanted one of the goose's golden feathers, but when she touched it she could not take her hand away. Soon her two sisters came along, and trying to free her, also found themselves stuck. Before long a parson and a sexton foolishly did what the one before them did and five people followed Simpleton's goose like a kite's tail. Continuing on his way, he came upon a kingdom where a king had promised marriage to his daughter if the young man could make her laugh.

When the princess saw Simpleton carrying a goose with five people trailing behind, she laughed. Unfortunately, the king did not like the name Simpleton for his daughter's husband and made him do three tasks before being given her hand. Everyone around Simpleton was mired in habits. Only the princess, the prize of the story, broke free of habits and took joy in life by laughing. Time and again fairy tales show the futility of repeatedly doing the same thing.

I felt I had moved away from grieving's bad habits. I seldom visited the cemetery, had regained enough humor and happiness to shrug off being a martyr and cut back on drinking. Still, there was a shadow that needed lifting. Some people say there is heaviness on the heart. I felt an invisible but still realized diffusion throughout my body that I wanted gone so I could return to a previous lightness. I'd been at this grieving stuff for a long time and I was weary. Weary but not finished. There was something to be absorbed.

I was happy, but underneath I wondered what was wrong. What didn't I understand? When I was around other people I didn't think about it, but when I was alone or faced with thoughts of the future, I was aware of a force. I no longer felt like caving into grief with spontaneous tears, and I knew I had much to be grateful for, but something was stuck.

When the sleeping mind is fully relaxed maybe it unravels thoughts and emotions that are stared at without a clue during the day. Sleep may be when the body and mind are most open to spontaneous healing and new understanding. In the dark of a winter morning my sleep ended by unwinding into a peaceful clear feeling edged with love. Through the cosmos of sleep I have experienced a peace so great that upon waking, I feel blessed by true presence. I felt touched by a new understanding I was unable to name.

It was like being parched from thirst and having a long drink of clear, cool, spring water. Though I didn't understand where the work was done, the details of nutrition and biology, or how I was physically replenished, I knew I was.

Slowly, I understood I was nourished from death's aftermath. The heavy diffusion I felt was not sorrow. It was unacknowledged knowledge that was collected piece by piece. It was as if a teacher had placed his hand on my shoulder and said, "Do you understand?" When I finally looked him in the eye and said, "Yes," the hand was removed and the knowledge was consciously mixed with the physical, mental and spiritual essence of who I am. It is now body history and will stay with me through the time of my existence.

Neeld's experience was similar to mine. "Suddenly, I felt a shift occur in my body; there was an actual physical alteration. Something released inside me. This shift was immediately followed by an inexplicable sense of well-being, of calmness and serenity. The vague foreboding—the sense that 'something is not right; something bad is about to happen,' which had been a constant presence in my life since Greg's death—had left me. Instead, sitting there as if in a round of sky and trees and light and earth, I felt in touch with something elemental, strong, ineffable."

Campbell states myths suggest something still deeper. "The talismanic ring from the soul's encounter with its other portion in the place of recollectedness betokens that the heart was there aware of what Rip van Winkle missed; it betokens too a conviction of the waking mind that the reality of the deep is not belied by that of common day. This is the sign of the hero's requirement, now, to knit together his two worlds." Grieving is at a natural end and life is regained.

Heroes can wonder what the value is of the difficult time they have spent in grief's journey. In *Down by the River*, Charles Bowden follows the family of Lionel Bruno Jordan in El Paso, Texas after his brutal murder. Jordan had a tight-knit family and many relatives grieved terribly for him. His niece, Brigitte, witnessed an intruder photographing the body at the funeral. "She knew, deep down inside, [there was] someone who wanted a photograph of Bruno dead, a corpse framed and ready to mount." The horrors and realizations Brigitte faced to find peace were not an easy path.

Knitting together this world of horror with peace and joy is confusing. Kali, destroyer and creator, offers a hand through the havoc to look beyond "all limited conceptions, boundaries and rules." The hero's journey has brought the mourner to the point of reuniting everyday life with all its sorrows to more profoundly live in the joys. The knitting together is being peaceful with touching the edge of eternity's chasm of where we came from and where we will return.

The story has come full circle. Grievers believe a part of them died with the loved one. Now, they reach the point of being reborn from the ashes. The phoenix that rises from the ashes is a recognized story of creation's cycle of death reviving itself to new life. It is a symbol in cultures as diverse as Egypt, India, Japan, and throughout the Americas.

Instead of ashes, other stories tell of the rising of the sun from night, and still others wake as did King Muchukunda when prodded by barbarians who found him in his cave after his sleep of eons. Unable to comprehend the king's magnificence, the barbarians immediately fell to ashes. At last, fully awake, King Muchukunda began to serve his savior, Lord Vishnu.

Rebirth is a reminder that everyone is in the chain of birth, life, and death's repeating pattern. Leeming writes: "The hero faces death and dies for us. In so doing he holds out a promise of new life through his sacrifice. He thus also teaches us something of the positive nature of death as the catalyst for a new birth through the spirit. As always, the hero is the symbol of man in search of himself." The last sentence is the seed of promise for grievers.

Outward appearances don't always reflect what has been learned. Bowdon continues his story of Brigitte, who is now the mother of a young son she watches as she talks to Bowdon. He writes of her transformed thinking. "You learn to stop asking because you know and what you know is all you are ever going to know. And Bruno is murdered, cut down, a carjacking they say, something that happened down by the river, near that line, back then, in one of those places. The child is in the sunlight. Brigitte is talking. She knows better than to think there are answers. She knows better than to believe in vengeance. What she knows is this: the child is in the sunlight." This is what mends the duality of human life. Horror gives way to enjoy seeing fragile children dancing in the sun.

Odin hung from the sacred tree, Yggdrisil, for nine days and nights to gain the wisdom of the runes which he passed on to his people. After receiving the runes he says: "then I began to be fruitful and to be fertile, to grow and to prosper; one word sought another word from me; one deed sought another deed from me." As presented by scholars of myth, the boon sends classic heroes to teach others.

Through each hero's heart the blossoms of the lower branches now shows its fruit. It is time to realize what has been learned and how it has changed life. I learned about the following seven subjects, but I did not learn everything about them. Life meanders and twists, always giving further nuance and definition. Unfortunately, too, it is easier to write, than it is to always live within their warmth.

Life is a steady accumulation of experience which results in beliefs. It is often impossible, and I think unnecessary, to separate the strands of life of being a wife, mother, daughter, friend, business person, citizen and Jody's sister. Every role presents puzzles, decisions or illuminations that overlap. I found writing what I thought I learned gratifying because it became evident I had learned something, and that gave me a peace and sense of coming to terms. Others may express a changed self with art, music, service, or genuine cheer for others.

None of the heroes I read about claimed on the last pages to know everything or to have all the answers. Divine heroes ascend to glory beyond human understanding. Human heroes recognize what they learn from trials and carry it into transformed lives.

The Deep Abiding – *A sea of peace serene*

The deep abiding is a feeling of wholeness and peace binding a person to God and the universe. Buddhist monks, Christian mystics, Native American shamans and other religious people define it as being as one, the deep abode, ecstasy, transported, entering the void. It may last for measurable time but usually, if experienced at all, it is fleeting. It seems its real power is in surprising us with a moment nearing comprehension, just long enough for a deep realization or personal revelation without turning us to ashes with Semele.

Semele was a lover of Zeus, and was soon to give birth to their child. Zeus' wife, Hera, heard of the expected child and visited Semele with the purpose of destroying the mother and baby. Taking on the visage of Semele's trusted maid, Hera convinced her the man who fathered her child couldn't be trusted as the god he said he was if he wasn't willing to show his true self. Zeus was very fond of Semele, and wishing to protect her from his godly brilliance, he only visited her as a mortal, but persuaded by Semele's pleading, he appeared in full glory. Hera was correct in predicting Semele would not be able to stand the brilliance, as she immediately turned to ashes when she looked upon him. Quickly, Zeus saved the prematurely born half-god and half-man, Dionysus. Semele would have been better off if she had been pleased with living and loving within her capabilities.

It is natural to desire illumination and full knowledge of the unknown, but step-by-step slow realization is the more sure-footed way to understand important truths. After Norse Frithiof finished rebuilding Balder's temple he stood leaning on his sword with memories of childhood and years of being a Viking passing before him. In tranquil spirit, resting from the labor of good work, he felt inner change. "Soon melted human vengeance, every human hate, as melts the sleeted armor from the mountain's breast, when smiles the spring-time sun. A sea of peace serene, of silent rapture, then swept o'er his hero-soul. He seemed to feel the heart of nature tuneful beat against his own, as if he were impelled to press the universe in his fraternal arm, and peace confirm with each created being in the night."

Dideon describes: "Setting the table. Lighting the candles. Building the fire. Cooking. All those soufflés, all that crème caramel …. Clean sheets, stacks of clean towels, hurricane lamps for storms, enough water and food to see us through whatever geological event came our way. These fragments mattered to me. That I could find meaning in the intensely personal nature of my life as a wife and mother did not seem inconsistent with finding meaning in the vast indifference of geology ...."

Nando Parrado was often asked how he was so successful in living a peaceful, productive and happy life since his harrowing time in the Andes. "I tell them I am not at peace in spite of what I suffered, but because of it. The Andes took so much from me, I explain, but they also gave me the simple insight that has liberated me and illuminated my life: Death is real, and death is very near."

Castenada's Don Juan relates, "Only as a warrior can one survive the path of knowledge, because the art of a warrior is to balance the terror of being a man and the wonder of being a man." Wonder, terror, that death is near, the grace of small tasks and the peace of silence are common threads describing the deep abiding. And each one is experienced in small step-by-step illuminations.

Grief's journey walks the traveler toward transformation and self renewal. When Judy Wolf's teen-age son died her childhood religion no longer served her new beliefs, and she became an interfaith minister. "[T]o walk gently next to your brothers and sisters, offering them compassion—to companion them in their passion."

Psychiatrist Gordon Livingston who knows theory and experience says, "Our constant challenge is not to seek perfection in ourselves and others, but to find ways to be happy in an imperfect world. We are impeded in this effort if we cling to an idealized vision of the past that insures dissatisfaction with the present."

For me, the deep abiding is being comfortable believing I don't know the "true" meaning of life or what exists beyond it, and it doesn't matter that I don't. My responsibility is to love, be grateful, live and work well within the beliefs I do have.

Non-profits and Activists – *I know something about the misery of man*

After a comfortable childhood and advantaged youth, Buddha spent ages twenty-nine to thirty-five searching for truth. When he came to his insights, he declared, "I don't know about the mystery of god, but I know something about the misery of man." This classic hero's journey ends with the hero returning from trials ready to teach and be of service. The stories of Christ, Muhammad, Buddha, and many religious leaders follow the hero's journey of seclusion while learning or being taught, followed by service. Mythical King Arthur was taught by Merlin before becoming king. Fictional Luke Skywalker became a leader after he learned from the supernatural Obi Wan Kenobi.

Grief's journey has taken detours and mocked established order with everything seeming to happen at once in dark corruptions of order from death's chaos. Involvement in non-profits or being an activist is often leaped into during early grief. The topsy-turvy experience of the grieving hero often creates the quirk of putting boons before apotheosis.

The same week Candy Lightner's daughter was killed by a drunk driver, she began hatching ideas for Mothers Against

Drunk Driving. Cindy Sheehan became an activist by protesting the Iraq War soon after her son Casey died saying, "Why would I want one more mother – either Iraqi or American – to go through what I'm going through?"

The dying person can charge the witnessing survivor with working for a cause. Susan Van Komen enlisted her sister, Nancy Bruden, to educate women about breast cancer. In 1982 Bruden founded the Susan G. Komen Breast Cancer Foundation that has given millions to research.

Establishing a non-profit or becoming an activist while unresolved emotions rage has many pitfalls. Offering to volunteer time or giving money is a gentler beginning. Volunteering time allows grievers to become familiar with the issues as students Buddha, King Arthur and Luke Skywalker did. Commitment can be expanded as healing occurs, and there is space to withdraw support if that is best.

But like Lightner, Bruden and Sheehan, many mourners are overwhelmed with emotion, and while actively grieving they establish a non-profit or become activists. It seems an altruistic gift to fight the cause of a loved one's death, but the grieving hero has much to consider before plunging into responsibilities because the cruel reality is: This is starting a business.

Three years before Jody's death, on the Friday before Labor Day Weekend, Sam came home from work declaring he had logically laid out the reasons he should have a raise, but he was refused, so he quit. He had worked in printing, had a talent for art and was eager. I could add a column of numbers, learn to typeset and buy printing. We hadn't any entrepreneurial experience. Optimism, resolve and the need to make money were all we had.

After three years, a few fights, a car repossession, a second mortgage on the house, needing to put a twenty dollar winter coat in layaway at K-Mart for Zac, and buying a three dollar thrift store raincoat, my only coat for years, our noses popped up for a little air. Only enough to get current with bills. The worst of this was when Jody was suffering the most deeply, and I know my self-involvement, however well-intentioned, reduced my very limited capacity to help him. The exhausting experience of starting a business was one more reason I didn't rush into altruistic work.

The list of hazards is long: Personal grief becomes public and displayed to strangers who must hear the story of death to support the cause. Death is a constant presence that can be overwhelming and a griever's style and sincerity will be open for scrutiny and judgment. Observers may wonder where the griever is in the continuum of motivation from healthy altruism to a public display of secret shame or guilt. The lives of family and friends are affected, and their style of recovery may be helped or hindered.

Running a non-profit requires a commitment of constant thought, daily planning, and years of dedication. Impersonal city, state and federal government regulations impose rules of business. Grief is transformed to tax forms, employee issues and marketing. Like any new business, it demands unexpected attention and a grieving founder cannot quietly leave if interest, need or ability evaporate.

There's more. Supporters expect sincerity and attainable goals. There are events to run smoothly, a board of directors to be organized and managed. Previous career goals, income and other interests of the griever before the death may be risked beyond the point of recovery. All this is at a time when new mourners are vulnerable to turbulent emotions and will be whammied by impersonal business building necessities. Lastly, a potential danger is if it is unsuccessful, it becomes one more thing to mourn, another disappointment to the heart.

An alternative to founding an organization is to volunteer and support a similar one. Get the feet wet. Learn the ropes. When I did advising on business startups, I always suggested this to people who wanted to start a business unrelated to any previous work. Many people observe from a distance how an industry works, quickly assume that piles of money (or legislative power) wait to be made, and believe they know enough.

Grievers can believe everyone should be empathetic and supportive of their cause. It's easy to think everyone sees this tragic situation, so of course they will help. People may be empathetic but not supportive. This includes friends and family who stood at the burial with just as many sincere tears. They may be committed to other groups or causes or not have enough time or money to spare.

Even people who are grieving because of similar reasons will choose not to help. A self-preserving reason is, it is not healthy to be around the cause because it keeps them in deep martyr-like grief. They may help financially but they heal best privately and don't want their name associated. They are bearing their burdens as well as they can and perhaps more successfully. Others who have gone through grief are recovered enough to have a full, energized and good life focusing on subjects important to them, and they may not be interested.

Candy Lightner wrote in her biography, "I believed my work with MADD was a great way to [grieve]. But I was wrong. As an activist I was far more attuned to the legislative process than I was the grieving process .... My attention as a mother should have gone to my other two children, but I avoided that, too." No one can question the success and necessity of MADD. Lightner was instrumental in changing a nation's thinking about drunk driving, but the out of whack order of grief's hero journey was costly to her and those still in her life.

Cindy Sheehan said, "I am going to take whatever I have left and go home. I am going to go home and be a mother to my surviving children and try to regain some of what I have lost." She was a brave woman, and regardless of politics, it is admirable she valiantly stood up for a child and a nation's future. Then, when it was time, she returned to her life, family and friends who needed her. No one is guaranteed a positive result from any decision, but I know and respect the damaged heart of a brave griever.

A griever with dedication and solemn unshakable purpose to transform society is to be admired. She saves lives and provides others with a light in the dark to follow. It can be a healthy way out of grief that honors the loved one and benefits society, turning private loneliness to accomplished action.

Court systems create activists. Sitting in court while a perpetrator of a loved one's death seemingly slips through justice's grasp can make the system seem anything but efficient and just. These sufferers may not start a non-profit, but working through the criminal justice system makes them an activist, and very often puts them on difficult public display. High profile cases turn grievers into fodder for the news when they are accosted in the halls of justice for a comment on the day's events.

Dutifully attending every court appearance or avoiding them altogether is not to be judged by outsiders. Reasons are personal and for the health and healing of the grievers, it should be understood they can change their participation any time they wish.

As fidgety children Jody and I waited for what seemed hours in a wide hall in a Los Angeles County government building. Two days before Grandma Spiking had been called and told her son, Wayne, was dead, shot in a lover's quarrel by the woman he was engaged to marry. Jody and I lounged on the wooden bench, sat up and swung our legs, walked up and down the hall, tried to see out a window across from us. The wide wood doors at last swung open and Mother, Donna and Grandma walked out. Grandma's face was ashen and haunted. A last stop through bureaucracy's maze was identifying the body on the morgue slab as her son.

It took many years before I pieced together more of what must have hurt besides the schizophrenia and earlier shock treatments. Wayne contracted infantile paralysis (polio) as a four-year-old and she was advised to make him comfortable in a wheelchair. She found a doctor who, against the medical practice of the time, thought daily exercise of the legs could restore walking. Mother has told me of the many times she remembers Grandma massaging his legs and the evenings they spent in the living room urging him to walk again, until at last he did.

She must have also remembered the short painful life of Donna's twin brother, Dale, who was born with numerous disabilities and lived only eleven months. That day in Los Angeles when details of her son's murder were spoken burned something very precious and deep within.

The steady accumulation of unhealed tragedy in a family can move suffering members to seek anonymity. Mikal Gilmore wrote, "I had told my close friends about what had happened with Gary—I felt I owed them a chance to decide whether they wanted to be the friend of a murderer's brother—but I hadn't told any of the editors or journalists I worked with. I still thought maybe I could keep enough of this horrible truth buried somewhere, so it would not spill over into the rest of my life and corrupt whatever dreams I might still have."

Gilmore shoulders a burden much larger than mine from people's reactions when society's finger tilted to us as we grieved the deaths of our brothers. It is my belief, too, that the wall of silence around Wayne, his life and death that enclosed my family like see-through wrap, was meant to protect his memory and lessen society's judgment. I learned through this sad journey that what grief means to the griever has little to do with how it is publicly judged.

Compassion – *Odysseus' smile*

After years of absence Odysseus returned to a land plundered and a home invaded. There was reason to angrily strike out in revenge, but during a battle to reclaim their homeland, Telemachos asked his father to show mercy to an enemy. At this moment Odysseus gave his first smile throughout the years of his sojourn. Smiling, Odysseus said, "Cheer up, my son has saved your life. So you shall know, and tell other men, that doing well is far better than doing ill."

If I were an artist, I would paint entwining, slithering morning glories to symbolize compassion. The lovely fragile vine with heart-shaped leaves glide upward and outward in graceful silent invasion. Mother planted it one summer by the back door of the house on N Street. It was only heart leaves for weeks when it suddenly burst. Every morning I went out to see the bright blue funnels greeting the sun, enchanted by how they protectively rewound at the coming of the day's heat. Now, I fantasize that is how compassion shields itself from brutality.

Compassion entwines through life, giving glimpses and opportunity of itself, but only rarely and fleetingly bursts forth. I first noticed compassion the summer of my twelfth year. A girl a year older moved into an apartment across the street with her widowed mother and younger brother. Margaret was born Catholic, but her mother converted to Mormonism and they moved to Salt Lake from California. Margaret was decidedly more worldly and physically developed than me, and she introduced me to a very different group of boys who drove cars and motorcycles. They informed me one afternoon I was too young to join them while they also discussed the size today and possible size tomorrow of my chest. Two suggested I'd be a knockout at sixteen but the others said I just didn't have it in me. Mother discouraged the friendship, but Jody and Margaret's brother were also friends and there was little to be done about their proximity.

During the summer Margaret and I noticed a very old hunched woman ever so slowly making her way up N Street from South Temple. Once a week she made the difficult physical walk up the gentle incline of our street to continue into the cemetery to her husband's grave. Young and innocent of death and how adults believed in it, my understanding of the true need for the somber visits was shallow. One hand held a cane while the other stiffly held potted pansies. A spade's handle poked out of the pocket of the heavy black coat she wore in July. We began greeting her and as thoughtless children aware of strength over a frail old adult, we were questioning nuisances. Her smell of age, waste and dirt surprised me and I asked Margaret if we should give her cans of chicken noodle soup from our cupboards.

The decision was no and the relief of conscience freed me to be more intrusive in my questions about her life, husband and why she visited. It was about the fourth week I noticed Margaret's uneasy looks and urgency to let the woman quietly go. She refused to meet her the next week which baffled me because I thought we were being friendly. I watched the woman's slow progress up the street and walked toward her when she was on my block. About five feet away I suddenly felt a wave of resistance, but I continued closer and started talking. The woman was short answered and stared straight. I looked down at her from my five feet. Then I knew.

My innocence held no virtue. My curiosity no right. Only the woman held rights to her story. I had put her in the same position I felt in school when Mormon children approached me. Theirs was not an offer of real friendship and with this woman, neither was mine. I stepped away from her path.

I have not found relief in compassion, only a quiet recognition that when its frail petals open, I think and observe differently. There is no way back, nor do I want it.

Odysseus was warned by the goddess Circe of the sirens who bewitch passing sailors with melodious song. The notes were so sweet and seducing that they spoke to each man in his deepest heart. Dante is told in *The Purgatorio* by a siren, "[F]ew indeed who taste how well I satisfy would think to stray." Norse mythology has Lorelei, an immortal water nymph who lives on the Rhine River. She, too, sings spellbinding songs that speak so intimately to the listener's heart that they become her willing victims. It is never made clear what the beautiful maidens sing, though it is evident it speaks to the needs, yearnings and deepest beliefs of each passing man.

In the framework of the griever's hero journey, the hero must also turn away from the siren who reminds us of the comforts of grief's justifications, angers and hurts. It is easy to stay seduced by what we want to hear or what we have always heard and believed. Changing an opinion about someone or something can feel like previous reasoning was wrong and we are weak because there is a change of mind. Especially if another person or idea we had condemned or trivialized now looks worthy of mercy. Circe's warning caused Odysseus to have himself bound by strong rope so he could not follow the sirens and he safely avoided their seductions.

A preacher of compassion predated Jesus and Muhammed in Persia. Born around 650 B.C., Zoroaster, is attributed with the homily, "good thoughts, good words, good deeds." Some believe his teacher was the Hebrew prophet, Jeremiah, who counseled him in his years of retreat. Zoroaster later called that time as being in the "sacred waters of compassion."

Compassion can be lonely in a crowd, but it is not lonely in the heart. I looked into the face of a mother of a friend of Jody's holding hate and anger that felt directed at me. It was after her son died of a drug overdose and before Jody died. Jody had spent time at her house with her family during his teen years. They had been a lonely boy's surrogate family and I'm sure they treated him well. I knew it when I walked fearfully to their door and knocked. Jody had been with them for weeks and I wanted him home though I had nothing to offer. He and Mother had fought and Jody retreated to his friend's family where I'm sure he unloaded his heart in ways he never did to us.

When the woman opened her door I asked to talk to Jody. She left me standing outside, where I peeked around the living room of this man, woman and several children. I was grateful they gave him the experience of a whole family and ashamed I wanted him home. Jody came to the door and we walked to the front yard to talk. My only argument for his return, "You belong with us." He came home two days later.

When I saw her after her son's death, I was met with one of the most agonized, hateful looks I have ever experienced. I had no defense and could only walk away. Occasionally she came to mind and I would let thoughts roll about. She came to Jody's funeral. Her face had cleared a bit. For a second's fraction I thought there would be an understanding of pain. When she looked at me I saw depths of a mother's grief through what I also interpreted as satisfaction.

I felt a quizzical blend of beginner's compassion and unfolding self-revelation. I looked at the mother, while my brother lay in his coffin behind me, and felt empathy. I understood, at least in part, and I was saddened for her. I recognized the anger she sent my way and the look of satisfaction. I recognized them because anger and satisfaction were emotions I'd experienced. Her fight with her panorama of emotions was not with me, though she may have thought it was. I was her target that moment, but they didn't hit. I knew her feelings too well and could see through them. Their power was against her.

What her look did do was give me worming space through fragmented ends of thinking, with a chance to imagine. Why would she bother with me, a person with whom she had exchanged only a dozen or so simple sentences? If I were writing Jody's story I could tell a different one than mine. It would have more hurts received than love felt. I could name some of the hurts but I will never know them all. I would tell the story of being the youngest and therefore, the most innocent. As the only male I would be lonelier. I wouldn't know at fourteen when I stayed at a friend's house my mother's full history, disappointments or angers. I wouldn't know my sister's fears, inadequacies or youthful blindness. But I would know I was staying, for now, in the safety of a home that accepted me and kept me safe. When I returned to the mother and sister, the family I was leaving would know I was a good child who faced unfair odds with people who were not managing well.

His stay would leave history's tracks in the family. For them it would be a story of their generosity and love, uncomplicated by the history of his family he couldn't know or tell. For him, they would be a secret source of power and belief he was mistreated and misunderstood. The manchild would return to his blood and become as his blood, not knowing how to save himself, not knowing how to learn and turn away from his sirens of sadness. He would not hear the cries or see the efforts by the mother and sister as they lived in the questions of their lives and held their hands out as far as they were able. Perhaps he would hold out his hand. Perhaps he would not.

Stephen Levine wrote, "It is not just our isolated healing but the healing of everyone who is so confused by uncontrollable impermanence. Let this be our conspiracy of healing—a conspiracy of the shared heart."

Trying to be poetic and positive, I call compassion an entwining invasive vine with heart-shaped leaves and a fragile flower, but what it really feels like is discovering my hand is in the entrails of the dead and I am sickened, bereft, alone and ugly to the universe. Yet, as I leave the dream and lift my hand, I discover a small thing of beauty that needs my care if it is to survive.

Redemption – *Recovering rightful heritage*

Religious and mythical heroes are redeemed, honored and returned to rightful rule after their trials. Abraham watches over the gates of hell, Jesus Christ returns to his rightful place with God. Buddha enters Nirvana in perfect harmony with all things. Hercules ascends to heaven and King Arthur is in Avalon. Odysseus is restored as king. After rebuilding Balder's temple, Frithiof is hailed as king and given his long-awaited bride. The story of a grieving human who mends a life can feel very small and alone if compared to these. Their stories are epics told in traditions so heroic and magnificent that the underlying, simple principles can be overlooked.

Before Jody's death my life story was told haphazardly with

one event following another following another with careless reasoning and interpretation. After his death it was told in nightmare fragments that stood out, unrelieved by forgotten transition scenes giving depth. Slowly, I turned new and more penetrating light behind me. As I pieced together what I had learned, I realized there were bits to be recognized from childhood.

I believe fairy tales often give morsels of knowledge and wisdom toned down to the ability of human beings to understand. In a Russian tale, Vasalisa was given a doll by her dying mother to keep in her pocket and use as intuition. I received three gifts as a child that helped me mend intuition.

The first was from a man who lived in the horseshoe-shaped adobe apartments where we lived in Venice, California. I was playing with my imaginary friend, Henry, when the man asked who I played with. I pointed to behind the evergreen growing by our front door where my shy friend stood. I introduced them and the man began saying hello to both of us when he passed by. On Valentine's Day he gave me a box of Whitman's chocolates to share with Henry.

On a summer morning in Utah when it is a dry oven, I was given the second gift. When I was seven Father picked Jody and me up to visit Grandma Lois for the day. We stopped at a grocery store to buy whipping cream for dessert, and while waiting in line, Jody and I eyed a carousel of cellophane wrapped toys. Stiff as a toothbrush, an eight-inch doll dressed in pink with pink hair and blue eyes stared at me. When he asked if I wanted the doll I hesitated, but said yes. He looked at it, fumbled with the bag, cleared his throat and asked if I wanted the one next to it. I looked at the nondescript, chubby, baby doll with brown hair and shook my head. He bought the pink doll and a miniature car for Jody. That was the last day we saw him for twelve years and the last time we saw Grandma Lois. She died in a car crash in the early morning hours of Mother's Day two years later. Pictures were on the front page of the *Salt Lake Tribune* when I picked it up for Mother early Monday morning. No one had called to tell us.

Donna gave me the third present. Sitting on steps from Grandma Spiking's house to a garage, we were playing with dolls. During changing clothes, combing hair, pretending where they might be going, I noticed Donna's distraction. She was bored and for the first time I knew she was tending instead of playing with me. Her waist was thinning below a growing chest. She wore a wide felt skirt with a poodle appliquéd on it and she sat among so many petticoats they made noise when she moved her legs. That morning I had watched her outline her lips with orange lipstick enhancing the copper-red of her hair.

Donna fingered the hair of her doll, Tony. The dusky red was a deeper color then her own, but she was the only doll we had ever seen with red hair. The doll's pre-pubescent shape was mature enough to pretend she was a woman, but I could see Donna's shape was rounding in soft generous curves that made Tony childlike. When she asked if I wanted Tony that day, she gave a fragment of her childhood to me without restriction on how to care for the doll that most looked like her.

Other than three charming memories, none of these gifts meant anything until years later as I sat on my bed folding socks. Late afternoon light was filtering through the blinds and the house was quiet. Suddenly, Jody's voice moved around me in the diffuse, disembodied sun. "I'm leaving you now, Beckie. You're strong enough." Jody's voice left the now emptier air and I felt an evaporating presence I hadn't been aware of, but now felt lost.

O'Hara felt a relinquishing new peace from such a visit by her murdered son as she sat at a beach. "'Mom, I'm so happy!' I looked at him and cried, 'How can you be happy without us? I miss you so much son.' Then, he said again: 'Mom, I'm so happy.' He stayed with me awhile until I felt at peace."

Reviewing and sorting revealed another memory. With Sam's encouragement when we were dating at the age of nineteen, the two of us decided to visit my father's brother living near Oakland and find out where my father was. I lied to Mother, saying I was going alone to visit Margaret, again living in California. Before leaving, I told Jody why I was going and asked if he wanted me to say anything for him. He answered no, he was not interested and I treated his answer as face value. We found my father married and living in San Francisco where he managed the construction on the public transit system, BART, at a financial district stop. Awkwardly, Sam and I met my father and his gracious southern belle wife, Chamsie.

I scrimped enough to save within pennies the amount for

my first airplane flight to visit my father for five days before Christmas. Again, Jody said nothing. Chamsie and Father came to Utah for three days the next June and I urged Jody to meet him. Everyone shook hands and we were civil. For two years we all kept in phone and mail contact. Then our father somehow vaporized and we did not see or hear from him. Jody and I never talked about it. I've wondered why and I think it was just too painful. Words would have verified what we both believed. We'd been assessed and failed. Eight years later our father called, three years before Jody's death.

In the early morning, the day after Jody's last Christmas, I drove to pick him up and take him to the airport. He was to visit our father, then living in Missouri. When I arrived, I knocked on the door. It was quiet. I knocked again and then knocked louder. At last he came, rousing himself from sleep. In fifteen minutes we were out the door and on our way.

When the phone rang three evenings later I felt dread before answering. I had never heard the emptiness in Jody's voice I heard that night. I took the phone around the corner, into a laundry room, and started talking as fast as I could. "Don't let him bother you. You're fine. You're good. I know. I know. It's too much. But we're okay. Don't let him bother you." I knew what it was. Our father's star quality. His larger, forever larger than ours life, with work that showed him the world, bonuses, real gold jewelry, suede jackets, a new Jaguar car. We were standing too close to our heritage and we were not prepared to meet it. We understood its desires, but, like Semele, not how close we could stand by the fire.

When Jody was alive, our father, Jody and I were attempting to mend bridges and be friends. Jody's death changed my view of childhood from "effort being worked on" to "recorded failure." The gift of belief from the man who gave Henry and me chocolates, the pink doll's foreshadowing, Tony's promise, and my part in bringing our father's, Jody's and my hands together, changed from life experiences to grow from to near irretrievable losses.

Consciously or unconsciously, the hero pays a self-imposed debt of grief. There is a gaping hole in life where maybe the right thing was done and maybe it wasn't, but the griever survived when another didn't. How is the world made even and square again? Or just survivable? We continue to settle our scores and suffer by our standards. Perhaps evening the score is inborn and perhaps it is a habit from childhood when we were required to pay for our indiscretions by time outs, no allowance or endured spankings.

Viktor Frankl chose the very difficult work of encouraging survivors of concentration camps after World War II to return to healthy, productive lives without their scars dominating the future. He was encouraged by Dostoyevsky's words. "There is only one thing that I dread: not to be worthy of my sufferings." In *Man's Search for Meaning*, Frankl writes of captives in the camps who shared food and cared for other prisoners though they suffered as much. He tells of the struggles of survivors to settle ruined lives and hearts and how they worked to redeem their lives to themselves. He believes this effort of self-redemption is the meaning of Dostoyevsky's words. To feel suffering, learn from unbearable experiences and continue living with a greater heart and inner strength.

When we've fully grieved and there is a rebuilding of life, moments of redeeming passage present themselves. The hero knows the depth of the hurt and the sincerity of care and effort life has required since the death. A balance is struck and the deepest insides let the hero know there is no longer, if there ever was, a need to suffer. Now there is time to slowly look around with renewed vision, and experience life in a deeper way. Life has new light showing greater depth, contrast, shadow and luminescence.

When the condominium sold, we found a good house and I began writing. Years later, I can say I am published. I have written books, stories, opinion columns, essays and I will continue to do so though financial rewards are humble and the best years of my career building have passed. I now look at artists sitting alone in airless booths in summer heat at festivals selling their art and writers of original stories never accepted for publication, and I understand. It can simply be the need of the work for oneself, the need to remind ourselves who we are.

If I were writing a crafted story I would write how a little girl was taught about imagination when a man gave her and her imaginary friend chocolates. The pink doll would be explained as a cheerful quirky symbol of the need to continue when a parent's story is away from the girl. She would learn the appearance and disappearance of people in life is to be accepted. Lives intersect, swirl, often barely touching and then separate, all while the music of life plays in compositions beyond understanding. Tony would be conscious awareness of impending sexual possibilities passed through generations of women.

I could make a fictional story tender as a young girl learns about herself. But my part in the story of my brother too slowly meeting his father is a weight with consequences my youth and needy self didn't understand until it was too late.

Memory, belief in imagination, the disappearance of people, and the use of sex and womanhood converged, grappled and finally blended in quietude. All of these things I have struggled with through life and since Jody's death. Only slowly, in life and writing, were they, in various ways, regained and redeemed.

Forgiveness – *Grace for Cupid*

Oz gave the Tin Man a heart, the Scarecrow his brain and the Lion courage, but was unable to help Dorothy. "Dorothy said nothing. Oz had not kept the promise he made her, but he had done his best, so she forgave him," wrote Baum. Dorothy forgave when others would have been angry or despondent. For the rest of their lives grievers will watch others as they enjoy time with parents, spouses, children, or siblings. Happy for her friends, Dorothy finally learned to use what was hers all along. She used the power of the shoes to return to a house damaged by a tornado, yet still the home she wanted.

The people I believed needed forgiving were our parents,

Nameless, Jody and me. From the beginning, I felt thrown off center with Mother. She was the one I immediately wanted with me, the person who best understood Jody and our shared sorrow. When I spent the night the day of his burial, and listened while my life split open, rivers of resentment leaked away and out into the night. That loss of resentment, when all mental barriers were down, lightened something inside that, for all its difficulties, has made grief's journey easier.

A remaining parent, whether through death or divorce, often receives the brunt of a child's anger, hurt, resentment and everyday childhood detritus. The absent parent, however, is seen as relatively innocent and receives yearning and desire, shrouded in mystery. At least that was the gist of my experience that led to a high water mark of resentment and anger against Mother in the teen-age years. Before our father's reappearance, I realized my faulty reasoning and consciously worked at not judging either of them, but not judging is not the same as forgiving. I had decided Nameless was ancient history that didn't need attention, but Jody's death revived what I had tried to forget.

Then, not surprisingly, I heard the small aggravating voice pipe up that is so dismissive and sure of itself. "Rebecca, what does forgiveness mean?" Playing with self-pity as much as forgiveness, I thought about that for a year or so.

I knew polite society promoted forgiveness. Confused about what that meant, I tossed ideas around. Was there a difference between a real hurt and a perceived hurt? Was I sure there was a "wrong" to be forgiven? Specifically, what needed forgiving? Can there be forgiveness when someone doesn't want it or isn't present to receive it? Does forgiving imply a duty to go on as though nothing happened or to believe that all is happening precisely as planned? Or something else? Is forgiving spineless compromising or weariness? What does never forgiving do? What good is it to the forgiver and forgivee? I wanted to know what I was getting into. I sporadically apologized in rambling self-centered speeches without audience or understanding.

An imaginary ghost audience listened to all my questions and lifted dismissive wrists to turn me away. They were bored with my repetitive effort to out-think them in my defense. That what-does-forgiveness-mean sentence scraped like sandpaper against my ear. Ambivalence to forgive was wearying. Finally, I understood the absurdity in the Spanish proverb I long ago clipped from a forgotten magazine, "If I die, I forgive you; if I live, we'll see."

I wanted conversational flow of feeling, reasoning and looking in a face to work a deal. I wanted interaction with an engaged partner as I'd learned was the give and take of marriage. I wanted to hear "what you did" and "what I did" to erase guilt and answer questions. I wanted commitment to well-being and recognition of agony. I wanted my brother to "feel my pain." Maybe I thought I could give my pain to him like I had my childhood marble collection.

Forgiving my parents was a slow loss of steam. I hurled out angry thoughts about their divorce, but over time I got bored. I knew why they divorced. I knew their personalities. I knew Father left us. I knew Nameless was Mother's regret. I knew Chamsie was a good wife and woman for my father. I knew our parents did what they thought was right at the time and neither of them meant to be cruel to their children. In time, neither of them seemed fair targets. They began to feel oddly innocent, as bumbling, foible-ridden accessories, and I saw them as I wanted to see myself and Jody, people who made mistakes and were redeemable.

"All right," I answered the voice. "What does forgiveness mean?" A time followed when I would switch radio stations and hear a discussion on forgiveness or look at a newspaper and be staring at an article on people across the world holding candlelight vigils of forgiveness and love. Viktor Frankl's book of WWII survivors poked its spine four inches above other sale books so I bought it. There was a dream of an exquisitely beautiful woman in a green dress. I was walking with a man who was leading me along a path while telling me things I needed to know. When he saw my interest in the woman he smiled and said, "She is you to learn from." Dozens of small events shook me to consider and reconsider.

Over time, pain led to thought, led to consideration, led to annoying self-assessment, led to unexpected understanding, led to awareness, led to forgiveness, led to peace. As with other issues, my first genuine step was to surrender. To quit trying to lay out rules. I accepted there would never be a climactic tying of loose ends or end-of-thriller story conclusion.

Observing details helped. In a class Mother and I took, I sat at an angle from her. I watched her in a moment she was forcing concentration, trying to learn. That mother's face had led my childhood, been my barometer, always signaling what to do, how to act, when it was time for peace, fun or watchful silence. Now she was willing herself to understand. She looked awed and determined to comprehend the words and dissect meaning. The face I so often held responsible reflected the endless search of all who seek.

She scrimped dollar by dollar to always feed us well, sent us to camp when it meant sacrifices for her, yet never realized a father was missed, or how she was being fought for. One eye was open, another closed, as she groped her way through tiring, single parenthood. She didn't have it easy.

My parents shared an expression. During my father's last visit to Salt Lake, two months before his death, he was intently watching television with absorbed delight on his face. It was the same look Mother had when I took her to the airport to leave for a month. Jumping from the car, rushing to the trunk for the luggage, there wasn't always time for both a hug and a kiss before she turned to disappear inside the terminal three hours early. She had the look leaving Salt Lake for foreign countries, he had it rediscovering U.S. life after living in Borneo's jungle. The jigsaw puzzle was too much for me. My response to realizing their similar expressions was surprisingly protective and maternal, allowing another leaking away of resentment.

When Chamsie called to say my father was not doing well

after his operation for blocked arteries, I flew the red-eye to Birmingham, Alabama. Her mother insisted I have time alone with him. He had a small space with machines that semi-circled a nurse station and was closed off by hanging sheets. We stuttered, not knowing what to say. By now we both knew we spoke most eloquently in intonation, body movement and presence, not English. As I sat by his head it was the first time I'd had the freedom to study his hairline and forehead so closely since I was five. I first noticed it in Twentynine Palms when Mother was heavy with Jody's birth. I studied its angles on a Saturday morning while he peacefully slept, a jutting shoreline with waves of worry, tension and laughter going to shore. There was no appreciation for a sleeping parent and I grabbed both eyelids, opening them suddenly and cruelly. In the hospital, I sat by his head and watched the now deeper waves carrying the heaviness of life gone by to the large forehead's white hairline.

"I'll never understand Jody," he said as we heard the humming machines. I looked in his eyes, listening. "I thought I was doing the best thing for both of you." I answered slowly, "I know." "I thought Gloria would get married and you would have another father and you wouldn't need me." I patted his arm, unsure what to say. I also had wanted that, and knew it was another reason I felt such bitterness for Nameless.

There was a time I would have happily recited a list of feelings and opinions to my father; when life was the result of his actions, before I became entangled in choices. I bent and kissed that loved forehead for the first and last time.

Don Juan looked with "kind, clear and penetrating" eyes at Castaneda and said he didn't have any personal history. "One day I found out that personal history was no longer necessary for me and, like drinking, I dropped it." I have a life's history, but when its interpretation didn't support how I wanted to think of myself, I revised it as Don Juan added, "little by little."

If traumatic history is not put into perspective, but instead defines us, it can swallow a lifetime. A patient told Levine, "My fiancé was killed in a plane crash, and I closed down to love. I said I'd never marry. And I never did. It took twenty years for me to forgive him for abandoning me."

I remembered what I really, to the gut of me, believe about God. God took Jody in at the moment of death and forgave him, perhaps while shaking His head at the silliness of children. He may have arrived damaged, weak and in need of solace and nursing, but his pain and loneliness were over. That was the most promising view of God I could imagine and feel comfortable believing.

Zeus forgave his son, the eternal trickster Cupid, when Cupid asked permission to marry the mortal Psyche. "Art thou to ask indulgence at my hands! [I] myself have been turned into a bull, a swan, or what not, through thy frolicsome roguery. But we cherish thee kindly as the spoilt child of Olympus, for all thy faults; and if I grant thy prayer, be mindful of the grace thou has ill deserved."

I was quicker to forgive my parents than Jody and me.

Perhaps I expected our life choices to be more responsible. Plus his intention of death laid bare the inadequacies of Mother's and my love. When he died, he handed the gauntlet of picking up life's broken pieces to us. If he is resting in peace that is good, but what I wish for him is what I told myself to do--rest in learning and loving. With that, I forgave both of us.

I don't have any special knowledge or information on religious or spiritual insights of forgiveness. But I do believe lives are shaped as much by what is done to us as by how we interpret it and act upon it. I make choices of reacting to people and their acts every day. Those choices create my life and what I think about it.

So I take full responsibility for singing *The Wicked Witch is Dead* to Donna the morning I saw the obituary for Nameless in the paper. Mother was out of the country and Sam and Zac didn't appreciate the dark humor I felt without remorse or bitterness. I was disappointed when Donna was horrified, but the billowing breeze of honesty I had never fully expressed was so freeing, I surprised myself by truly letting him go and wishing him a forgiven happy ever after wherever ever after is. Smiling with savored pleasure, I collected remaining photos I had of him and generously mailed them to his daughter with a reasonably kind and polite note, no less.

Eventually, I answered the question, "Rebecca, what does forgiveness mean?" For me, it is realizing everyone's humanness, including mine. When I can consider another with wry, affectionate, tranquil or rousing jousting humor, I know I've forgiven. I believe the deepest benefit of forgiveness is to the forgiver, though it seldom gives answers. What it gave me is more peace within myself. Painful as his family history is, Gilmore in the end wrote, "Our lives go on. We have to imbibe the pain, face the memories and forgive what we can. All in all, not the worst truth to learn."

Joy – *Mwindo's sorrow*

When traumatic death reaches down and rips a person's emotions out of her chest and stomach, swings them around on a stick and throws her alone on the floor to ponder what it all means, a surrounding feeling is sometimes joy.

The Prophet is a very slim book by Kahlil Gibran, who was born in Lebanon in 1883. A copy of it was given to me by a friend when his wife died and he cleaned out her books. Gibran was poetically straightforward and lovely. His chapter on *Joy and Sorrow* is sixteen lines long. Three of the lines are:

Some of you say, "Joy is greater than sorrow," and others say, "Nay sorrow is the greater."

But I say unto you, they are inseparable.

Together they come, and when one sits alone with you at your board, remember that the other is asleep upon your bed.

On the morning of her children's deaths by car accident, Isadora Duncan recalled "[T]he sight of my children, so rosy and lovely and happy, I had such a great emotion of joy that I suddenly jumped out of bed and began to dance with them, all three of us bubbling with laughter."

On the morning of Jody's death, there were two reasons I didn't ask him to lunch. Besides a desire to spend time writing, I was scheduled to pick up my mother-in-law for a mid-afternoon doctor appointment and I didn't think I should spend more time away from the office.

When we returned to her house Sam's brother, Steve, made small talk as Lupe disappeared into the bedroom. I admired his natural ease with his mother as she weakened. He talked to her warmly and normally, easing her pain far more than my stifled tears.

I left them and began driving to a last business stop. Loose thoughts of dead people spontaneously passed through my mind. I was untouched by my grandfather's death when I was four. Grandma Lois was a kind person I remembered affectionately. The Christmas before she died I bought a tin printed with roses that held sachet I never was able to give her. When I was in high school, I opened the holiday wrapping it still had and sniffed, but there was no longer a scent. Whatever happened to Uncle Wayne, who played with me at Grandma Spiking's? Yes, he was dead but what became of the person, the essence, the soul of the young, beautiful man who resembled James Dean? Near enough to feel the wind of death's shrapnel, Sam's Uncle Ralph had died of cancer within six months of our marriage.

I thought of Peter, a man I worked for at age twenty, who mentored me by his presence and a few words. The kindness in his eyes belied his crisp white shirts, cufflinks and expensive suits. He appeared a healthy, virile, handsome successful lawyer in his thirties who was a husband and devoted new father. It seemed an unknowable cosmic trick that he withered from cancer. Finally, though still alive, there was Lupe. Periodically she was given a reprieve with enough strength to enjoy life, but we knew it was temporary. The cancer was spreading, pinching life away bit by bit.

I suddenly felt unreasonably happy. Husband, son, family, work, business, everything. There was a surprising moment of pure and total elation that was a rumbling, uncontrollable gushing from my insides feeling like waves of gratitude I wasn't inclined toward. Spontaneous and specific, I knew I was thankful for the life I was living.

Traffic was whizzing by as I drove, but for seconds it seemed almost without my power as I felt floating presences. Several seemed familiar as in a dream just wakened from, others were not. A strong male voice whispered, "Remember this happiness." Within the hour I knew of Jody's death.

Parrado's transcending moment was eleven days after the crash when he heard on the small radio the search for them was called off. Cold, hungry and miserable, "suddenly out of nowhere, I was jolted by a surge of joy so deep and sublime that it nearly lifted me bodily from the floor." He remembers the sure feeling he would survive. "Notice this! Notice this! There is joy still," the universe can yell at us in the darkest moments.

The next time I felt joy was a week later. The funeral was over, my father on his way back to Indonesia, and Mother was floating down Idaho's Snake River. I was making dinner and reached for an avocado on the kitchen counter and held a knife to it for slicing. The feel of warm, roughened skin over nourishing, soft fruit, the sharpness of the blade ready to make sure cuts to the seed, the hunger of my body that did not feel hunger but hadn't eaten very much in a week, were noticed in a long moment. Nature gives. No matter our intent, desire, awareness, worthiness. Nature gives. I felt a very small sliver of understanding and as I did, I was grateful and an uncontrollable joy moved through me.

It seems to be the nature of life that clear sharp emotions can change us forever. It also seems natural that the feeling softens and mutes until the power must be consciously remembered or it can be forgotten. Romantic love, deep sorrow, the births of loved children, reaching long sought career and sports goals. Each one brings a cluster of heightened emotion that can sear to the bone, and turn to ash.

Native American shaman Aua told of his initiation. "I would sometimes start weeping, without knowing why. Then suddenly, for no good reason, I would be filled with a great inexplicable delight...." Closeness of sorrow and joy feel odd and uncomfortable, as if where one exists, the other can not. Joy feels as a self-serving unfaithfulness while grieving a loved one. How can joy intrude on the purity of sincere sorrow? How can sorrow be real if there is joy?

When the African hero Mwindo was born, his father sent men to kill him since he wanted only daughters. As they attempted to bury him, they saw he was protected by heavenly spirits and good fortune. Knowing his father's murderous motives, he immediately transformed into a second birth, "Most wondrously, Mwindo was born laughing and also speaking already a man among men."

Sorrow and joy do meet in grief. They show life's duality that can confuse and disorient. We separate them, believing they define totally different circumstances that should not intrude on one another. This is why joy is seldom mentioned in the beginning of grief books. When it is discussed, it is stuck here, in the back under conclusions, as a shameful detail of catastrophe.

In *Women Who Run With the Wolves*, Estés states the Grimm Brothers name the male child born to the maiden in *The Armless Maiden* Sorrowful because he comes from loss. In the Goddess traditions of the tale, the child is a spiritual gift of what she has learned from loss while visiting the underworld and is named Joy.

Lost as Sophie was in her sorrows and her need to annihilate herself with her lover, Nathan, she instinctively placed joy around her. Navy surplus pink paint covered her apartment walls. "[S]plashing the room with complementary hues of orange and green and red—a bright carnation bookcase here, an apricot bedspread there.... I wanted to burst out laughing at the way she imbued that dumb Navy camouflage paint with such joy and warmth. And there were flowers.... daffodils, tulips, gladioli...."

The joy I felt cutting into the avocado was complete, leaving me torn I felt it in such grief. Only later did I piece joy and sorrow together and come to believe the flashes of joy and awareness on the day of Jody's death, and as I cut the avocado, were encouragement to live well again.

There isn't a conclusion about joy I took from grief. Joy is a force of being. Now I realize its close association with sorrow, and though they don't always travel together, they know each other like old enduring lovers.

Closure – *Gilgamesh finds an end*

Fairy tales end with a lesson or reuniting. Dorothy learns the pleasure of helping others, the power of asking for what she wants, and the strength of knowing she has always had the power to return home. Vasalisa learns the strength of intuition and is willing to share the light with her sisters. The Armless Maiden is united with the masculine in life. All had loss, abuse, fear or deep loneliness, but they worked their way through them and learned to live well.

Clinicians define closure differently. Gordon Livingston's grief over two sons was a sorrowful hero's journey but in the end he returned with more wisdom to his profession of helping others. Yet, he says, "I learned an abiding hatred for the word 'closure,' with its comforting implications that grief is a time-limited process from which we all recover." Kübler Ross and Kessler write, "No matter how you work at feeling your feelings fully, you never really find the closure that you hear about or see in movies. But you do find a place for loss, a way to hold it and live with it."

Philosopher Alan W. Watts words an approach and applies a cure in *The Wisdom of Insecurity*. "The pain is no longer problematic. I feel it, but there is no urge to get rid of it, for I have discovered that pain and the effort to be separate from it are the same thing. Wanting to get out of pain is the pain; it is not the 'reaction' of an 'I' distinct from pain. When you discover this, the desire to escape 'merges' into the pain itself and vanishes."

Most people listen, respond to the words they understand and absorb what they can for a personally defined closure. Gilgamesh felt weariness. "He stopped, realizing he had not come this far to hear himself recall the failure of his grief to save, but to find an end to his despair." In a passionate good-bye to Dido, Aeneas tells her he was visited by a god in a dream and told to stop distancing himself from his life by grieving and start leading his men to Italy. "No longer set yourself and me afire. Stop your quarrel. It is not my own free will that leads to Italy."

Human beings struggle with how to live with grief and loss. Nan Watkins wrote, "After Peter was gone, I realized I had been privileged to see the full arc of his life, from birth to death. Normally a mother does not see the end of her child's life. The child's arc is left open, unfinished, a question, when she dies.... Yet I had glimpsed the full arc of my son's life and felt comfort in that. Burying his ashes was a ritual not unlike the evening rite of tucking him in bed as a child, only this time, it was for eternity."

Very often when traumatic death occurs the media wants statements from relatives and friends. Unthinking and unknowing, the media too often suggest the finding of a body or the capture of a criminal will bring closure. In the beginning, the closure new mourners want is to walk into the untouched bedroom of the beloved and see them peacefully sleeping instead of on a morgue table. They want closure of the god-awful time they are trapped in. Two forces cannot occupy the same space, and in the life of the new mourner trauma's explosion is in full detonation. There is no closure on something expanding right before the eyes.

Anyone expecting closure in the beginning will not find it. What they will experience are events that mark time but do not give relief. The first event was when I fell asleep on the first night with a sleeping pill and a glass of wine. A coffin closed forty-eight hours after his death. There were events of cleaning out his clothes, unmaking his bed, cleaning his car and closing finances. There were his first unattended Thanksgiving, Christmas, my birthday, his birthday, Mother's Day and mother's birthday in that slowly endured order. At last, the first anniversary of his death and burial offered its weak "closure."

There is deep and sorrowful need to see a body. The day between the death and funeral Donna told me it was important to see Jody's body so I would know in my innermost self he was dead. Otherwise, she said, I might see his face superimposed upon strangers and believe he was still alive. I did see his body and I touched him while I was alone with him in the room thirty minutes before the funeral. It was not closure, though my aunt was right. It was a ripping open that defined the surreal as real, though it did not prevent me from seeing his face upon men of similar age, coloring and build.

The hero's ultimate task is to attain a reasonable peace with pain. For me, there is peace and gratitude Joseph Jarman Phillips II was my brother, regardless of the end. I love him still and I want to keep the dearness of his memory. Closure stalls, memory remains.

What I experienced with my mother-in-law, grandma and father seems a gentler way for survivors. Death may not be any easier, but there is less room for misunderstanding and a better opportunity for peaceful acceptance.

Writing helped grief's spiral lift ever further up and away. First, I wrote painful disjointed haphazard notes that often were not kept. Later I wrote a long rambling book-length letter that gave fresh air to wounds. Eventually, this work surfaced. A friend who is a nurse and therapist, had both parents die before she was twenty-four and an older brother not many years later. She told me it was expected that with each writing recovery would move forward in a natural progression that others satisfy in different ways.

While I was writing this book, another friend suggested it was probably a good cathartic exercise. I answered, perhaps. I believed I was settled enough that Jody's death was only one more subject in a list including marriage, motherhood, career, traveling, inner self, and friends. Though, of course, thoughts lurk or I never would have thought of this at all.

I knew I had learned much on the subject of Jody's death that might be useful to others, but I was hesitant to write because I knew how much work and thought it would take. I knew what I learned was not unique, nor was what I suffered. I was near putting it aside when I experienced the moment of realizing grief's parallel story with the walk of the traditional literary hero. There was a surprising simultaneous feeling of inner grace for myself that could be a lift in the spiral. I felt peace without writing these pages, but it was an inspiration to begin.

I wanted to show the similarities to the hero's journey everyone experiences through grief. I wanted to put a name to what Mother, Sam and Zac went through with me as they experienced their hero's journey. And I wanted to thank them for passing through it with me.

So, perhaps I am finishing my story of having returned from the hero's journey, and as the scholars say, mending my two worlds while clearing the path for others to use. If I have made some small part of grief easier to bear, I will be pleased.

Closure is gaining peace by merging grief's explosion with time and acceptance. It is a screen door where monsters no longer gather, but memories are free to come and go.

The Hero's End of the Journey

During childhood walks in the cemetery, Jody and I saw evidence that babies who lived only a few days were still missed twenty years later. Drooping peonies, roses and chrysanthemums hung over the deeply etched words, *Till we meet again*. Surnames etched over the names of husbands and wives on four foot high black granite faced the rising sun over the Wasatch Mountains. A name and birth date of someone still living was alongside the deceased's with space for a death date. I wondered about the devotion survivors practiced years after deaths. Perhaps it cultivates a friendship with the ultimate end all humans face.

Survivors of traumatic death often lose knee-jerk fear of it. Perhaps never a friend, death is an acknowledged fact of life and we have been close enough to feel its serene indifference. Most people believe in a happy reunion following death with religious beings or family and friends. An imagined cheery reunion has comforts. Picturing the beloved in a happier, better place allows mourners peace. This peace can be for the deceased, but it is also comforting to believe whatever angers, hurts, disappointments or failures were in the relationship, the ultimate story ending is a good one.

The circle is a common symbol of life. Christianity, expressed in Jesus's life, is based on completing a circle with resurrection heralding life after death. In the Book of Mark, 16:1-20 Jesus is gone from the sepulcher and shows himself to Mary Magdalene. "After that he appeared in another form unto two of them...."

Buddha taught that all life circles in reincarnation and transcends through a soul force. Goddess Kali is the motherly nurturing symbol of the relentless circle of life in the karmic beliefs of Hinduism. Even in the glitz of Hollywood it is respected with the theme song to *The Lion King* in *The Circle of Life*.

Myth explains life in circular movement and resurrection. The winter solstice celebration with a yule log and feast was held in honor of the Norse god, Frey, who ruled sunshine, fruitfulness, and summer's prosperity. On the solstice, Frey's sun spirit was set free to fight the frost giants that brought Mother Night. Persephone's travels marked the Greek circle of seasons. Reverence for cycling nature and rebirth corresponds with earliest beliefs.

Nightly, Odin took his fallen warriors to Valhalla to drink and eat to satiety from an ever self-renewing boar. The warriors woke every morning to new life, died daily in their battles and at night were whisked away by Odin. When I first read this it seemed another primitive bloody tale of yore. It can be understood that way, but underneath there is also hope, optimism and understanding of what the human spirit so often needs. There is metaphorical bloodshed of the spirit as people live through life's challenges at every level. Yet, humans strive for renewal to return again and fight the good fight, live the good life.

What stage of grief the griever is experiencing may make a difference in how the personal circle of life is imagined. My opinions changed through time. In the beginning, when shock and passionate grief were tremendous, I imagined a tearful emotional scene with Jody of two tormented, regretful souls who now realized how little they understood on earth. There would be sincere hugging, flowing tears and declarations of new awareness with abounding love. It was a dramatic scene requiring sniffles and handkerchiefs.

The scene was revised when shock subsided and routines regained. I'd had time to think about responsibilities, regrets and the purpose of human life. I was angrier, sadder for specific reasons, confused and frustrated by an inner life that was turned upside down. I was angry and sad Jody lost out on life's opportunities. Equally, I was angry and sad Mother and I were left with a heavy emotional shackle that was not easily dissolving. My disappointment gushed out to his surprise and hurt. His anger and loneliness flowed out of him as though he were made of it until I suffocated. I could not make a reunion comforting in the overwhelming emotion.

Eventually, an imagined reunion was peaceful, accepting

and loving. Jody and I nodded our heads in new awareness and quietly forgave each other. There was gentle laughter as our eyes met with clear guileless love in a deeper communion and transformation for both of us.

Mother and Grandma Spiking's beliefs were, of course, sprinkled on me and I came to believe we are all part of an evolving story we likely don't understand. Should they be correct that grief and unresolved issues of the living tie the dead to us in unhealthy emotional strangleholds, I have released Jody. I am peaceful enough that I will not hold him to me at the expense of his or my growth. He is free to be without entanglement in my life and death, and well on his way to being established in whatever the universe holds for him.

Grief's hero journey takes the griever through many turns and circles of thought until, at last, in awareness of an apotheosis and a claiming of the boon there is a deeper, abiding belief and peace. The hero's journey of grief is complete, though it may never be finished. There is now full acknowledgment of inner growth. At the end of the journey through the path of the lower branches, no one claps or gives the newly arrived griever, who is now a hero, a silver loving cup to take home. But, the griever is transformed, as any hero is, into a more fully developed and realized person.

Still, there is a last request. Utnapishtim and his wife, the Scorpion couple guarding the gate of Gilgamesh's underworld, had lived through grief and listened to every story passing before them. When Gilgamesh asked to visit his dead father,

Utnaphishtim hesitated. "His wife whispered to him saying: He has come far. Have you forgotten how grief fastened onto you and made you crave some word, some gesture, once?" Understanding and comforting others in a journey that is theirs alone, can be as small as a word or as large as years of listening. Though a griever's journey may be completed, it is a kindness to express comforting words and gestures to others.

The newly recognized hero who makes it to the end of an aware journey remembers Odysseus' dead mother's words, "Make haste back to the light; but do not forget all this...." Merlin gave the scrolls containing the story of King Arthur's life to an abbot at a monastery, saying, "Keep it safe for those who are not yet born, or they will deck him in their own dreams, their minds will mirror a false image; they will not see his reign as it was: a fine and shining enterprise, a reaching out to God." The hero's journey always involves learning that deepens the hero's heart, understanding and knowledge.

Traveling Between Two Worlds – *Learn until our brains all rot*

Religious and mythical heroes travel with ease between earthly life and the mysteries of universal truth without compromise to either. "[N]ot contaminating the principles of the one with those of the other ... is the talent of the master," wrote Campbell in his conclusions of the journey.

Yahweh of Judaism, Christ of Christianity, Allah of Islam, Vishnu of Hinduism, walk in many realities and dimensions without losing orientation and direction. In countless disciplines and pantheons this ability is usually attributed, as Leeming writes, to a "permanent status in recognition of his inherent divinity—his real self."

Heroes have weathered the dangers, loneliness, questions, sorrows and angers through the hero's journey, and now a stronger self is felt. Elie Wiesel became very clear his career would be writing about the Holocaust. When interviewed he said, "That is who I am; take me or don't take me, but that is who I am." Carol Pearson writes, "We feel the size of our souls." An internal equilibrium has enlarged with mental and emotional growth and returned with a peace that means a well-recovered hero no longer needs assurance in the same way.

Yahweh, Christ, Allah, Vishnu, Mwindo, Buddha and Odin returned from their journeys with a deeper understanding and were willing to share their knowledge, but all any of them could do was point the way and be of service. It remains with human beings to respond. Merlin was a magician who traveled between two worlds as he raised Arthur to be king. Sadly, he realized he was only playing his appointed part and was unable to protect Arthur from his choices. Grievers who feel the weight of responsibility should remember gods and magicians only help, they do not decide. That power was with the person we love and now it is with us.

Many beliefs describe humans as students searching for lost parts of ourselves to make us more whole and able to continue. With humor and goodwill, it is implied in Harry Potter's school

Blossoms of the Lower Branches

song at Hogwarts. "Bring back what we've forgot, Just do your best, we'll do the rest, And learn until our brains all rot."

After the first year of school Harry Potter returns to the Dudleys. "Uncle Vernon, still purple-faced, still mustached, still looking furious at the nerve of Harry, carrying an owl in a cage in a station full of ordinary people." The returned grief hero does not carry an owl, but like Harry he has learned a few tricks, and stepped into a new skin of the self, though surrounded by a world of innocence.

With deeper understanding of the blossoms of the lower branches the hero re-considers the rewards of the higher branches and how they fit into life. The worldly possessions of things, money, and social status have a value and place the hero now walking in two worlds can better steer to his real needs.

The hero no longer needs empathy from others to deal with grief's lifelong shadow. It is sweet should it come along, but there is understanding so deep that it doesn't need verification. There is no longer a comparison of the hero's life to others. If a spouse died, there is happiness for others who have theirs, if a child has passed, there is happiness for those who have never lost theirs, and if a sibling died, there is pleasure others enjoy theirs. Yet, experience lives in the aching tenor of voice between Mother and me when I call on Jody's birthday. We talk easily about the loveliness of the April day, and we do not suffer or talk about Jody. But when I say good-bye and "I love you," she has answered, "and love to Jody, too."

When we were children she would tell long tales over dinner that she was a banished princess daughter of The Netherlands' Queen Juliana. Enraged because her daughter married a commoner, Mother's sympathizers whisked her away for her own safety. But she understood court intrigue and knew her true consort was searching for her, and would soon rescue all of us. We only had to wait. I would have believed her if Donna and Grandma Spiking had not existed. A mother's words echo deeply when spoken in the tones that rocked us to sleep in her arms. When I was in high school I asked her about Wayne, saying his death was an awful story. She stopped what she was doing, turned to look directly at me and said, "Rebecca, the love always survives."

Virgil relied on reason to lead Dante through purgatory. To finish the journey, Virgil relinquished Dante's care to Beatrice who stood for love. Traversing between reason and love and knowing where each is needed is traveling between two worlds. Every hero will reach the end of his grief story with a different ending. Traveling between two worlds is looking backward on life's history and forward to the future with acceptance of each one's griefs and joys. Then, it is continuing with reason and love along the untamed and still winding path through life.

Blossoms of the Lower Branches

Suggested Reading and References

Abbey, Edward, *Desert Solitaire*, Simon & Schuster, New York, 1990.

Abrahams, Roger D., *African Folktales*, Pantheon Books, New York, 1983.

Afanas'ev, Aleksandr, translated by Norbert Guterman, *Russian Fairy Tales*, Pantheon Books, New York, 1973.

Alighieri, Dante, translated by John Ciardi, *The Purgatorio*, New American Library, New York, 1961.

Andersen, Hans Christian, translated by Tiina Nunnally, *Hans Christian Andersen Fairy Tales*, Penguin Books, New York, 2004.

Ariès, Philippe, *The Hour of Death*, Barnes and Noble, USA, 2000.

Armstrong, Karen, *Muhammad, A Biography of a Prophet*, Harper Collins, New York 1992.

Arnold, Sir Edwin, translator, *Bhagavadgita*, Dover Publications, New York, 1993.

Arnott, Kathleen, retold by, *African Myths and Legends*, Oxford University Press, Oxford, 1993.

Baldwin, James, *notes of a native son*, Beacon Press, Boston, 1957.

Baum, L. Frank, *The Wonderful Wizard of Oz*, Harper Collins, New York, 1900.

Becker, Ernest, *The Denial of Death*, The Free Press, New York, 1973.

Berry, Wendell, *Hannah Coulter*, Counterpoint, Berkeley, 2004.

Bierhorst, John, *History and Mythology of the Aztecs, The Codex Chimalpopoca*, translated from the Nahuatl, University of Arizona Press, Tucson, 1992.

Blum, Ralph H., *The Book of Runes*, St. Martin's Press, New York, 1993.p

Bowden, Down by the River, *Drugs, Money, Murder and Family*, Simon and Schuster, New York, 2004.

Brooks, Polly Schoyer, *Beyond the Myth, The Story of Joan of Arc*, Harper Collins, New York, 1990.

Caldwell, Sarah, Kali, *The Slayer of Illusion*, Mandala Publishing, California, 2003.

Camus, Albert, *The Stranger*, Alfred A. Knopf, New York, 1988.

Campbell, Joseph, *The Hero with a Thousand Faces*, MJF Books, New York, 1949.

Suggested Reading and References

Campbell, Joseph, *Myths to Live By*, Penguin Books, New York, 1993.

Carlisle, Nate, *Hoping for resolution*, The Salt Lake Tribune, July 11, 2008.

Castaneda, Carlos, *The Art of Dreaming*, Harper Paperbacks, New York, 1994.

Castaneda, Carlos, *Journey to Ixtlan*, Simon & Schuster, New York, 1972.

Coomaraswamy Ananda K. and Nevedita, Sister, *Myths of Hindus and Buddhists*, Dover Books, New York, 1967.

Didion, Joan, *The Year of Magical Thinking*, Alfred A. Knopf, New York, 2005.

Doka, Kenneth J., Editor, *Living with Grief After Sudden Loss*, Taylor & Francis, Pennsylvania, 1996.

Duncan, Isadora, *My Life*, Liveright, New York, 1955.

Estés, Clarissa Pinkola, Ph.D., editor *Tales of the Brothers Grimm*, Quality Paperback Book, New York, 1999.

Estés, Clarissa Pinkola, Ph.D., *Women Who Run With the Wolves*, Ballantine Books, New York, 1992.

Feinberg, Linda, *I'm Grieving as Fast as I Can, How Young Widows and Widowers Can Cope and Heal*, New Horizon Press, New Jersey, 1994.

Frankl, Viktor E., *Man's Search for Meaning*, Beacon Press, Boston, 1992.

Gilmore, Mikal, *Shot in the Heart*, Doubleday, New York, 1994.

Glubb, Sir John, *The Life and Times of Muhammad*, Cooper Square Press, New York, 1998.

Guerber, H.A., *Myths of the Norsemen, From the Eddas and Sagas*, Dover Publications, New York, 1992.

Haar, J.T., *King Arthur*, Crane Russack, New York, 1973.

Hamilton, Edith, *Mythology*, Little, Brown and Company, New York, 1999.

Harper, Marvin Henry, *Gurus, Swamis, Avataras*, The Westminster Press, Philadelphia, 1972.

Harrison, Kathryn, *While They Slept, An Inquiry Into the Murder of a Family*, Random House, New York, 2008.

Hart, Joseph, *Trauma? Get Over It*, Utne Magazine, Kansas, July-August 2006.

Suggested Reading and References

Hijuelos, Oscar, *Lunch at the Biltmore*, The New Yorker, New York, January 17, 2005.

Hinds, Jess Decourcy, *'I'm Sorry' Shouldn't be the Hardest Words*, Newsweek, May 28, 2007.

Holmes, Ernest, *Science of Mind*, Dodd, Mead and Company, New York, 1938.

Homer, *The Odyssey*, translated by H.W.D. Rouse, A Signet Classic, New York, 1999.

Jones, David M., *Mythology of the Aztecs and Maya*, Southwater, London, 2003.

Jung, Carl G., Editor, *Man and His Symbols*, A Laurel Book, New York, 1968.

Kübler-Ross, Elisabeth and David Kessler, *On Grief and Grieving*, Scribner, New York, 2005.

Kushner, Harold S., *When Bad Things Happen to Good People*, Avon Books, New York, 1989.

LaPlante, Matthew D., *Soldier was torn between duties to family, country*, Salt Lake Tribune, Utah, July 21, 2005.

Leeming, David Adams, Mythology, *The Voyage of the Hero*, Oxford University Press, New York., 1998.

Lehrman, Sally, *The Nature of Nurture*, Utne, Ogden Publications, Topeka KS, July-August 2008.

Levine, Stephen, *Unattended Sorrow, Recovering from Loss and Reviving the Heart*, Rodale, USA, 2005.

Lewis, C.S., *A Grief Observed*, Bantam Books, New York, 1976.

Livingston, M.D., Gordon, *Too Soon Old, Too Late Smart*, Marlowe and Company, New York, 2004.

Mandelbaum, Allen, *The Aeneid of Virgil*, A verse translation, Bantam, New York, 1971.

Malory, Sir Thomas, translation by Robert Graves, translation of Sir Thomas Malory, *LeMorte d'Arthur*, Bramhall House, New York.

Mason, Herbert, *A Verse Narrative Gilgamesh*, First Mariner, New York, 2003.

Meyers, Jeffrey, *Robert Frost*, Houghton Mifflin, Boston, 1996.

Moffat, Mary Jane, Editor, *In the Midst of Winter*, Vintage, New York, 1992.

Moss, Robert, *Conscious Dreaming, A Spiritual Path for Everyday*

Suggested Reading and References

Life, Three Rivers Press, New York, 1996.

Nadle, June Knights, *Mortician Diaries*, Inner Ocean Publishing, Maui, 2006.

Neeld, Ph.D., Elizabeth Harper, *Seven Choices, Finding Daylight After Loss Shatters Your World*, Warner Books, New York, 2003.

O'Hara, Kathleen, M.A., *A Grief Like No Other, Surviving the Violent Death of Someone You Love*, Marlowe & Company, New York, 2006.

Ovid, *Metamorphoses*, translated by Mary Innes, Penguin Books, New York, 1955.

Parrado, Nando with Vince Rause, *Miracle in the Andes*, Crown Publishers, New York, 2006.

Pearson, Carol S., *The Hero Within*, Harper & Row, San Francisco, 1986.

Prenshaw, Peggy Whitman, Editor, *Elie Wiesel: Conversations*, University Press of Mississippi, Jackson, 2002.

Puhvel, Jaan, *Comparative Mythology*, The Johns Hopkins University Press, Baltimore, 1987.

Raglan, Lord, *The Hero*, New American Library, New York, 1979.

Rouse, W.H.D., Gods, *Heroes and Men of Ancient Greece, Mythology's Great Tales of Valor and Romance*, Signet Classics, New York, 1957.

Rowling, J.K., *Harry Potter and the Sorcerer's Stone*, Scholastic Inc., New York, 1998.

Sanders, Catherine M., *Surviving Grief and Learning to Live Again*, John Wiley & Sons, Inc., New York, 1992.

Sheeler, Jim, Final Salute, *A Story of Unfinished Lives*, Penguin Press, New York, 2008.

Smith, Huston, *The Religions of Man*, Harper and Row, New York, 1986.

Spiegel, Maura and Richard Tristman, editors, *The Grim Reader: Writings on Death, Dying, and Living On*, An Anchor Book, Doubleday, New York, 1997.

Stewart, R.J., John Matthews, *Merlin Through the Ages*, A Blandford Book, UK, 1995.

Swedenborg, Emanuel, *The Spiritual Life / The Word of God*, Swedenborg Foundation, New York, 1971.

Suggested Reading and References

Tegner, Esias, translation of Shaw, Clement B., A.M., *Frithiof's Saga, A Legend of Ancient Norway*, The Translator, Chicago, 1908.

Terkel, Studs, *Will the Circle Be Unbroken? Reflections on Death, Rebirth and Hunger for Faith*, The New Press, New York, 2001.

Thomas, Henry & Dana Lee Thomas, *Living Biographies of Religious Leaders*, Garden City Books, New York, 1959.

Treadway, David, C., Ph.D., *Dead Reckoning, a therapist confronts his own grief*, BasicBooks, New York, 1996.

Trillin, Calvin, *Alice, Off the Page*, The New Yorker, New York, March 27, 2006.

Untermeyer, Louis, *Robert Frost's Poems*, Washington Square Press, New York, 1946.

Villoldo, Alberto and Erik Jendresen, *The Four Winds, A Shaman's Odyssey into the Amazon*, Harper and Row, San Francisco, 1990.

Viorst, Judith, *Necessary Losses*, Fawcett Gold Medal, New York, 1986.

Vogler, Christopher, *The Writers Journey: Mythic Structure for Writers, 3rd Edition*, Michael Wiese Productions, California, 2007.

Waterman, Jonathan, Editor, *The Quotable Climber*, The Lyons Press, Connecticut, 1998.

Waters, Frank, *Mexico Mystique, The Coming Sixth World of Consciousness*, Swallow Press, Ohio, 1975.

Watkins, Nan, *East Toward Dawn, A Woman's Solo Journey Around the World*, Seal Press, New York, 2002.

Watts, Alan W., *The Wisdom of Insecurity*, Vintage Books, New York, 1951.

Wiesel, Elie, *Night*, Bantam, New York, 1982.

Wolf, Judy, *Spiritual Life Rafts, Women's Stories of Profound Loss, Courage and Healing*, Shim Institute, Book Printers of Utah, Salt Lake City, UT 2008.

Wurtzel, Elizabeth, *Bitch, In Praise of Difficult Women*, Doubleday, New York, 1998.

www.ingramcontent.com/pod-product-compliance
Lightning Source LLC
Chambersburg PA
CBHW031234290426
44109CB00012B/291